Postcolonial London

'In recent years, postcolonial studies has begun to focus on questions of how space is represented within what were once seen as "imperial centres". This book links this new focus with questions which open up the "national" and thereby addresses issues which have always been important, such as the extent to which our visions of the national have been built on migrant and diasporic, colonial and postcolonial identities. Thus we are forced to question the extent to which London has always in a sense been a transformative "postcolonial" space not only after Empire, or after immigration, but before.'

Susheila Nasta

Postcolonial London explores the imaginative transformation of London by African, Asian, Caribbean and South Pacific writers since the 1950s.

Engaging with a range of writers from Sam Selvon and Doris Lessing to Hanif Kureishi and Fred D'Aguiar, John McLeod examines a cultural history of resistance to the prejudice and racism that have at least in part characterized the postcolonial city. This resistance, he argues, bears witness to the determination, imagination and creativity of London's migrants and their descendants.

McLeod's superb study is essential reading for those interested in British or postcolonial literature, or in theorizations of the city and metropolitan culture.

John McLeod is Lecturer in English at the University of Leeds. He has written on postcolonial literature for a variety of publications, including *Wasafiri*, *Interventions* and *Journal of Commonwealth Literature* and is the author of *Beginning Postcolonialism* (2000).

Postcolonial London

Rewriting the metropolis

John McLeod

Routledge
Taylor & Francis Group

LONDON AND NEW YORK

First published 2004
by Routledge
2 Park Square, Milton Park, Abingdon, Oxfordshire,
OX14 4RN

Simultaneously published in the USA and Canada
by Routledge
29 West 35th Street, New York, NY 10001

Routledge is an imprint of the Taylor & Francis Group

© 2004 John McLeod

Typeset in Goudy by The Running Head Limited, Cambridge
Printed and bound in Great Britain by TJ International Ltd,
Padstow, Cornwall

British Library Cataloguing in Publication Data
A catalogue record for this book is available from the British Library

Library of Congress Cataloging-in-Publication Data
McLeod, John, 1969–
    Postcolonial London : rewriting the metropolis / John McLeod.
        p. cm.
    Includes bibliographical references and index.
    1. English literature—England—London—History and criticism.
2. Authors, Commonwealth—Homes and haunts—England—London.
3. English literature—20th century—History and criticism.
4. Commonwealth literature (English)—History and criticism.
5. Authors, English—Homes and haunts—England—London. 6. London
(England)—Intellectual life—20th century. 7. Postcolonialism—
England—London. 8. London (England)—In literature.
9. Postcolonialism in literature. I. Title.
    PR8478.M38 2004
    820.9'32421'09045–dc22   2004002062

ISBN 0–415–34459–X (hbk)
ISBN 0–415–34460–3 (pbk)

For Liz Ekstein

Contents

Acknowledgements

One book, many obligations. My biggest debt is to the undergraduate students who have taken my module, 'Postcolonial London', in the School of English at the University of Leeds since 1996. The influence of their discussions, disagreements and imaginative explorations of writers and issues will, I hope, be felt throughout the following pages, and many of my ideas are indebted to their enthusiastic and stimulating engagement with texts. *Postcolonial London*'s merits are as much theirs as they are mine (suffice to say, its weaknesses are solely my responsibility).

Shirley Chew first encouraged me to pursue my interest in postcolonial London in the classroom and, later, on the page. Her wisdom and generosity remain inspirational. I have also benefited enormously from the input and insight of David Richards, whose support for my career continues to be a valued and vital source of strength. His friendship is precious and dear, and I have much to thank him for. Elleke Boehmer and Bart Moore-Gilbert offered intellectual, moral and practical support, as well as their time. I am especially grateful to Professor Boehmer, and to Catherine Batt, for helping me think creatively about my personal investment in postwar representations of London. I am also indebted to Caryl Phillips for inviting me to New York in October 2001 to give the Lucyle Hook Lectures at Barnard College, Columbia University, where I had the invaluable opportunity to share my work with, and learn much from, a new constituency of students. And I am most grateful to Bernardine Evaristo for memorably introducing me to Notting Hill, her willingness to provide some personal information which I use when reading her work in Chapter 5, and her supportive enthusiasm for my research over several years.

I owe a major debt of gratitude to Alison Creedon, James Procter and Andrew Warnes, who gave up their valuable time to read this book at manuscript stage, offered expert advice, and made many helpful suggestions. In particular, I benefited tremendously from the imagination and keen intelligence of Dr Procter whose guidance was characteristically judicious and generous. I would also like to thank Routledge's anonymous readers who offered much constructive criticism and sharp comment. *Postcolonial London* would not have appeared without the steadfast support and enthusiasm of Liz Thompson at Routledge, and I consider myself extremely lucky to have worked with such a generous, committed and skilled commissioning editor. A debt of gratitude is also owed to Rosie Waters, who offered considerate encouragement at an important stage of this book's development.

I have learned much from the expertise of my postcolonial literature colleagues at Leeds, past and present, especially: Sam Durrant, Lynette Hunter, Peter Morey, Julie Mullaney, Stuart Murray and Brendon Nicholls. I am especially grateful to Dr Murray for his input into my work on Janet Frame. My doctoral research students Ingrid Gunby, Dave Gunning, Caroline Herbert and Abigail Ward have also impacted purposefully on the development of my thinking. And I remain particularly grateful to the following for their words of advice, cheerful support and entirely welcome distractions during the writing of this book: Julie Adams, Mark Batty, Stuart Davies, Peter and Shirley Ekstein, Rachel Evans, Tracy Hargreaves, Trevor Hayward, John and Jo Huntriss, Rick Jones, Robert Jones, Alex Nield, Francis O'Gorman, Martin Rushworth, Lisa Shaw, David and Facey Williams. Susanne Pichler kindly shared with me her work on Buchi Emecheta, from which I learned much.

Thanks are also due to the administrative staff in the School of English at Leeds, especially Sue Baker and Pam Rhodes. I am extremely grateful to the School of English and the Arts and Humanities Research Board (award ref. AN 8998/APN 14010) for granting me an extended period of research leave in 2002–3 during which time this book was finished.

Of course, I would have achieved nothing without the love and support of such wonderful parents, Veronica and James McLeod, and our family: Linda, Brian, Caitlin, Lydia and Madeleine. Above all, Liz Ekstein has helped me in more ways than I can name or she can imagine. Her patience with my work extends far beyond the call of duty, while her input into its development has been incalculable. This book is for her, with much love.

An early version of a section of Chapter 2 previously appeared as 'Naipaul's London: Mr Stone and the Knights Companion' in *Moving Worlds: A Journal of Transcultural Writings*, 2.1 (2002), 42–50. I am grateful to Angela Royal Publishing for granting me permission to quote extensively from Bernardine Evaristo, *Lara* (Tunbridge Wells: Angela Royal Publishing, 1997) in Chapter 5.

Introduction
Locating postcolonial London

One afternoon, in May 1955, the anthropologist Sheila Patterson took a journey to Brixton in South London. Turning down a side-road away from the main shopping street, she was 'overcome with a sense of strangeness, almost of shock'. In the familiar environment of a South London street, she was surprised to find that 'almost everybody in sight had a coloured skin':

> waiting near the employment exchange were about two dozen black men, most in the flimsy suits of exaggerated cut that, as I was later to learn, denoted their recent arrival. At least half of the exuberant infants playing outside the pre-fab day nursery were *café noir* or *café au lait* in colouring. And there were coloured men and women wherever I looked, shopping, strolling, or gossiping on the sunny street-corners with an animation that most Londoners lost long ago.
>
> (1965: 13)

Patterson's shock at the London she sees emerging just off the main shopping thoroughfare, down an innocuous side-street, bears witness to a new London community in its interstices and hitherto neglected locations. Its transformative potential is adumbrated by the uses the newcomers make of urban space, liming Brixton's streets and turning the street-corners into sociable sites of community and communication that perhaps recall similar locations in Kingston, Bridgetown or Port of Spain. There is another London being created here, one which admits the times and places of overseas to the supposedly humdrum heart of the aged British Empire, creating a novel environment which also epitomizes the perpetually changing milieu of city living.

Yet some of the difficulties faced by these latest Londoners are suggested by the queue which has formed outside the employment exchange, and the fact that this neighbourhood seems enclosed by an imaginary border which

Patterson crosses when she turns off the high street and confronts a scene of 'strangeness'. These difficulties are partly social and economic, but also bound up with modes of perception and representation. Patterson's disorientation stems from her inability to read the scene of what should be familiar and unspectacular, namely 'a fairly typical South London side-street, grubby and narrow, lined with cheap cafés, shabby pubs, and flashy clothing-shops' (13). In the struggle to render the source of her disconcerted feelings, the newcomers are granted an almost prelapsarian innocence: they stroll happily in the sunshine and display an animation which most Londoners lost 'long ago'. Her diplomatic attempt to describe the multiracial children playing outside the nursery with recourse to French (so bizarre to the twenty-first-century eye) cannot escape the racializing optic it wishes to eschew, while also raising the issue of miscegenation frequently found in discussions of New Commonwealth immigration at the time (Webster 1998).

Patterson's study of Caribbeans in Brixton, *Dark Strangers,* crystalized several contradictions on the part of those keen to understand how London was changing as a consequence of migration and settlement in the immediate postwar years. On the one hand Patterson made an important attempt to expose and address many of the difficulties facing newcomers to the city, such as their expectations of London nurtured from afar and the prejudicial attitudes they found in employment and housing which reflected the infamous 'colour bar' of which Learie Constantine had written a year before Patterson travelled to Brixton (Constantine 1954). She also recorded the survival strategies and initiatives of Caribbeans in 1950s London, such as the 'pardner' associations of which the Trinidadian novelist Sam Selvon wrote humorously in his Brixton-based novel *The Housing Lark* (1965). On the other hand, Patterson's study also revealed the extent to which, in the 1950s and 1960s, Caribbeans were within, but not a part of, London's economic and social fabric, while her vocabulary often intimated something of the imaginative assumptions and barriers that would impact centrally upon the lives of London's newcomers for many years to come. Brixton's diasporic peoples, like many other new Londoners from countries with a history of colonialism, would be subjected to a series of attitudes which frequently objectified and demonized them, often in terms of race, while questioning their rights of citizenship and tenure in one of the world's most historically cosmopolitan cities. The perpetual identification of these peoples and their families as 'strangers' in, rather than citizens of, London bears witness to the profoundly polycultural character of the city in the postwar years and to a number of reactionary responses at the levels of state and street which refused to accept the newcomers' legitimacy and rights of tenure.

Almost forty years later, the poet and playwright Gabriel Gbadamosi described the pleasures of driving into 1990s Brixton, turning off London's major thoroughfares and heading for the excitements of its market. Here, he exclaimed, one finds streets moving 'with a different flow':

> Go up Coldharbour Lane, especially in summer, Electric Avenue or Atlantic Road, and you enter the Bermuda Triangle of Brixton market, one of those places where you pass from the fluent curses of the London traffic to the stop-start acceleration of shouts in the street, stand-offs and stylish getaways. As the road slips from mainstream London road culture it hits an interchange with the pulse of Jamaican street life, the go-slows of Lagos . . . There is a buzz of community, of jostling preachers, socialist newspaper sellers, street vendors and hustlers, an exchange and display of often very singular identities.
>
> (1999: 185)

Gbadamosi's mapping of Brixton echoes Patterson's – he too situates Brixton in juxtaposition to London's 'mainstream' – yet the sense of place is entirely different. Here is a vision of Brixton articulated from the other side of Patterson's vista. Gbadamosi offers a reading of these streets that is visceral and knowing rather than anthropological and shocked. In talking of the 'Bermuda Triangle' of the market he toys with the notion of Brixton at the end of the century as a dangerous location, a racialized ghetto in the minds of too many Londoners; yet it is the heady excitements created by Brixton as a cultural crossroads which Gbadamosi wishes to lay bare, where the pulse of Jamaican street life is inflected by the 'go-slows' of Lagos. Epitomized by its market which 'pulls London, Africa and the Caribbean into itself' (185) Brixton appears as a vibrant transcultural site of exchange: of voices, memories, musics, rhythms, ideas and politics, where new communities have been created from its transnational human traffic. Brixton harbours a perpetual process of 'interchange' in London, one that is continually created from the legacy of postwar migration, settlement and diaspora.

For Gbadamosi as it was for Patterson, the challenge facing those concerned with London is 'to read the signals of and responses to movement among people making sense of their experience in a new place' (185–6). *Postcolonial London* is my attempt to respond constructively to Gbadamosi's challenge and read critically the ways in which those who have arrived from once-colonized countries in London and their descendants have since the 1950s represented their experience in a 'new place' which, by their very presence, has itself been made new. In this book we engage with the visions and versions of the city which Londoners such as Gbadamosi have created. What, I ask, has been made of the city by these Londoners in their creative endeavours, often in the midst of seemingly insurmountable hostility, prejudice and, most bleakly, violence? What has London meant for them, and how have they rewritten its meanings? How have their cultural energies helped reimagine London, nurturing new ways of regarding and living in the city, and to what extent have their creative initiatives resourced modes of resistance at large? How has living in, and writing about, London enabled new ways of thinking about regional, national, diasporic and transcultural identities?

First and foremost, then, *Postcolonial London* is a book about change: cultural, social, political, aesthetic. Change is never easy, of course, and many of the changes to London intimated in this book have occurred in the midst of discouraging and difficult conditions. As John Eade reminds us, for example, 'Black and Asian settlers from former British colonies have played the major part in creating London's multicultural society, but it is they who experience some of the highest levels of poverty and discrimination' (2000: 2). The writing of these and other Londoners often bears stark witness to the subaltern lives and fortunes of those rendered other or marginal in a frequently hostile and unwelcoming city where prejudices towards newcomers have been, and still can be, found within employment, housing, government and the Metropolitan Police. Yet as we shall see, their writing offers alternative and revisionary narratives of subaltern city spaces which do not easily succumb to the demands of authority.

Since the end of the Second World War, the urban and human geography of London has been irreversibly altered as a consequence of patterns of migration from countries with a history of colonialism, so that today a number of London's neighbourhoods are known primarily in terms of the 'overseas' populations they have nurtured. Whitechapel and Tower Hamlets boast significant Bangladeshi communities; Brixton has long been associated with Jamaican, Trinidadian and Guyanese settlers; Southall has significant numbers of Indian and Pakistani peoples; Earl's Court is renowned for its Australians and New Zealanders; Hampstead is a centre for South Africans in London; Clapham and Balham are home to many with links from Ghana. It is estimated that 300 different languages are readily spoken within the boundaries of the British capital. Although this mapping of London makes tidy a number of different cultural constituencies whose members perpetually move through the city and interact with others, it none the less gives an indication of the patterns and histories of settlement which characterize London at the beginning of the twenty-first century. *Postcolonial London* is my attempt to explore critically and closely some selected examples from a much wider body of texts which take as their subject the lives, struggles, disappointments, achievements, conflicts and creations of such peoples in the city since the 1950s.

In exploring the cultural endeavours of the writers in this book under the heading 'postcolonial London', I am using a term which has enjoyed occasional currency in postcolonial studies but which has yet to be precisely rendered or adequately explored (Nixon 1992; Jacobs 1996; McLeod 1999; Ranasinha 2002). In this introduction I want to specify exactly what is meant in my articulation of 'postcolonial London', and why it may prove a productive conceptual tool. Paul Gilroy has argued that '[t]he postcolonial character of contemporary London has a simple facticity which leaves it not really amenable to debate' (1999: 57). Yet the 'simple facticity' of postcolonial London is no guarantee of visibility when the history of London society or culture is narrated. It is not just the case that, as Whisky Sisodia stutteringly suggests in Salman Rushdie's *The Satanic Verses* (1988), '[t]he trouble with the Engenglish is that their hiss hiss history happened overseas, so they dodo don't know what it means' (343); there also remains a troubling lack of acknowledgement of the history which has happened *within* the imperial metropolis as a consequence of colonialism and its aftermath (which Rushdie's novel, of course, attempts to confront). As Laura Chrisman has recently argued, British colonialism created a complex 'interplay of the metropolis and imperialism' (2003: 22) in which events and people from overseas made an impact at the Empire's administrative heart. It was not simply the case that London as the centre of the Empire stood in powerful contradistinction to the colonial margins. As Jonathan Schneer has shown in his fascinating study *London 1900: The Imperial Metropolis* (1999), although London's built environment and public spectacles cheerfully celebrated the grandeur and fortunes of British imperialism, the city was also affected by the endeavours of those who had arrived via the international routes opened by imperial traffic. Elleke Boehmer's exploration of resistance to Empire nurtured through the transnational encounters of the late nineteenth and early twentieth centuries calls attention to London as a significant site of dissident thought, where intellectuals and radicals from colonized countries created interdiscursive modes of resistance through their interaction. As she vividly demonstrates, 'London, pullulating with secularist, anarchist, socialist, avant-garde, and freethinking circles . . . thus formed an important meeting ground for Indian, Irish, African, and Caribbean freedom movements' (2002: 20). Boehmer demonstrates how the South African intellectual Sol T. Plaatje fashioned his forms of oppositional expression in 'the cosmopolitan London of the 1910s and 1920s in which elites from different colonial contexts were able to mingle and exchange opinions in clubs, salons, and debating halls – in effect to experience different forms of cultural and political self-representation' (153). So by the early decades of the twentieth century, London's role as the metropolitan heart of the Empire meant that, as

C. L. Innes explains, it was also the 'the heart of resistance to empire' (2002: 167). It was in 1930s London that a number of influential intellectuals and radicals – such as Kwame Nkrumah, George Padmore, Jomo Kenyatta, Amy Garvey and Ras Makonnen – formulated their own opposition to Empire through their interactions with themselves and other political groups (Geiss 1974; Gikandi 2000; McLeod 2002a).

For these reasons, it is important to proceed with an historical understanding of London as a much more complex and conflicted location than that implied by the totalizing and abstract concept of the undifferentiated colonial 'centre'. As Laura Chrisman remarks, such a view 'leads rather easily into the problematic notion that this unit has a unitary consciousness', serving 'an aestheticisation of space that obscures as much as it illuminates the operations of imperial cultures' (2003: 6). London occupies a particularly significant place in the evolution of postcolonial oppositional thought and action, and has long been an important site of creativity and conflict for those from countries with a history of colonialism. The social and cultural changes we explore in this book might be thought of as representing the latest phases in a much longer and complex history, to which they are in part indebted.

Indeed, the presence in London of individuals and communities from overseas is as old as the city itself, and might be considered to constitute its definitive characteristic. In the early 1990s the Museum of London embarked upon a project titled 'The Peopling of London', the aim of which was to call attention to 15,000 years of settlement in the city. In claiming that 'immigration from overseas has been a persistent theme in the city's history' (Merriman and Visram 1993: 3), the project proposed that the ancestry and present existence of both London and Londoners was most accurately conceived of in terms of multicultural diversity. Anna Marie Smith has pointed out that '[t]he black population in London numbered between 15,000 and 20,000 in the late eighteenth century – almost 3 per cent of the total population of the city' (1994: 134). Further evidence of London's multicultural and multiracial diversity can be found in Gretchen Gerzina's study of eighteenth-century black peoples in the city, *Black London* (1995), Stephen Alomes's account of the postwar 'expatriation' of Australian creative artists to Britain in *When London Calls* (1999), and Sukhdev Sandhu's anecdotal and chatty survey of black and Asian London writing, *London Calling* (2003) – as well as historical studies of Britain's diaspora populations by such figures as Peter Fryer (1984), Ron Ramdin (1999), Rozina Visram (1986, 2003) and James Walvin (1984), in which London features as an important location. Yet these endeavours and achievements, both before the Second World War and since, are still to be fully acknowledged at large. As Paul Gilroy demands in his essay on

London, 'we have to produce histories of the city in [the twentieth] century which allow the presence of diverse colonial peoples and their stubbornly non-colonial descendants far greater significance than they have been allowed in the past' (1999: 60). For these reasons, *Postcolonial London* joins with the work of those above and responds to Gilroy's demand by focusing attention upon the heterogeneous, diverse and polycultural character of the city's society and culture. It does so partly in a spirit of critical admiration for the cultural creativity of the period – evidenced by the work of figures such as Lord Kitchener, Colin MacInnes, Janet Frame, Linton Kwesi Johnson, Bernardine Evaristo and others – but also to support politically the contestation of London as defined in terms of racial, ethnic and cultural purity which has often resulted in the hostile subjection of those descended from countries with a history of colonialism to unacceptable experiences of racialization, exclusion and discrimination.

In speaking of postcolonial London, then, I am in part attempting to make visible a number of contexts resulting from colonialism and its legacy which have contributed to the social and cultural fortunes of London since the end of the Second World War. These include the postwar impact 'at home' of the waning of Empire and formal decolonization; the relatively large-scale movement of peoples into London from countries with a history of colonialism; the establishment of London-born transnational communities often regarded to be 'strangers' to London in equal measure to their migrant parents or grandparents; and the transition from London as 'imperial metropolis' to a globalized and transcultural 'world city'. The historical facticity of postcolonial London is certainly a major element foregrounded by the term. However, I also intend it to be responsive not only to historical or sociological phenomena but also to the imaginative endeavours of aesthetic creativity. As important as its declaration of 'facticity' is the term's attempt to articulate novel and divergent ways of regarding and representing London. In other words, 'postcolonial London' does not factually denote a given place or mark a stable location on a map. It emerges at the intersection of the concrete and the noumenal, between the material conditions of metropolitan life and the imaginative representations made of it. It is as much a product of 'facticity' as a creation of the novels, poems and other texts explored in this book.

In order to conceptualize postcolonial London in this way, let me say more about how I understand each part of my phrase before making some claims about the validity of their conjunction. In writing of London I am engaging with a location which might be conceptualized as inseparably tangible *and* imaginary. As Julian Wolfreys defines it in his thought-provoking study of London culture, London 'is not a place as such' but also '*takes place*' (1998: 4) in the representations made of it. My approach to

London in this book is similarly informed by a sense of the city simultaneously as a physical location 'as such' and also produced, experienced and lived imaginatively. James Donald's work on the modern city helpfully conveys a sense of the city fashioned at the conjunction of the material and the imaginary:

> ways of seeing and understanding the city inevitably inform ways of acting on the space of the city, with consequences which then in turn produce a modified city which is again seen, understood and acted on. It is not just that the boundaries between reality and imagination are fuzzy and porous. In the development of cities can be discerned a traffic between the two, an economy of symbolic constructs which have material consequences that are manifested in an enduring reality.
>
> (1999: 27)

To this line of thought, it is not possible to conceive of representations as simply mimetic of, determined by or antecedent to urban realities. Donald invites us to consider the ways in which perceptions of the city influence urban change and how people come to live within cities with recourse to symbolic constructs. In using the suitably urban metaphor of traffic, he conveys something of the scale and complexity of city life which takes place amid the inseparable relations between the material and the invented. Cultural production constitutes a vital part of the imagining of the city and, as Donald suggests, has the potential to impact upon the understanding of urban reality. As he importantly explains, '[i]t is not that the images are over here, on the noumenal side of representation and text, as opposed to the phenomenal space of the city over there. The reality of the city emerges from the interplay between them' (41).

Donald's sensitivity to 'the creative but constrained interchange between the subjective and the social' (18) which takes place in the city is influenced by his reading of the work of a number of thinkers of urban life such as Walter Benjamin, Georg Simmel, Robert Park, Henri Lefebvre and Michel de Certeau. The influence of de Certeau is especially prevalent – especially his work on walking in the city found in *The Practice of Everday Life* – to the extent that Donald mounts a spirited defence against those who consider de Certeau's thinking to be flawed by its tendency towards binarisms or its breathless poeticism. Despite these criticisms, de Certeau's essay, 'Walking in the City', offers several important resources for the conceptualization and exploration of postcolonial London which are worth exploring. Much of de Certeau's thinking rests upon his juxtaposition between the 'Concept-city' of officious discourse, where all is rational, planned and functional, and the spatial practices of those who invent a 'metaphorical' city in the 'proliferating illegitimacy' of their unplanned, individuating and 'surreptitious creativities' (1984: 96). The Concept-city is understood specifically as a synchronic 'place' that de Certeau distinguishes in terms of orderliness and stability in which 'the law of the "proper" rules' (117). Contrastingly, a 'space' has none of the 'univocity or stability of a "proper"' (117). It is defined as a diachronic and heterogeneous location of migration, mobility and instability, an 'effect produced by the operations that orient it, situate it, temporalize it, and make it function in a polyvalent unity of conflictual programmes or contractual proximities' (117). It is akin to 'the word when it is spoken . . . modified by the transformations caused by successive contexts' (117). By regarding the movements of city dwellers in terms of speech acts, with each spatial journey through the city constituting its own destabilizing narrative in conflict with the obligations of place, de Certeau offers a resistant grammar of city living where the concrete, regulated and panoptic certainties of authority are contested by the brigandly, spontaneous and subversive contingencies of spatial practices. If the map is the defining representation of the Concept-city which colonizes space in order to produce a static depiction of the city as place, then the wanderings of those who tour the city write new scripts of city-space in the delinquent narratives of their passage. 'What the map cuts up', de Certeau writes, 'the story cuts across' (129).

De Certeau's work on the spatial stories of city living, although perhaps too conveniently schematic, remains enormously suggestive as a point of departure for the conceptualization of postcolonial London. It crucially recognizes that cities are crucibles of power, and that city dwellers are constantly in negotiation with factors which attempt to regulate and police their lives. Their activities contribute to the subversive practices of everyday life as tactics of resistance and survival: 'Innumerable ways of playing and foiling the other's game . . . that is, the space instituted by others, characterize the subtle, stubborn, resistant activity of groups which, since they lack their own space, have to get along in a network of already established forces and representations' (18). The antic and stubborn stories which create the 'metaphorical' city are always scripted in relation to the Concept-city which attempts, but fails, fully to contain them. As de Certeau importantly remarks, stories engage with the determinations of both places and spaces and carry out 'a labor that constantly transforms places into spaces or spaces into places' (118). Hence, representations of postcolonial London bear witness to modes of authority which attempt to trap London's newcomers and their families in a particular mapping of the city (if not erasing them from the map entirely), regulating their movements and placing their activities under surveillance. But these texts primarily give expression to the improvisational, creative and resistant tactics of those who make possible new subaltern spaces in the city. Postcolonial London, then, stages the contest between the authoritarian, regulated and policed 'place' of the city and the insubordinate, contingent and ultimately creative innovations of 'space'.

It will be clear by now, I hope, that while acknowledging the agency of the imagination in mediating and shaping urban reality, I do not wish to proceed with the relaxed notion of urban space which collapses material forces into the two-dimensional weightlessness of postmodernist representation where issues of power and authority conveniently evaporate. Although Iain Chambers claims that the metropolis is '*as much* an imaginary reality as a real place' (1990: 54, emphasis added), his postmodernist approach tends to emphasize the saturation of images which occurs in the city and results in the evacuation of a sense of stable reality (and hence contradicts his view of the city existing as a concrete entity 'as much' as it is noumenal): 'Literature, cinema, television, video and advertising have accustomed us to environments that are no longer geometrically organized by streets, buildings, parks, boulevards and squares. The media, and the images of the metropolis they offer, provide us with a city that is immaterial and transparent: a cinematic city, a telematic hyper-space, the site of the modern imaginary' (54). One might ask exactly to whom he refers when using 'us' in these sentences. Chambers's vision of the city is as abstracting and non-referential as 'the telematic hyper-space' he discusses in which all sensitivity to facticity disappears. Postcolonial London will not be found here.

The dangers of proceeding with a postmodernist notion of the metropolis in terms of 'telematic hyperspace' have been outlined in the collaborative work of Michael Keith and Malcolm Cross concerning racism in the postmodern city. They acknowledge the noumenal aspect of city living in their comment that 'the postmodern city, if it exists at all, incorporates a way of seeing as well as a way of being' (1993: 2). Although they agree that the city 'is an imaged urbanism as well as a historical product' (8), their attention to the role of race in the metropolis powerfully demonstrates how imagined divisions and hierarchies can impact upon urban social relations. Using the phrase 'the racialization of space' (3) to explain the ways in which certain peoples and neighbourhoods are defined pejoratively through the optic of race – and hence are 'placed' in terms both of the built environment and their imagining at large – Keith and Cross pursue the ways in which social and semiotic processes combine to construct unequal experiences of city life. The centrality of race to the fortunes of contemporary cities cannot be underestimated: 'Contemporary urban form incorporates a set of racialized values which structure the architecture of power in the city' (11). These values contribute to the maintenance of a racialized underclass and the construction of racialized ghettoes perceived as sites of criminality and danger. The postmodernist city of telematic hyper-space actually contains 'tacit social orders which potentially naturalize the putative existence of a racialized other whose claims to redress are rendered suspect by a set of racial characteristics which may begin with subtle models of second-class citizenship and stretch to the crudest articulations of genetic criminality' (11).

In speaking of London in this book as both a location 'as such' and that which 'takes place' in representations, my intention is to approach postcolonial London writing in relation to the social and material inequalities that have in part resulted from the city's divisive architecture of power. In the chapters which follow I shall be concerned with the ways in which the cultural initiatives of postcolonial London confront different schematics of the city's architecture of power, and suggest the possibility of making new spaces in London where the subaltern contingencies of everyday life contest and dismantle authority. Of course, race is not the only authoritative discourse of power with consequences for London's diaspora communities, and nor do such modes of domination emerge exclusively from outside their bounds. As we shall see on many occasions, but especially in Chapter 3, diaspora neighbourhoods are capable of creating and perpetuating their own forms of coercion. In addition, although the subaltern creation of new spaces in London may be the subject of several of the texts explored in this book, the attitudes of the writers involved may not always be entirely supportive, as my exploration of V. S. Naipaul's representations of London in the 1960s will reveal. Although de Certeau's thinking problematically suggests that the operations of power in the city can be grasped in terms of a binary struggle between panoptical modes of authority and tactics of resistance on the ground, it is better to conceive of power as much more supple, complex and intricate – as Michel Foucault terms it, 'a complex strategical situation in a particular society' (1990: 93). London's diaspora communities are not immune from pursuing internally their own forms of compulsion which mobilize hierarchies of gender, sexuality, age, class, caste and other social categories of identity; while structures of state authority are by no means inevitably or perpetually oppressive. Jane M. Jacobs's understanding of the city captures very well the sense of postcolonial London as a contested terrain and site of potential transformation for which I am aiming. As she explains in her work on the imperial legacy in London, Perth and Brisbane, cities are 'promiscuous geographies of dwelling' (1996: 5) where complex structures of power are constantly insisted upon, revised, contested, renegotiated and resisted: 'Precisely because cities are sites of "meetings", they are also places which are saturated with possibilities for the destabilization of imperial arrangements.

This may manifest through stark anticolonial activities, but also through the negotiations of identity and place which arise through diasporic settlements and hybrid cultural forms' (4). The operations of power, like modes of 'destabilization', are numerous and always changing. There is no one singular process which fixes 'tacit social orders' into place, just as there is no singular mode of resistance or means of negotiation. As Homi K. Bhabha describes it, in such 'cramped conditions of cultural creativity . . . claims to cultural authenticity and sovereignty – supremacy, autonomy, hierarchy – are less significant "values" than an awareness of the hybrid conditions of inter-cultural exchange' (2000: 139). It is with a conception of London as a vexed space of inter-cultural exchange, as emphasized in Gabriel Gbadamosi's rendering of Brixton market, that I proceed in this book.

Jacobs's focus on the propensity within cities for the renegotiation of 'imperial arrangements' takes us to a consideration of what I intend by 'postcolonial'. As is well known, postcolonial, postcolonialism and postcoloniality are highly contested terms which have enjoyed considerable critical attention from many quarters in recent years (Ashcroft, Griffiths and Tiffin 1989; Ahmad 1992; Moore-Gilbert 1997; Gandhi 1998; Loomba 1998; San Juan 1998; McLeod 2000; Quayson 2000; Ashcroft 2001; Huggan 2001; Young 2001). Although it is not possible to explore these debates in depth here, it is worth observing that several disagreements concerning the postcolonial revolve around its advocacy of, and potential for, meaningful change. On the one hand there are those such as Bill Ashcroft for whom 'postcolonial' describes the agency and capacity for transformation of once-colonized peoples who have been, and may well remain, subjects of colonial authority. For Ashcroft (who quotes de Certeau favourably in his work), 'the range of strategies, the tenacity and the practical assertiveness of the apparently powerless' (2001: 17) make possible acts of transformation which ceaselessly contest the operations of 'imperial power' (55). The postcolonial, then, describes valuable protean forms of resistance, disruption, agency, contestation and change. However, Graham Huggan's exploration of the postcolonial as a potentially exoticizing and disabling concept checks much of the enthusiasm and utopianism of Ashcroft's approach by warning that the postcolonial may well function to repackage and fetishize the seemingly disruptive energies of cultural difference within the familiar and manageable category of the exotic. In mounting this argument, Huggan makes a distinction between postcolonialism and postcoloniality. The former can be understood conventionally as an 'anti-colonial intellectualism that reads and valorises the signs of social struggle in the faultlines of literary and cultural texts' (2001: 6). Postcoloniality, on the other hand, 'is a value-regulating mechanism within the global late-capitalist system of commodity exchange' (6). Each is bound up with the other, creating a contemporary situation where 'post-colonialism and its rhetoric of resistance have themselves become consumer products' (6). The postcolonial exotic, hence, emerges at a 'site of discursive conflict between a local assemblage of more or less related oppositional practices and a global apparatus of assimilative institutional/ commercial codes' (28). It follows, then, that all forms of postcolonial resistance and counter-value are always readily commodifiable by global capitalism as exotic spectacle. And although Huggan retains some faith in the ability of the producers and consumers of postcolonial culture to intervene and challenge the depoliticizing propensity of commodification through acts of 'strategic exoticism' (32), his argument more often than not casts doubt on the agency of postcolonialism as a disruptive and resistant discourse to free itself from the exoticizing propensity of postcoloniality.

My understanding of the postcolonial resides somewhere between these two attitudes. In a similar fashion to Bill Ashcroft, I argue for a notion of the postcolonial which is connected to successful modes of resistance and transformation – and indeed this book aims to provide several such examples. That said, Ashcroft might at times think more deeply about the effectiveness of his examples of postcolonial transformation to disrupt the systems of power/knowledge in which they are contained. Sadly, even if oppressed peoples intend and attempt resistance at a local level, it does not always follow that their tactics have significant global impact. Huggan's alertness to the ways in which postcolonial culture in recent years has com-fortably and successfully entered academic institutions and the global marketplace is timely and instructive, and adds weight to the views of those critics who declare a worrying complicity between postcolonial critique and global capital – such as E. San Juan, Jr., for whom post-colonialism is 'a peculiar excrescence of the geopolitical climate in the metropolis' (1998: 10) and little more than the pathetic 'pseudoresistance' (11) of a cosmopolitan intellectual elite produced by global capitalism that has nothing critical to offer those still suffering from colonialism's practices in either the present or the past. Even if Huggan would no doubt question the voracity of San Juan's argument – which unforgivably dismisses the intellectual struggles, successful forms of resistance and transformative achievements of postcolonial artists and intellectuals at a stroke – and is careful to maintain a faith in the transformative potential of the postcolo-nial, the tenor of his argument makes one ultimately wary of its capacity for meaningful change.

The work of Simon Gikandi and Stuart Hall is useful here in negotiating between these contrasting positions, maintaining a faith in the possibility of postcolonial transformation while remaining alert to the continuing unequal relations of power – social, cultural, economic – with which the postcolonial is inevitably bound up. Gikandi defines postcoloniality as 'the term for a state of transition and cultural instability' (1996: 10). This state is generated by the appropriations of and resistances to the culture of colonialism which continues to resonate during and after much postwar decolonization. In these terms, the 'post' in 'postcolonial' describes a condition 'in which colonial culture dominates the scene of cultural production but one in which its face has been changed by both its appropriation by the colonized and the theoretical oppositionality it faces in the decolonized polis' (14). In the context of London, the culture of colonialism still has agency as one of several meaningful determinants; but its face has been changed by, on the one hand, the resistant spatial practices which have emerged within the city by those who have contested the conditions in which they have been forced to live, as well as (and more depressingly) the evolution of *new* forms of racial and cultural differentiation that continue to divest power from London's racialized peoples and keep them in 'their place'. It is important to acknowledge these complex relations without tending towards either an overconfident notion of postcolonial transformation or a gloomy disillusionment with the postcolonial's political effectiveness. As Stuart Hall puts it, the postcolonial 'does *not* mean that we have passed from a regime of power-knowledge into some powerless and conflict-free time zone. Nevertheless, it does also stake its claim in terms of the fact that some other, related but as yet "emergent" new configurations of power-knowledge relations are beginning to exert their distinctive and specific effects' (1996: 254). Many of the writers whose work we consider in this book arguably contribute to the imagining of the new 'power-knowledge relations' which resource social and cultural change in the city.

Having elaborated upon my conceptual understanding of both the postcolonial and London, let us place these terms together and take stock of the semantic resonances of 'postcolonial London'. It must be acknowledged that the deployment of this term involves a degree of risk. An articulation of the postcolonial in relation to a significant Western metropolis, which might be regarded generally as the beneficiary of imperial power rather than as a site of subjugation and exploitation, potentially deflects critical attention away from the economic, social and cultural circumstances in countries with a history of colonialism. If postcolonial studies is primarily the study of such locations, in speaking of postcolonial London I am in danger of recentralizing the Western metropolis. When proceeding with a perception of London in terms of the postcolonial we must be careful to note that its postcoloniality is not at all commensurate with sites of colonial settlement in once-colonized countries. But as we have seen, it would also be inappropriate to consider London as solely the undifferentiated colonial 'centre' or immune from the consequences of Empire, its resistance and its decline. As Ania Loomba has argued, postcolonial studies shows how 'both the "metropolis" and the "colony" were deeply altered by the colonial process. *Both* of them are, accordingly, also restructured by decolonisation' (1998: 19). It is entirely legitimate to try to understand how this restructuring has impacted upon the metropolis. With this in mind, then, I would suggest that 'postcolonial London' may be considered a conceptual stratagem intended to foreground the consequences of metropolitan restructuring *as they have been represented* by writers who have arrived from, or who have ancestral links with, countries with a history of colonialism. As a way of regarding metropolitan culture it foregrounds the subaltern agency and activities of those who have struggled to settle owing to the architecture of power which creates mappings of the city in terms of officious 'place'. It admits the facticity of London's colonial and diaspora histories to the study of cultural production, and also recognizes that the experience and understanding of the city cannot free itself from imaginative and discursive modes. It engages enthusiastically with the cultural endeavours explored in the following chapters, but does not prematurely celebrate London as a tolerant, democratic or hybrid location. It names a frequently utopian subaltern aesthetic which emerges from the representations made about the city, yet remains absolutely bound up with the sobering social conditions and relations which are expressed in London's divisive architecture of power.

The utopian slant of postcolonial London writing requires more comment. Sallie Westwood and Annie Phizaklea have suggested that there exists 'a deep rupture between the poetic and experiential and the sociological and economistic discourses which have sought to render migratory processes intelligible' (2000: 4). In their view, popular cultural representations of the migrant figure have fallen foul of problematic romanticizing tendencies 'which are curiously at odds with the ways in which sociologists and economists have tried to conceptualize and analyse migration' (4). In *Postcolonial London* my reading of the cultural texts I have selected attempts to avoid cheerleading 'the pleasures of difference' (3) and steers clear of the thoughtless romanticization of migration and settlement. Cultural creativity should not be considered outside of London's insoluble and unforgettable social conflicts. But I also want to sustain a notion of cultural creativity as a critical, resistant and – above all – utopian political pragmatic activity. Aesthetic practices are not confined or fully determined by the social circumstances within which they emerge. The resources which cultural creativity may offer the pursuit of political and concrete change are extremely valuable and can be too quickly dismissed as solipsistically poetic and experiential. In a discussion of the cultural dissidence of racially subordinated peoples, Paul Gilroy has referred to the 'politics of transfiguration'

(1993a: 37) which are discovered in utopian imaginings of 'qualitatively new desires, social relations, and modes of association' (37). The creative endeavours of such peoples frequently function '[b]y posing the world as it is against the world as the racially subordinated would like it be' (36). The postcolonial rewriting of London as a utopian space of cultural and social transformation is often engaged with a transfigurative politics. Time and time again in this book we shall encounter texts in which the capacity to rewrite the metropolis is not simply enabled by social privilege or an escape from social experiences, but a groundbreaking and -making act of proleptic imagination which suggests new models of social possibility. Such utopian vistas refuse to accept the predominant mapping of London as an imperious place for newcomers and their descendants. They daringly imagine an alternative city in which divisive tensions are effectively resisted, and progressive, transformative kinds of social and cultural relationships are glimpsed. As we shall see, such projections are often inspired by the popular cultural energies of everyday life in London – its dance halls, music, street-culture and so on – where received models of race, identity and belonging begin to break down. In the work of Colin MacInnes, Linton Kwesi Johnson, Hanif Kureishi and others, for example, the articulation of utopian visions of London which take seriously the possibilities of diasporic living are frequently bound up with the critical advocacy of youth. This is not, of course, to presume that new versions of London spring into concrete existence immediately when they are voiced, or that the social divisions of the city magically disappear at the moment when they are semiotically challenged in novels, films, songs or poems. I do not wish to pursue an unrealistic culturalist approach to the mystical effectivity of postcolonial London writing, but I would like to suggest that such projective, utopian impulses possess a transformative potential which contributes to and resources the changing shape and experiences of London's 'facticity'.

There is one further configuration impacting on the articulation of postcolonial London in this book which requires comment: the vexed relationship between city and nation. As the capital city of the British isles and seat of state authority, London is imagined to possess a particularly important relationship with the nation. The slippage between London, England and Britain as corresponding terms can be unhelpful, perplexing and extremely difficult to resist, but is worth questioning in order to lay bare the disjunctive relationship between capital city and nation which informs many representations of postcolonial London – and which makes the study of postcolonial London resolutely *not* the equivalent study of postcolonial England or Britain. To proceed first with the relationship between England and Britain, consider Paul Gilroy's account of their connection:

The term 'English', which is so often mistakenly substituted for [British], acts as a partial and manifestly inadequate cultural counterpart. The disjuncture between the two terms is a continual reminder not just of English dominance over Scots, Welsh and Irish people, but also that a British state can exist comfortably without the benefit of a unified British culture. The idea of an authentic cultural content of our national life is therefore constructed through an appeal to Englishness rather than Britishness. It is around this concept that the difficult tasks of creating a more pluralistic sense of national identity and a new conception of national culture revolve.

(1993b: 75)

Gilroy's distinction between the British state and an English national culture at its service indicates the cultural hierarchies which have operated in Britain in the postwar decades, with the creative endeavours of the other British nations considered to be of local or minor 'fringe' interest. The visions of national culture which have emerged from the articulation of a mystical sense of Englishness have tended to be remarkably exclusive. The representation of the English countryside as epitomizing the unspoiled essence of Englishness has a long history and – coupled with postwar initiatives in the so-called 'heritage industry' – has made a pastoral vision of England a major aspect of English national culture which has continued to the present day.

In contradistinction, notions of British culture have seemed more open to multicultural and transnational influences, yet in effect serve to protect the sanctity of Englishness from unwelcome interference. As Robert Young has pithily remarked, '"British" is the name imposed by the English on the non-English' (1995: 3). Or as Iain Chambers puts it, Britishness can be understood in two ways which in effect keep English and British safely apart: 'One, is Anglo-centric, frequently conservative, backward-looking, and increasingly located in a frozen and largely stereotyped idea of the national, that is English, culture. The other is ex-centric, open-ended and multi-ethnic' (1990: 27). In the postwar decades, the primary location of open-ended models of Britishness has been the city: the disruptive energies of British transcultural ex-centricity are deemed to be safely contained within the *cordon sanitaire* of urban limits, beyond which conventional models of Englishness remain untouched. As Gilroy argues:

Contemporary racism has identified black settlers with the cities in which most of them live and their cultural distinctiveness with its urban setting. Black life discovered amidst urban chaos and squalor has contributed new images of dangerousness and hedonism to the anti-urbanism of much English cultural commentary. How much less congruent is a black presence with the natural landscapes within which historically authentic English sensibility has been formed?

(1993b: 80)

In terms of national culture and identity, this scenario puts London in an interesting and productively conflicted position. On the one hand, London is the location where the British Government and so many state agencies have their national headquarters, circumstances which assist in the city's imaginative fashioning almost as a synecdoche for the nation. On the other hand, as a specifically urban location which has welcomed for centuries peoples from overseas, London's transcultural facticity has made possible new communities and forms of culture indebted to its history of 'peopling' which, in turn, come to pose a considerable challenge to the pastoral articulation of English national culture as representative. In this conception, London can be considered a profoundly disruptive location, incubating new social relations and cultural forms which conflict with the advocacy of a national culture or the pursuit of cultural nationalism. As Chapter 2 demonstrates, the disjunctions between capital city and nation have been abrasive, with the former enabling a confrontation with the imagining of the latter. If a certain vision of English national culture legislates against (in Gilroy's words) a more pluralistic concept of national identity emerging, representations of postcolonial London perhaps offer the means of challenging its exclusive and undemocratic characteristics and opening up exclusionary national categories through an attention to the social and cultural possibilities of transcultural exchange.

For example, in responding to a question about the resurgence of English nationalism in the 1990s Hanif Kureishi looked to London as solving the quandary of his own struggle with national belonging: 'suddenly you see London and you think it can belong to us, it doesn't belong to the English, it's international . . . [Y]ou can claim London as your own' (Moore-Gilbert 1999: 9). Coming from the South London suburbs as the child of a Pakistani father and an English mother, Kureishi clearly regarded London as making possible the opportunity of new forms of identity and belonging which contrasted with the sense of exclusion beyond the city's limits. 'I find going to the country[side] terrifying', he continued, 'because you always feel excluded. One gets very bad paranoia' (9). For some, living in and writing about London affords an opportunity to intervene in, critique and contest the received notions of culture and identity that impact nationally *as well as* locally, even though national and local culture is not coincident. Enabled and energized by London's transcultural traffic which perpetually traverses national borders, postcolonial London texts can constitute centrifugal subaltern significations that legislate against the consolidation of illiberal models of national culture and identity. City and nation are set at odds.

The following chapters are best considered as affording five particular opportunities for reading critically and patiently a select body of significant texts, rather than constituting an exhaustive or seamless narrative which summarizes the period covered and its conflicts. They open up a number of different vistas on the city at important moments of social and cultural contestation, and each has at its heart a recurring motif or key metaphor. In Chapter 1 I explore the consequences of Caribbean and African migration to London in the 1950s, from the arrival of the SS *Empire Windrush* to the Notting Hill riots of August and September 1958, in terms of the utopian visions created in Sam Selvon's novel *The Lonely Londoners* (1956) and Colin MacInnes's novels *City of Spades* (1957) and *Absolute Beginners* (1959). These writers imagine the potential for new forms of community and identity in the city often nurtured by the popular cultural energies of the decade. Specifically masculine and inspired by the youthful 'spatial creolization' of London, such visions have at their heart festive images of song and dance, the energies of which are mobilized to inspire new social visions of London's transcultural changes. Crucially, although the fortunes of the city's newcomers are often plotted as proceeding from expectation to disillusionment in the 1950s, I suggest that these utopian and often optimistic visions of London articulated during a period of mounting tension and hostility represent a significant and often forgotten achievement when regarding the cultural output of the decade, as well as constituting politically potent cultural responses to the decade's enduring problems.

In Chapter 2 I consider the representation of London in a number of texts written during the 1960s by three self-consciously literary figures who arrived in London after the Second World War with the intention of becoming successful novelists. In their work, the conflict between received models of Englishness and the new cultural and social possibilities of London receives an ambivalent welcome and is often expressed through images of the city's insubstantiality and weight, especially bomb-sites and ruins. In V. S. Naipaul's writing of the time, especially his novel *Mr Stone and the Knights Companion* (1963), the postwar changes to London are portrayed as upsetting received notions of English identity and civility which Naipaul nurtured and admired from afar. In Doris Lessing's *In Pursuit of the English* (1960) and Janet Frame's *The Edge of the Alphabet* (1962), contrariwise, such changes afford the possibility of challenging the legitimacy and authority of English national culture which is deemed to service colonial prejudices towards those arriving from colonized countries. In writing about London, Lessing and Frame discover subversive ways of opening

exclusionary models of England and Englishness to some of the transformations of the immediate postwar years.

The operations of gender preoccupy Chapter 3 in which I examine the
writing of three figures, Buchi Emecheta, Joan Riley and Grace Nichols.
Their work, which spans the 1960s to the early 1980s, calls into question
some of the utopian and optimistic visions of London explored previously,
especially in Chapter 1, by male artists, as well as outlining some of the different ways in which black women have experienced and responded
imaginatively to metropolitan life. Two related recurring motifs are stasis
and arrested movement, as each writer explores differently the particular
difficulties for women in moving freely in the city's spaces. In Emecheta's
novels *In the Ditch* (1972; rev. 1979) and *Second-Class Citizen* (1974), and
Joan Riley's *Waiting in the Twilight* (1987), the difficulties of settling in
London are compounded by attitudes to gender, so that women find themselves stuck as second-class citizens in London's diasporic neighbourhoods.
None the less, and as Nichols's collection *The Fat Black Woman's Poems*
(1984) especially suggests, it is possible to imagine tentative yet emancipatory visions of London where female agency is able to contest the coercive
demands of the city at large and the specific neighbourhood in question,
suggesting resources which resist the problematic construction of migrant
women in London.

In Chapter 4 I explore the representation of the incendiary riotous conflicts of 1980s London, in an attempt to read critically the representation
of violence in the dub poetry of Linton Kwesi Johnson, Hanif Kureishi's
film *Sammy and Rosie Get Laid* (1988) and Salman Rushdie's novel *The
Satanic Verses* (1988). Of particular interest is the extensive use each writer
makes of images of fire. In exploring Johnson's work as engaging with the
London of so-called 'second generation' settlers in which the streetwise
combination of poetry and music sounds its own signature as an urban
cultural creation, I explore the ways in which his careful representation of
fiery resistance in London establishes its legitimacy, righteousness and vali-
dation as an act of meaningful political resistance indebted to the history
and culture of Caribbean anti-colonial insurgency. In Kureishi's film there
is also a sympathetic exploration of youthful riotous protest as a significant
subaltern challenge to the officious policing of the city, yet a certain squeamishness remains towards those who eschew the creative and pacifistic
possibilities of popular culture in favour of incendiary protest. Finally,
in my reading of Rushdie's *The Satanic Verses*, a novel most frequently
connected to the celebration of London's transcultural and heteroglot
character, I question Rushdie's problematic representation of popular
protest as contradicting the supposedly translational vision of London he
elsewhere promotes.

Finally, in Chapter 5 I consider the representation of 1990s London as a purposefully transcultural location in David Dabydeen's *The Intended* (1991), Fred D'Aguiar's collection of poetry *British Subjects* (1993) and Bernardine Evaristo's prose-poem *Lara* (1997). Beginning with a consideration of the sense of optimism about London as a multicultural and hybrid city that pervaded much opinion at the end of the decade – as evidenced by the reception of Zadie Smith's novel *White Teeth* (2000) – I turn to the work of three figures who offer more sceptical and troubled visions of contemporary London while also finding in its transcultural contemporaneity the source for determined creativity, muted celebration and continued resistance to the city's social conflicts which have not disappeared. These depictions of London are frequently figured through images of water. They call attention to the social and cultural problems which endure into a new century while also looking forward to the refashioning of London as a transcultural space of social possibility at the turn of a new century. As Bernardine Evaristo writes in *Lara*, 'the future means transformation' (1997: 139).

Let me make two important concluding remarks concerning the historical and cultural shape of this book (which inevitably cannot cover adequately such a potentially wide field in a single volume). As will be clear from the above, *Postcolonial London* proceeds in a loosely chronological fashion from the 1950s to the end of the century. This arrangement, combined with the examples from Patterson and Gbadamosi with which I began, suggests something of the changes to London across the period, in terms both of the experiences of the city and of the kinds of representations made about it. As Gbadamosi's travelogue exemplifies, diasporic Londoners have taken control not only of the spaces in which they have found themselves but also of the agency to make their own representations about the city and their experiences. But it would be wrong to conclude that London's postcolonial history generally proceeds happily from postwar exclusion and struggle to multicultural inclusion and millennial chic. Four years before Patterson published her study, in May 1959 an Antiguan carpenter, Kelso Cochrane, was stabbed to death in North Kensington by six white youths. Six years before Gbadamosi published his essay, in April 1993 a young black South Londoner, Stephen Lawrence, was murdered by five white youths in Eltham. The killers of each victim have never been convicted. Let us be clear: much has been achieved, both socially and culturally, in combating the unacceptable social attitudes which have spoiled the experience of London for many newcomers and their descendants; yet there remains more to be done. Although change has occurred in London in the decades between the 1950s and the 1990s, often for the better, many problems, prejudices and conflicts remain. So, although *Postcolonial London* attempts to be sensitive to change, as I suggested earlier, it does not presume or glibly promote an emancipatory narrative of London's diasporic communities.

Second, the cultural representations we shall explore in this book refer us to a number of different historical trajectories that cannot be readily totalized into one common story of arrival and settlement. The factors which affected the arrival and fortunes of Caribbeans in London is not necessarily commensurate with that of South Africans, Australians or South Asians. Similarly, the different London neighbourhoods to which the cultural texts explored in this book take us – Brixton, Notting Hill, Kentish Town, Balham, 'Brickhall' – open several vistas on the city which do not readily aggregate into a common view of London. London is the location of many different localities and neighbourhoods, and appears differently when viewed from Soho or Willesden. There are as many different postcolonial Londons as there are postcolonial Londoners perhaps, and far too many visions of the city to explore adequately here. That said, one of the most persistent issues which emerges across a number of different postcolonial London texts is race, not least because race became an increasingly influential discourse in many reactionary responses to both London's and Britain's postwar transformation. The new communities established by Sri Lankans, Jamaicans, Nigerians and other migrants have in the past been pejoratively represented under the singular racial category of black, with differences of ethnicity, culture, location and religion ignored. This in turn has impacted upon the ways in which white newcomers to London from Canada, Australia, New Zealand, South Africa and Ireland have been perceived and accepted in the postwar city. As Kathleen Paul has demonstrated in her excellent study of the 'whitewashing' of Britain in the postwar years, 'formal definitions of [British] citizenship increasingly have had less influence than racialized images of national identity. Thus skin color and the races which were presumed to follow came to be perceived as natural dividers of people' (1997: 189). Although it is difficult to identify typical or indicative experiences when exploring the social and cultural history of postcolonial London owing to the divergent trajectories involved, officious metropolitan responses to the settlement of diaspora communities have tended to ignore many newcomers' cultural and historical differences and mobilized instead the homogenizing modality of race. For these reasons, the articulation and critique of race in postwar London constitute a central preoccupation of this book, not least because Londoners who are descended from a number of countries with a history of colonialism have found it difficult to avoid the social and cultural consequences of racializing assumptions throughout the period. As we shall see subsequently, race as a divisive social and cultural discourse has impacted widely in London, from the ways in which space is cognitively mapped to the policing of the city's streets.

As Kathleen Paul has put it, 'it is the nature of migration to remake a society and the fate of societies to be remade' (vx). In what follows, I explore an important body of cultural texts and consider the visions of London which they negotiate from a number of often conflicting points of view. Rather than registering London's remaking with strangeness and shock as Sheila Patterson did when she turned a corner in Brixton in 1955, there are other ways of approaching London's postwar transformation which aim – as this book does – to make sense of postcolonial Londoners' remaking *on their own terms* as well as engage critically with the valuable and transformative representations they have made.

1   Making a song and dance
Sam Selvon and Colin MacInnes

'Calypsos sung at Lord's', reported *The Daily Telegraph and Morning Post* on Friday 30 June 1950. Underneath a photograph of nearly a dozen jubilant West Indian cricket fans dancing on the grass at Lord's cricket ground, the newspaper's reporter described the vivid scenes of jubilation which had followed the previous day's historic victory by the West Indies over England in the Second Test, the first to happen on English soil:

> the invading spectators formed in a group and, led by a guitarist, broke out into a rhythmic calypso (a West Indian impromptu song) extolling the great achievement of their team.
>
> Other spectators, instead of hurrying to the gates, stood silent and amused. Above the continuous hum of excitement from West Indians at the far end of the ground the words of the calypso carried across the hot air:

> *This match will stir our memory.*
> *We hope it will be noted in history;*
> *All through our bowling was superfine,*
> *With Ramadhin and Valentine . . .*

The same exultant party later continued its celebration down St John's Wood-road and out of sight. Then Lord's, the green arena deserted, once more returned to its characteristic calm and dignity.

The calypso, known both as 'Cricket, Lovely Cricket' and 'Victory Test Match', was composed at the game by Lord Beginner (Egbert Moore), a popular figure in the calypso tents of San Fernando and Port of Spain in Trinidad since the late 1920s (Rohlehr 1990). Legend has it that Lord Beginner arrived in London with his friend and fellow calypsonian Lord Kitchener (Aldwyn Roberts) aboard the SS *Empire Windrush*, which docked at Tilbury on 22 June 1948, with 492 Caribbean migrants aboard seeking a new life in London. Kitchener was also at the Test Match. In a recent interview he recalls what happened when the jubilant West Indian supporters slipped out of the reporter's sight:

> I went there, with a guitar. And we won the match. After we won the match, I took my guitar and I call a few West Indians, and I went around the cricket field, singing. And I had an answering chorus behind me, and we went around the field singing and dancing. That was a song that I made up. So, while we're dancing, up come a policeman and arrested me. And while he was taking me out of the field, the English people boo him, they said, 'Leave him alone! Let him enjoy himself. They won the match, let him enjoy himself.' And he had to let me loose, because he was embarrassed. So I took the crowd with me, singing and dancing, from Lords [*sic*], into Piccadilly in the heart of London. And while we're singing and dancing and going to Piccadilly, the people opened their windows wondering what's happening. I think it was the first time they'd ever seen such a thing in England. And we're dancing in Trinidad style, like mas, and dance right down Piccadilly and dance round Eros. The police told me we are crazy. So, we went a couple of rounds of Eros. And from there, we went to the Paramount, a place where they always had a lot of dancing. And we spend the afternoon there, dancing and having a good time.
>
> (Phillips and Phillips 1998: 103)

Although Lord Kitchener's memory might be misleading – it was Lord Beginner who composed the calypso – it brings into view several vital elements of postcolonial London writing of the 1950s. Of particular importance is the role of popular cultural activity in the reimagining and reconstruction of London. The reference made to the Paramount, a popular dance hall situated in Tottenham Court Road in London's West End, indexes a number of London entertainment venues burgeoning in the postwar years which featured Caribbean- and African-influenced music and dancing, and where Londoners old and new encountered each other across the identitarian divides of race and gender. These locations, concentrated mainly in West London, were essential in helping facilitate the promise of social change. In spilling beyond the boundaries at Lord's, dancing around the pitch and into the streets, Lord Kitchener's dance captures something of the transgressive and festive creativity of music and dancing in 1950s London. It is a spontaneous moment of 'spatial creolization', where the sound, motion and energy of other times and places – the road marches and carnivals of Trinidad, the dynamism of the Paramount – shape a new passage through the city. Its itinerant route tethers the officious 'calm and dignity' of Lord's cricket ground with the subcultural joviality and energy epitomized by dancing at the Paramount. In Michel de Certeau's terms it is a spatial practice analogous to the subversive act of walking which confronts the operations of authority with the contingency and inventiveness of a spontaneous trajectory:

> the long poem of walking manipulates spatial organizations, no matter how panoptic they may be: it is neither foreign to them (it can take place only within them) nor in conformity with them (it does not receive its identity from them). It creates shadows and ambiguities within them. It inserts its multitudinous references and citations into them (social models, cultural mores, personal factors).
>
> (1984: 101)

In making a song and dance both in and about London, the metropolis is transformed by the manipulative and citational acts of newcomers who negotiate space in terms of the social, cultural and personal factors from other times and locations – 'Trinidad style'. A new channel in the city is opened where Lord's and the Paramount become stages on the same convivial journey, part of an impromptu calypsonian circuitry which wires up London in unanticipated ways.

In addition, Lord Kitchener's dance reveals a recurring tension in representations of 1950s postcolonial London, where music and dancing are asserted as forming a creative kinesis in conflict with authority's powers of arrest. The dance can only happen with the help of those English who cajole the curmudgeonly policeman attempting to arrest its movement, while the *Telegraph* report also mentions 'the ground staff [who] darted out from the Tavern side and barred [the spectators'] route across the wicket with posts and ropes' as the jubilation spilled over from the stands. The dance is a threat to the officious ordering, controlling and policing of lives in the city, where borders – both physical and imaginative – are actively and anxiously regulated.

The utopian visions of a hybridized and multicultural London to be found in the fiction of Sam Selvon and Colin MacInnes draw upon singing and dancing which were bringing old and new Londoners together in the 1950s influenced by Caribbean calypso, American pop, African music and jazz. In the energies, encounters and social relations subsequently suggested, each writer found the inspiration for daring, hopeful projections of London where the city's divisive architecture of power was effectively contested. The difficulties faced by newcomers to London in securing decent accommodation and employment have been well documented and the resultant picture is often gloomy, with their efforts often thwarted by racism and prejudice on the part of landlords and employers (Glass 1960;

Patterson 1965; Webster 1998). Several postcolonial writers bear witness to the racism, violence and torment they and others experienced during the decade, and offer a bleak, sombre view of the city that demythologizes the colonial myth of London as the heart of a welcoming site of opportunity and fulfilment for those arriving from the colonies. Yet despite the cruelty of urban life experienced by newcomers, London is also daringly imagined as making possible a utopian social blueprint where the prejudices and hostilities encountered on the street might be conquered. At the heart of such utopian visions – which appear in postcolonial London writing of the decade but are rarely acknowledged – resides the festive spirit of popular cultural life considered to facilitate alternative forms of contact beyond divisive social categorization.

As we shall see, Sam Selvon's short fiction and especially his novel *The Lonely Londoners* (1956) turn frequently to calypso for the resources which influence a vision of London as something other than the terrifying experience of objectification, economic hardship, racism and loneliness. In his novels *City of Spades* (1957) and *Absolute Beginners* (1959), Colin MacInnes, an enthusiast of music hall, pop songs and teenagers, offers visions of an inclusive, cosmopolitan London built upon the emergent popular cultural activities of the city's African and Caribbean newcomers, yet threatened by economic hardship, police hostility and – in *Absolute Beginners* – race riot. Each writer is engaged in a double activity of presenting London as both 'place' and 'space': bearing witness to forms of urban authority which attempt to secure London's newcomers in a certain mapping of the city, but also prizing the agency of those whose determined attempts to open new spaces in London expose the city's plasticity and deliver it up to the democratizing possibilities of spatial creolization. Yet there are important differences. Whereas Selvon's visions of London stem from an ultimately sympathetic and knowledgeable care for the Caribbean folk in London, MacInnes's work, despite its anti-racist aspirations, struggles initially to overcome a series of problematic and objectifying representations of black peoples in London. Only in the closing paragraphs of his masterpiece, *Absolute Beginners*, does a potentially progressive popular cultural vision seem to emerge.

Lord Kitchener's dance routes itself through a specific West London milieu which would become familiar with other acts of spatial creolization in the 1950s, stretching east–west from Soho to Notting Hill, bordered by Hyde Park and Bayswater Road to the south and Harrow Road to the north. The arrival in West London of newcomers from once-colonized countries after the Second World War had a significant impact on an area of the city already distinguished by a long history of transcultural settlement. According to Jerry White, at the turn of the century Soho was known as London's

French quarter, and as the century progressed it also boasted significant Cypriot, German, Italian, Polish and Russian Jewish communities. In the 1920s the Big Apple Club in Gerrard Street (later to become the hub of London's Chinatown) catered specifically for black men in London, while in the 1930s there was a black Londoners' café in Great White Lion Street. The establishment particularly of Caribbean migrant communities after the war made a significant impact upon an already diverse locale, especially as regards its available pleasures:

> The West Indian migration from 1947 rapidly began to work its magic on London's night life. The migrants' musical traditions rooted quickly – calypso was especially suited to informal small-scale performance venues like cafés, clubs and pubs. Their capacity for enjoyment created its own leisure industry of drinking and gaming clubs, with appropriate annexes for casual sex, and a passion for noisy parties that did not always go down well with the neighbours.
>
> (2001: 338–9)

This Soho-based activity would soon spill over to create a new pleasure district nearby to the north and west, in Notting Hill. As testified by Charlie Phillips's photographs reproduced in *Notting Hill in the Sixties* (1991), certain of London's streets would undergo sensory transformation. Phillips's photographs capture several supermarkets with stocks of African, Caribbean and Indian foodstuffs (such as Basmati rice, Jamaican bananas and Barbados raw sugar) on display on the pavement. Coupled with the new forms of nightlife established during the decade, the sights, smells and sounds of these streets were quickly transformed.

Those who arrived in 1950s London had come to a location that was essentially mythic. As Mark Stein explains, many newcomers from the Caribbean had a 'romantic attachment' to the city conceived of as the metropolitan parent-state of the colonies, while the 'lingering effects of colonial education meant that the centrality of London was only beginning to be questioned by a larger number of colonial citizens' (2001: 158). Such venerated expectations of London can be found in Lord Kitchener's calypso 'London Is the Place for Me' (1948), written aboard the SS *Empire Windrush* and which he performed for the cameras on disembarking at Tilbury. Here is the calypso's refrain, and one of its verses:

> London is the place for me
> London this lovely city
> You can go to France or America, India, Asia or Australia
> But you must come back to London city . . .

At night when you have nothing to do
You can take a walk down Shaftesbury Avenue
You will laugh and talk and enjoy the breeze
And admire the beautiful sceneries of
London, that's the place for me.

Lord Kitchener's calypso is, of course, not about London at all but about a certain expectation or ideal of London when seen from afar. The myth it perpetuates about 'this lovely city' is one of fulfilment, friendship and freedom. Walking in the streets is a pleasure, and one can wander where one pleases with ease. The calypso's farcical sensibility and happy artifice, coupled with its brisk beat, jaunty tone and humorous optimism, cheerfully possess the city in song as an accommodating and unproblematic place 'for me'. There is a sense throughout that Lord Kitchener is having fun with London's signatures, its proper names and its famous sounds: the version recorded for Melodisc in 1951 begins and ends with the chimes of Big Ben played on the piano. This detail suggests something of the creative, creolizing energy of the decade. Big Ben's familiar chimes fall into the hands of a piano player in a calypso band who makes them an integral part of a new song that bears witness to the presence of Trinidadians in London.

The reality of London, of course, would often be very different from its expectation, especially as regards walking the streets or securing residence. Mike Phillips was a four-year-old when he arrived in London from Guyana on 3 January 1956:

> I had always possessed a mental map of the city which sketched out an outline of its institutions – Buckingham Palace. The British Museum. The LSE. The MCC. Parliament. The Foreign Office. Scotland Yard . . . All these were landmarks in the London I knew before I set foot in its streets, but during my initial encounter with the city, they might as well have been operating on the moon. The London I lived in seemed to have a different history, and to be organized around different elements.
>
> (2001: 30)

One of the most prominent metanarratives subsequently created about the 1950s depicts the decade as a journey from idealism to disillusionment where, as in Mike Phillips's memory, a mythic, illusory London is entirely destroyed by the 'different elements' which constitute the city's uninviting reality. I do not want to challenge this view of the social experiences of 1950s London; but we might like to consider the ways in which the initial idealism of many newcomers (which we find in Kitchener's calypso) was not vanquished by life in London but rearticulated in the face of such experiences as a means of subaltern resistance. The optimism of these early representations survived and became the inspiration for new hopeful visions of London which set against adverse social conditions the potentially transformative propensity of the migrant's initial optimism. Rather then positing hope and disillusionment as polarities or stages on a linear historical trajectory from expectation to disillusionment in representations of the time, they are perhaps better thought of as simultaneous tendencies which co-exist throughout the decade. The tenor of Kitchener's calypso and the celebratory dance at Lord's constitute a significant cultural achievement which anticipates the similar attitudes and responses of 1950s writers such as Selvon and MacInnes.

Selvon had arrived in London from Trinidad in 1950 with the ambition to be writer, but it was not his only passion. 'Let me tell you what I wanted to do, what I have always wanted to do', he once remarked in an interview. 'I wanted to be a composer. I wanted to write music' (Dance 1992: 232). Susheila Nasta has expertly acknowledged the influence of calypso on Sam Selvon's London writing, especially in its formal qualities: its burlesque satirical mode, its subversive irony, its anecdotal and farcical sensibility (2002: 78–9). What remains to be explored, however, are the consequences of calypso for Selvon's *social* visioning of London. As Stuart Hall has argued, the calypsos of Lord Kitchener and others

> became the first signature music of the whole West Indian community. The calypsos of the 1950s therefore must be 'read' and heard alongside books like [The] Lonely Londoners by Sam Selvon (also a Trinidadian) as offering the most telling insights into the early days of the migrant experience. They are still overwhelmingly jaunty and positive in attitude – this is the music of a minority who have travelled to a strange or strangely familiar place in search of a better life and are determined to survive and prosper.
>
> (2002: 11)

It is true to a certain extent that, in Nasta's words, 'the world of [Selvon's] Londoners [is] not gold, but grey', where his characters' lives are stifled and limited by the 'bleak reality of survival in an alien and alienating metropolis' (2002: 75). But there is an alternative vision of London in *The Lonely Londoners* which rewrites the city in terms of the jaunty, positive calypsos of the day, and which is too quickly passed over. Selvon projects a utopian vision, inspired by calypso, of an optimistic and inclusive London created by the city's newcomers.

As John Cowley explains in his account of the origins of calypso in nineteenth-century Trinidad, calypso represents 'part compromise and part defiance' (1996: 235) with European musical traditions and perceptions. Historically it draws upon a number of nineteenth-century sources: the dances of stickbands parading through Trinidad's towns during carnival (occasionally resulting in combat when the bands encountered each other), the masqued satires and sartorial songs of canboulay and carnival, the *bel airs* or drum dances, the *gayap* or work song. Calypso is the creative culture of the Trinidad folk and, for Selvon, embodied the principle of creolization in its combination of Anglophone and Francophone traditions with African influences. In his 1979 lecture 'Three into One Can't Go – East Indian, Trinidadian, West Indian', Selvon referred to calypso as the people's 'most popular and evocative means of expression' (1989: 222). The narratorial voice often used in Selvon's work is indebted to Trinidad Creole English (Wyke 1991) which, for Selvon at least, enshrined the creative and popular spirit of calypso. It is revealing that Selvon occasionally described his narrative voice with recourse to musical metaphors. He explained in an interview with Reed Dasenbrock and Feroza Jussawalla that 'I really try to keep the essence, the music of the dialect' (1995: 115), while in his essay 'Finding West Indian Identity in London' he described his experiments with language in a way which connected music with mobility: 'I found a chord, it was like music, and I sat like a passenger in a bus and let the language do the writing' (1995: 60). The image of the bus reinforces Selvon's understanding of his fictional discourse as a specifically public transport, a vehicle for the linguistic forms and functions of the folk.

Just as Lord Kitchener recast Trinidadian calypso in the streets of London, one of Selvon's best London stories is a reworking of a calypsonian theme. The short story 'Calypso in London' (1957) is a rewriting of 'Calypsonian' (1952) which transplants several elements of the latter tale from Port of Spain to London's East End. 'Calypso in London' concerns the miserable predicament of Mangohead, a migrant from St Vincent. Unable to find work, borrow money, enjoy female company or elicit a kind word from his landlady, Mangohead struggles to survive the biting cold of a London winter. After failing to get a job at a cigarette factory in the East End, he visits his friend Hotboy, a Trinidadian calypsonian, at an Indian tailor shop in Cable Street owned by Rahamut. His troubles have put him 'in a thoughtful mood, and while he meditating on the downs of life, he feel like composing a calypso that would tell everybody how life treating him' (1973: 127). Mangohead composes four lines of a calypso which he eagerly brings to Hotboy at the shop. Hotboy is not pleased to see Mangohead – he presumes he has come to borrow ten shillings, as he did last week – but he listens to Mangohead's calypso which contains reference to his miserable time in London. Hotboy suggests that the calypso might also raise topical public issues and he begins to hum a tune. Thinking that he might use it to rediscover his renown in London, Hotboy takes over the writing of the calypso and, while concentrating, he flippantly agrees to Mangohead's request of a loan of ten shillings having barely heard the question. Once he has finished writing the calypso he is outraged to learn that Mangohead has left with ten shillings given to him by Rahamut on Hotboy's behalf. Hotboy refuses to reimburse Rahamut, and the story leaves them arguing. Later we learn that Hotboy later sold the calypso, although the narrator has never heard it: 'I sure the number was really hearts, and would make some money for the boys if it catch on and sell' (131).

'Calypso in London' depicts many of the central concerns of Selvon's rendering of the city in the 1950s. His London is populated in the main by the male arrivants from the Caribbean, trying their best to survive in an environment which seems to conspire against them at every turn. The winter setting underlines their misery and hardship: Mangohead has to quit a job digging up roads in Hampstead as his hands have become frozen. There is no money and little company or help from others. He survives only by hustling his friend, which causes tensions between Hotboy and his employer. As Hotboy's role in the narrative proves, dreaming of a better life in London exposes one to moments of weakness and exploitation. Although the calypso is 'really hearts' it disappears and is never heard, and ultimately fails to fulfil its promise to bring Hotboy fame and fortune. The 'boys' appear as a loose community of self-seeking hustlers, dreaming of better days that will never come, surviving rather than living in London.

Much of Selvon's writing about London touches at some point upon the bleak reality of the city as an unwelcoming wilderness – in the novels *The Lonely Londoners* (1956), *The Housing Lark* (1965) and *Moses Ascending* (1975), the play *Eldorado West One* (1969) and the short stories collected in *Ways of Sunlight* (1957). Frequently we see male characters engaged in a seemingly futile quest for financial security, trying to get decent accommo-dation, suffering racial discrimination by white Londoners and exploiting the good nature of fellow Caribbeans. The misery of their London is best captured in 'Basement Lullaby' (1957), a short story set in Paddington which concerns two unhappy musicians, Bar 20 (whose name recalls a steelband from 1940s Trinidad) and Fred, who spend the narrative stopping each other from getting some much-needed sleep. They live in a cramped, dingy room 'under the earth' in a hellish space '[a]s if the whole world dead' (1973: 179), with their relationship driving them to a kind of mad-ness. The myth of a London of plenty is frequently rendered as little more than an optical illusion. At one moment in *Eldorado West One* Moses tells a reporter that 'sometimes in the night I see as if the Bayswater Road sparkling with diamonds. But then you look in truth you see is only stones and gravel that mix-up with the asphalt. *You* know of any London street what pave with gold?' (1988: 20). The night-time illusion of a diamond-studded London is a suitable hour for dreamers. Like Moses, Selvon's work often looks through the illusions of London to the unhappy 'truth' of a 'mix-up' limited world.

Although I do not want to diminish the purpose and power of Selvon's attempts at demythologizing the ideal of London as the comfortable, rewarding 'place for me', there is another vision of the city at large in his writing. As 'Calypso in London' also demonstrates, Selvon's characters are remarkably *creative* figures who make something of their lot, and of their city. Mangohead may be without warmth, affection and money; but he has his imagination and his language, and he uses these dynamically. The calypso he engenders with Hotboy gets him a 'cuppa and a hot pie' (1973: 130), but its agency does not stop there: Hotboy later sells it on, and one can imagine its subsequent fortunes in the city, being sold from person to person, enabling the buyer to afford a little sustenance. Mangohead and Hotboy give to Caribbeans in London a short-term means of survival that comes from within the community rather than from white, often racist employers, while its story of individual hardship and international affairs bears witness to the boys' experience of London *on their own terms*. The calypso has significant social and cultural agency: it reveals Mangohead and Hotboy as active, imaginative figures rather than passive victims. The calypso ensures their survival but also adds something to the city that was not there before – it is more than the 'cuppa' and pie for which it is initially exchanged.

In Selvon's 1950s writing, London is not purely a grey wilderness but also a worldly and creative space analogous with the calypso which Mangohead and Hotboy made for themselves at Rahamut's Indian tailors in London's Cable Street. An overriding tone of bleakness in Selvon's representation of London is something which is only securely established much later, in the late 1960s and 1970s, and particularly in *Eldorado West One* and *Moses Ascending*, each written significantly after events such as the Notting Hill riots and a number of public endorsements of racism by politicians such as Enoch Powell. According to Barbadian writer George Lamming, a friend of Selvon's who was also writing in and about London at the time, 'I think that the event that really started to twist feelings was what were known as the Notting Hill riots. 1958 was that critical moment when as it were, the wound opened very wide because attitudes in England on the question of race were very ambivalent' (1998: 8). If we read *The Lonely Londoners* squarely within the context of Selvon's post-1958 writing, some of the novel's more optimistic and visionary aspects identifiable with

the creative popular cultural energies of the 1950s and native to calypso
are in danger of being filtered out. There are several affirmative aspects of
Selvon's representation of London which, in this particular decade, are not
yet fully thwarted by disillusionment.

The Lonely Londoners is an almost exclusively West and Central London
novel, with the action occurring in and around Hyde Park, the Bayswater
Road, Marble Arch, Notting Hill Gate, Queensway, Piccadilly Circus and
St Pancras Hall. Episodic in structure, its narratorial centre of consciousness is split between Moses Aloetta, a world-weary veteran of the city, and
Henry Oliver or 'Sir Galahad' who arrives full of excitement at the prospect
of living in London. Each character conjures a different view of the city to
the extent that the novel fluctuates throughout between two visions of
London, gold *and* grey. These conflicting moods characterize the novel and
place it at a significant remove from other fictions of London written by
Caribbean migrants at the time, such as George Lamming's *The Emigrants*
(1954), Andrew Salkey's *Escape to an Autumn Pavement* (1960) and, a little
later, V. S. Naipaul's *The Mimic Men* (1967), which are much more tonally
consistent in their gloomy rendering of migrant life in London. In contrast,
The Lonely Londoners restlessly shifts between different views of the city
which modulate between affection and disenchantment, exuberance and
despair.

Like Lord Kitchener, Selvon's character Galahad arrives with a dream of
London as a place of prosperity, happiness and welcome. Indeed, when the
boat-train pulls into Waterloo he is asleep and has to be woken by a guard.
London will confront many newcomers to the city with a similarly rude
awakening, it seems, as Moses suggests when collecting Galahad from the
station: 'London will do for you before long' (1985: 35). As in 'Calypso in
London', London as an unwelcoming and brutal place is rendered primarily
through its inhospitable weather. *The Lonely Londoners* opens in winter
with a description of the 'fog sleeping restlessly over the city and the lights
showing in the blur as if is not London at all but some strange place on
another planet' (23). As Moses waits for Galahad on the platform of the
station he is 'stamping he foot' (32) to ward off the cold. The novel connects the winter to stasis – Moses is in danger of freezing like Mangohead
in Hampstead. The cold weather is frequently twinned with the newcomer's fear: on his first full day in London Galahad looks at the sun
through the fog, hanging in the sky like a 'force-ripe orange' (42), giving
no heat. He is profoundly disorientated and is filled with feelings of panic.
Most importantly perhaps, he is paralysed when he feels the hand of a
policeman on his shoulder: 'He just stand up there and he hear a voice say:
"Move along now, don't block the pavement"' (42–3). On many occasions
in the novel the characters are arrested by a sense of fear that severely

curtails their freedom of movement through the city. Fear is the affective manifestation of London's authority and prejudicial agency, with stasis the physical result of the characters' loss of control.

The predominant spokesperson in the novel for this view of London is Moses, who frequently presents a fearful view of the city to Galahad. In one conversation, set significantly in winter's 'bitter season' (122), Moses decries the 'lonely miserable city' (130) and talks of people dying alone in their rooms, their deaths only visible to the outside world when the milk bottles begin to mount up on the doorstep. For a moment London is rendered a necropolis, a terrifying city of the dead, as Moses declares his life to be inert: despite ten years in London he is 'still the same way, neither forward nor backward' (129). Fear and paralysis also emerge in his thoughts about London with which the novel concludes. He dwells upon the 'great restless, swaying movement that leaving you standing in the same spot' (141) and becomes weighed down with 'thoughts so heavy like he unable to move his body' (142). To counter the gloom, Moses frequently broods in his room and returns imaginatively to an idealised past in Trinidad where he can live again and 'lay down in the sun and dig my toes, and eat a fish broth and go Maracas Bay and talk to them fishermen, and all day long I sleeping under the tree, with just the old sun for company' (130). This remote view of Trinidad reverses the myth of London as a paradise when seen from afar, and is perhaps a dangerous romanticization of the island – especially when we remember the novel's anecdote concerning the Barbadian Five Past Twelve who was soaked in pitch oil and chased by a group of men for courting a Trinidadian woman in Queen's Park Savannah. For Moses the rose-tinted past of Trinidad is the only future he can envision. He remains stuck in the present, locked in a diabolical and arrested moment of time, dreaming of better days.

Juxtaposed with the cold immobility of Moses's London is the mood of 'summer is hearts', primarily but not exclusively associated with Galahad. When Moses waits for Galahad to arrive at the station at the novel's beginning, 'stamping he foot' to keep warm, his actions hint at the London associated in the main with Galahad: one of energy, circulation, movement, warmth. Like calypso, Galahad makes Moses move his feet. Galahad arrives with nothing from Trinidad, no baggage or goods and, famously, does not feel the winter's cold. Although he will, like others, experience the loneliness and fear of the bitter city as we have seen, he is not as controlled or vanquished by it as seems Moses.

Galahad's actions enable another view of London to be uncovered. Moses's London is frequently one of interiors. Although at times his basement becomes an important meeting place for the boys that James Procter rightly describes as 'an important repository for a group consciousness'

(2003: 46), we are also shown Moses brooding in his lonely basement, more crypt than room, with 'London and life on the outside' (Selvon 1985: 140). In contrast Galahad's accommodation is presented as a dressing-room for the city outdoors and through which he wanders with awe despite his early shock. He is frequently connected to the city's vitality. References to 'life' are abundant in the passages which concern him, and his hopeful view of London contests the gloomy realism associated with Moses. Consider the following passage which depicts Galahad dressed in his finery waiting to meet Daisy, his companion for the evening, at Piccadilly Tube Station:

> So, cool as a lord, the old Galahad walking out to the road, with plastic raincoat hanging on the arm, and the eyes not missing one sharp craft that past, bowing his head in a polite 'Good evening' and not giving a blast if they answer or not. This is London, this is life oh lord, to walk like a king with money in your pocket, not a worry in the world.
>
> Is one of those summer evenings, when it look like night would never come, a magnificent evening, a powerful evening, rent finish paying, rations in the cupboard, twenty pounds in the bank, and a nice piece of skin waiting under the big clock in Piccadilly Tube Station. The sky blue, the sun shining, the girls ain't have on no coats to hide the legs.
>
> 'Mummy, look at that black man.' A little child, holding on to the mother hand, look up at Sir Galahad.
>
> (87)

This view of London is, of course, idealistic and lacking in a degree of reality. Galahad's advocacy of 'life' is expressed erotically and bound up with his quest for sexual adventure which problematically objectifies women as 'craft' and 'skin' (Lord Kitchener, we recall, danced merrily around Eros after watching the cricket at Lord's). His view of London is marked and marred by his distinctly masculinist pursuit of heterosexual conquest. Selvon appears aware that Galahad's London is frequently a romanticization comparable with Lord Kitchener's 'London Is the Place for Me' (and indeed Moses's nostalgic vision of Trinidad). But there are important aspects in the passage which cannot be so readily dismissed. The 'life' celebrated here is linked to Galahad's movement in the city's exterior spaces, and his walking contrasts vividly with his moment of paralysis on his first morning in town. Like Lord Kitchener's dance, Galahad's ability to walk, and the confidence he exudes when circulating in the city (is it a coincidence that this passage is set at 'the Circus'?), represents a modest victory for himself – if not for the boys in general – over London's powers of arrest. It bears happy witness to the determination and agency of the migrants who are depicted throughout the novel moving through London. In walking 'like a king' Galahad considers himself, wittily, the monarch of all he surveys. His elation is fuelled by the fact that, in his eyes, he is fulfilling London's promise from afar: in London, and because of London, he has accommodation, food, money and possibly a sexual partner. Like Lord Kitchener he is possessed by the poetry of the proper name: to say the words 'Charing Cross' makes him 'feel like a new man' (84).

Selvon cannot allow Galahad's dreams entirely to come true, of course. The child's remark turns Galahad into the object of a racializing gaze which threatens to curtail his agency. The dream of London is, like the diamond-studded pavement of the Bayswater Road, a trick of the light and an error of vision. None the less, Galahad's determined quest for his dream and the possibilities and energies he creates along the way are prized by the novel, and Galahad remains at the end a vital counterpoint to Moses's weary pessimism. When Moses complains that the Old Year's Night celebrations in Piccadilly Circus lack the dynamism of Trinidad where there is '[f]ete like stupidness', Galahad disagrees: 'It good to lime out there every Old Year' (132). In response to Moses's depressing remark that because he does not receive regular deliveries of milk no one would know if he had died in his room, he bluntly declares, '[t]he best thing to do is to take milk regular' (131). Moses responds to this as a witty, trivializing remark – 'Laugh kiff-kiff if you want' (131) – but fails to see the underlying message in many of Galahad's suggestions, which is that Moses must actively *do* something about his situation. 'If you ain't do well is nobody fault but your own' (133), Galahad declares.

Moses's experiences of the city ironize Galahad's naïve adventurousness, but Galahad represents an approach to living in London which Selvon invests with value. There is, of course, an element of each character in the other: Moses indulges in some of the coasting and horseplay of Galahad and the other boys, and Galahad gradually develops a sense of realism about living in London. But they are yet to become like their namesakes in *Eldorado West One*, where Galahad has changed into an unsympathetic and exploitatative figure in league with a crooked white landlord, while Moses is little more than his obsession to return to Trinidad. If *The Lonely Londoners*'s propulsion is at one level from expectation to disillusionment, there is another dynamic at work which moves in the opposite direction: the novel begins on a 'grim winter evening' (23) but ends on 'a summer night [where] laughter fell softly' (142). This summer, and the laughter it contains, is a figurative rendering of the migrants' creative spirit in which, at this moment in the mid-1950s, Selvon continues to invest.

The potential social consequences of the migrant's creative calypsonian propensity is most fully explored in the episode of Harris's 'fete', one of the least discussed aspects of the novel. At the fete there is discovered a different kind of motion linked to music and dancing which does not necessarily leave one standing in the same spot. Held at St Pancras Hall and featuring a steel band playing calypsos in London, the fete is the only occasion where virtually all of the characters, male and female, are gathered together. It also welcomes white and black guests. In a similarly transcultural mood, the fete seems to beckon different times and places into the hall, making it a bouyant if fragile scene, the signature tune of which is calypso. As Simon Gikandi argues, Caribbean popular forms such as calypso 'are important because they challenge the very foundations of Eurocentric cultural codes and suggest an alternative hermeneutics' (1992: 96). St Pancras Hall begins to 'look like Saltfish Hall' (Selvon 1985: 115) in Trinidad, fusing the Caribbean and London, and also recalls 'the old Paramount' (120) in Tottenham Court Road, the terminus of Lord Kitchener's dance. The heady excitements of London's outdoors in the summer months also infiltrate the hall's interior: 'Like Marble Arch in the summer, any of Harris fete is a get-together of all the boys, wherever it happen to be' (114). In de Certeau's terms, other shadows are cast in St Pancras Hall, which is made into a space of ambiguity and melange. This collective space of enjoyment contrasts vividly with Moses's basement room, where the boys meet each week in the winter months to shelter from the cold, struggling for change to put in the gas meter and prone to Moses's occasionally gloomy and inhospitable moods.

Selvon transforms St Pancras Hall into an inspirational source of spatial creolization which derives its vibrancy from the creative kinesis of music and dancing. In one memorable moment two figures, Tanty and Harris, dance while the band play Tanty's favourite calypso, 'Fan Me Saga Boy Fan Me'. Tanty is a figure of the dynamism of the Caribbean past in London, and at one level she functions as a familiar gendered trope of the ways and knowledge of the motherland. Harris, contrariwise, has turned his back on his Caribbean past and attempts to 'play ladeda' by speaking 'correct' English and 'going to work in the city, bowler and umbrella, and briefcase tuck under the arm, with *The Times* fold up in the pocket' (111). Their dance to the calypso in London implies a strategy for creating and enjoying 'life' by suggesting the need to combine the possibilities of both past and present, the cultural resources of Trinidad as well as the transformative opportunities made available in London. Their dance recalls the 'part compromise, part defiance' which John Cowley argues is definitive of calypso. Along with Tanty and Harris, Five Past Twelve joins the dance with a white girl, as does Big City. As each couple dances the narrator significantly declares 'nobody ever get to find out' (118) the reasons why the girls agree to dance with the boys. Although there is certainly a sexual charge to the dancing, in St Pancras Hall the relations between men and women seem different from the anonymous, objectifying relations hitherto depicted in the novel. It is as if the occasion to indulge in new cultural activities in London, dancing to calypso, becomes a way of envisaging just for a moment a new kind of socially inclusive space which emerges from the creolizing promise of the dance-floor: tolerant, racially inclusive, pleasurable, mobile, negotiating between (rather than polarizing) past and present, inside and outside, the Caribbean and London. As Moses says to Galahad, 'the things that happening here tonight never happen before' (118–19). The dancing at St Pancras Hall can perhaps be read as the first tentative steps of a community composing itself – one which is inclusive of many different Londoners, not only Caribbean migrant men. It is a possibility best exemplified at the fete's end when Harris tells the boys not to be 'jocking waist' (122) and stand to attention when the band plays 'God Save the Queen'. Rather than the stasis demanded by obedience to the mother country, the prospect of dancing calypso style to Britain's national anthem suggests another kind of stance, where the pedagogical dissemination of national identity is brought into contact with, and changed by, the performative cultural resources of London's latest newcomers (just as the chimes of Big Ben become part of a new score: Kitchener's calypso, 'London Is the Place for Me').

The utopianism represented by the fete is the most important dream at the heart of *The Lonely Londoners*. The fete is, inevitably, a fragile and utopian space, where possibilities are glimpsed rather than new social relations cemented. Yet its depiction maintains Selvon's confidence in change as both necessary and possible: in a cruel, unwelcoming city, the ability to imagine the metropolis otherwise is a daring and vital act which keeps faith with the transformative propensity of migration as well as the initial hope and optimism which encouraged newcomers to travel. The myth of London as a metropolitan El Dorado is certainly one of the illusions disassembled by the novel, but the calypsonian creativity Selvon salutes maintains to the end the claim to tenure in the city sung by Lord Kitchener from the gangway of the SS *Empire Windrush*. The novel's narrative shape certainly recalls the structure of a calypso, with each ballad concerning the different characters acting as the verses of a longer composition punctuated by a number of familiar refrains: 'take it easy', 'what happening?', 'oh lord'. The characters' changing of names is a central calypsonian characteristic and suggests that Selvon's Londoners have, like calypsonians, the creative potential to compose (for) themselves in the fashion of Mangohead and Hotboy in 'Calypso in London'.

Moses's brooding about the unhappy situation of the migrants in London threatens to set the mood of the novel's final pages at some remove from the calypsonian vibe of the fete. Yet the creative and uplifting spirit of the fete can still be heard as the narrative closes in the 'laughter [which] fell softly' (142). It recalls, perhaps, the laughter which Lord Kitchener enjoys in Shaftesbury Avenue in 'London Is the Place for Me' that maintains the determination, optimism and hope of Caribbean newcomers. It also suggests the embryonic beginnings of a new voice in London, different from the 'kiff-kiff' laughter of survival often mobilized by Galahad and the boys as a means to endure the harsh reality of the city. This laughter seems to conjure both the satirical and sentimental moods of the calypsos in London at the time. Combined with Moses's sight of 'a tugboat on the Thames' (142) moving across the water, it forms a figure of imaginative fertility and mobility that will conquer the debilitating feelings of stasis and weariness. Although the novel closes in a predominantly sobering, melancholy mood, the soft sound of laughter acts as an important response to the heaviness of Moses's thoughts and a vital, unvanquished sign of creative hope for Selvon's Londoners. They have yet to bring into existence the calypsonian vision of London mooted in St Pancras Hall – but there remains *to the novel's end* a hopeful dream of change directly responsive to, rather than ignorant of, social realities. This is, I would suggest, the novel's most important achievement which marks it off from the contemporaneous London writing of Salkey, Lamming and Naipaul.

In 1931, seventeen years before Lord Kitchener, Colin MacInnes landed in London at Tilbury Docks. Aged sixteen, he was returning to the city of his birth which he had left in 1918 to emigrate to Australia with his mother and step-father. After a few months in London he settled in Belgium, subsequently travelling throughout the continent, visiting Paris, Florence and Nuremberg. After the war he settled in a number of locations in Central London – Regent's Park, Soho, Spitalfields. He maintained a sense of displacement in the city of his birth which he put down to his childhood abroad: 'Born in London, but not reared there for so many vital years, my feeling for the city has perforce become that of an inside-outsider: everything in London is familiar; yet everything in it seems to me as strange' (1962: xiii). MacInnes was, of course, a very different figure from Selvon. He had arrived in London at an earlier moment and as a consequence of a very different history. Whereas Selvon wrote from within the communities he depicted and attempted to mobilize the language of the folk which was also his own, MacInnes's visions of London were voiced from a position of displacement from both the language and the people about whom he wrote – African and Caribbean newcomers, London's affluent and energetic youth.

In a parallel fashion, however, MacInnes discovered in popular cultural activity in postwar London the potential for envisaging social change in the city, and he too dared to project utopian visions of London as a way of contesting prejudice and violence. He frequently celebrated London as a repository of dreams and applauded the city's seeming malleability:

> Considered purely as a creation of man, London is a largely shameful shambles; considered as a place in which men may freely dream, it is one of the happiest cities in the world. To give shape to this poetic mess – to form, in his mind's eye, the private city of his own imagination – each Londoner can create, in his thoughts, a city entirely his own.
>
> (1962: xviii)

MacInnes's remark is ostensibly a comment about the uncoordinated architecture of London which makes certain places, such as Trafalgar Square, seem 'higgledy-piggledy' and guilty of 'spiritual confusion' (xviii). Spectators must make what they will of London's diversity and muddle. But it also describes a creative process which is at the heart of his London novels, especially *City of Spades* and *Absolute Beginners*. In MacInnes's London fiction, inflexible and officious attitudes are countered with a new vitality, derived almost entirely from the popular cultural activities of migrants and the young. The battles which ensue, frequently between authority and youth, reveal MacInnes's London to be a contested space of conflict and creativity. The popular cultural activities of music and dancing were suggestive to MacInnes as potentially composing a new London where racial prejudice, often supported by state authority, might be vanquished. He was particularly inspired by the American pop music and jazz that he encountered in places such as the Paramount and the bars and clubs of Soho. Youth offered a subterranean, subcultural vitality which cheerfully rejected the officious world of adult authority. In the late 1950s MacInnes was one of its most important advocates.

In a late essay on the English novel, 'Bourgeois form for a bourgeois audience?' (1975), MacInnes praised those willing to step outside their immediate social circle and write about the lives of others. This involved writers eschewing detached 'research' and willingly changing their lifestyles: 'The writer of one group who aspires to describe another in fiction has thus to assimilate himself somehow to it by hazard or, more perilously, intention' (1979: 226). MacInnes was excited by the changes he saw in London after the war and lived, sometimes perilously, among its new peoples, patronizing its liveliest cosmopolitan spaces. He was no stranger to the Paramount, upon which he based the Cosmopolitan club in *City of*

Spades, and also frequented the Mangrove Restaurant which became a *cause célèbre* in 1969. One of the anonymous interviewees cited in *Notting Hill in the Sixties* recalls MacInnes's visits to the Notting Hill restaurant Fiesta One, which opened on the corner of Ledbury Road and Westbourne Park next door to a popular calypso club:

> The person who did Absolute Beginners[,] chap who died not so long ago, used to come into our restaurant, he was one of the gay people around the place. There were a lot of gay people around the place and he was one of them. Colin McInnes [*sic*] that was the bloke, a tall blonde person, wrote most of his books smoking dope in rooms with a lot of black people. Right. I knew Colin, I knew how he got his information and what he did, one didn't have to read Colin McInnes' [*sic*] books to find out about Absolute Beginners.
>
> (Phillips and Phillips 1991: 73)

MacInnes's enthusiasm for the vibrant new London emerging in Soho and Notting Hill was inflected by his private predilections, especially his sexual attraction to black men, and this must be balanced against his public support of new migrant communities. The Trinidadian film-maker Horace Ové, a friend of MacInnes, regards him as 'the first white to speak honestly to blacks, as an equal' (quoted in Gould 1993: 220). Yet there was another side to MacInnes's benign interest in black men which tended towards negrophilia, regarding them as either sexual objects or noble savages. Francis Wyndham believed that MacInnes had an 'anthropological' interest in Africans and Caribbeans: 'It was part of the way he looked at people, not individualistically, but as representative of this or that' (quoted in Gould 1993: 116). Similarly, Daniel Farson notes that MacInnes's passionate opposition to racism was compromised by his own racializing attitudes: 'Though he fought courageously for their rights, he could be as condescending to the black people he befriended as the worst type of English colonial bigot' (1993: 141).

In his public pronouncements at least, MacInnes embraced warmly African and Caribbean migration as firing London with a welcome vitality and as the latest stage in a longer history of arrivals fundamental to the life of the nation. Writing of Petticoat Lane (now Middlesex Street), MacInnes delighted in the transformation of the street into a carnival each Sunday morning owing to the cosmopolitan crowds which congregated at the market:

> The whole district is traditionally Jewish and, as well as the tourists from Continental Europe who flock on the Sabbath to the market,

there is a large element of those immigrants from Commonwealth countries who, in the past fifteen years, have settled in our midst – to the infinite pleasure of those of us who love the life and variety they have added to the capital, and the sour disdain of those who have forgotten that the very essence of the English nation – and more particularly, of its capital – is that we are a gloriously mongrel breed.

(1962: 23)

As this remark suggests, MacInnes had no time for those who opposed immigration or perpetuated racism. As a significant journalist for a number of major publications and a broadcaster for the BBC, he was an important anti-racist public figure during the 1950s and 1960s who attempted to challenge myths about newcomers in essays such as 'A Short Guide for Jumbles (to the Life of their Coloured Brethren in England)' (1956) and 'The New British' (1963). His love of 'life' is analogous with, but also some distance from, the similar advocacy of London's heady possibilities in Selvon's writing of the time. For Selvon 'life' is coterminous with the bright lights of the big city; for MacInnes it is, more problematically, part of his 'anthropological' view of black peoples and one of a series of problems which complicate his transformative vision of immigration and settlement in London.

City of Spades, *Absolute Beginners* and *Mr Love and Justice* (1960) were published in 1969 as one volume, significantly titled *Visions of London*. Commenting on the trilogy's title in his introduction, Francis Wyndham pointed out that 'the word "visions" suggests a subjective (and possibly even hallucinatory) approach to "documentary" material' (MacInnes 1969: viii). Certainly MacInnes's novels are marked by a tendency to document new London spaces presumably unfamiliar to the majority of his readership, who gain readerly access – in the words of Montgomery Pew in *City of Spades* – to a world 'where you've never set foot before, even though it's always existed just under your nose' (MacInnes 1993: 65). This view has tended to downplay the fictional qualities of MacInnes's work. Even his biographer Tony Gould has commented that MacInnes 'was a good writer, but not a great one . . . he was a better essayist than novelist' (1993: xii). Other commentators, such as Wendy Webster, have read MacInnes's work as directly symptomatic of the dominant ideological values of the day, without pausing to reflect upon his fiction as mediating critically the world it portrays (see Webster 1998: 48–9, 51–2, 104). It is unwise to read MacInnes's novels as little more than narrative vehicles for thinly veiled statements of his own opinions or for ideology at large. As we shall see, the subjective, hallucinatory elements of his fiction, although much overlooked, are vital. In his novels MacInnes both projects and interrogates his vision of the youthful cosmopolitan London he loved. His fiction facilitates an important degree of critical self-consciousness and self-questioning often missing in his essays. MacInnes's novels are much more subjective and artful than is often assumed, and engender an important third dimension unavailable in his non-fiction. For this reason they mediate an important analytical vision of postcolonial London in the late 1950s perceived from a position poised ambivalently inside and beyond the cultures and communal spaces they depict.

City of Spades is set within the bohemian London populated by those recently arrived from Africa and the Caribbean, as well as black American GI soldiers stationed in the capital. Its narrators, between whom the narrative alternates, are two relative newcomers: Montgomery Pew, a twenty-six-year-old white Londoner recently employed as Assistant Welfare Officer of the Colonial Department and representing state involvement in the lives of migrants; and Johnny Fortune, a youthful student of meteorology newly arrived from Lagos. Also significant is Theodora Pace, an Assistant Supervisor of Draft Planning at the BBC who becomes keen to make a programme on Britain's new black population. In particular, the novel focuses upon three centres of gravity for migrants in 1950s London: Soho in the west, Brixton in the south, and Whitechapel in the east. Its central characters each begin the narrative in West London, which epitomizes a vision of cosmopolitan pleasure and delight, but are pulled gradually east and south towards violence, economic hardship and – culminating in the trial of Johnny Fortune – the discriminatory rule of the British judiciary.

Early in the novel, Montgomery Pew visits the Moorhen pub as part of his attempt to explore the London spaces being created by the migrants whose welfare is the central concern of his new position. Outside the pub he hears a calypso sung by Mr Lord Alexander, possibly a fictionalization of Lord Kitchener:

> You leave your mother and your brother too,
> You leave the pretty wife you're never faithful to,
> You cross the sea to find those streets that's paved with gold,
> And all you find is Brixton cell that's oh! so cold.
>
> (MacInnes 1993: 47–8)

The juxtaposition of the Moorhen in the West End with the song's reference to the 'Brixton cell' indexes the novel's attempt to express spatially the hopes and impediments of migrants in London, whose journey to an illusion the calypso records. Johnny is eventually arrested on suspicion of pimping and soon languishes in his own 'Brixton cell', in prison. If the West End epitomizes the possibilities of a cosmopolitan London, Brixton reveals a less palatable vision. Frequently a setting for violence in the novel, Brixton becomes a spatial repository for disappointment, disillusionment and dangerous survival, a nightmare world which inverts the illusory promise of Soho.

London's pleasure zone, with its clubs, pubs and dance halls, is the source of MacInnes's social utopianism in *City of Spades*. It is a treasured and fragile space. Many establishments are constantly under surveillance by the police and threatened with closure. In particular, the Cosmopolitan club – based, according to Tony Gould, on the Paramount in Tottenham Court Road (1993: 120) – is the hub of this creative energy which so thrills Johnny Fortune on his first visit not long after his arrival in London:

> This Cosmopolitan dance hall is the nearest proximity I've seen yet in London to the gaiety and happiness back home.
>
> For the very moment I walked down the carpet stair, I could see, I could hear, I could smell the overflowing joys of all my people far below. And when I first got a spectacle of the crowded ballroom, oh, what a sight to make me glad! Everywhere us, with silly little white girls, hopping and skipping fit to die! Africans, West Indians, and coloured GIs all boxed up together with the cream of this London female rubbish!
>
> (MacInnes 1993: 49)

This passage presents simultaneously the possibilities and problems of MacInnes's hallucinatory vision of a reinvigorated, cosmopolitan London. On the one hand it constitutes a sensory, euphoric vision of overflowing joy. The crowd on the dance-floor creates a benign spectacle where the occasion of being 'all boxed up together' seems conducive to 'gaiety and happiness'. The Cosmopolitan nurtures a shared cultural enthusiasm for music and dancing, and opens a space where Africans, Caribbeans, Britons and Americans (white and black) encounter each other in a mutually gratifying location. Whereas Johnny and Montgomery first meet each other in the official location of Montgomery's office which places them as 'Jumble and Spade' according to the title of the chapter in which this meeting occurs, their equitable and enduring friendship is struck by their happening upon each other at the Cosmopolitan where they effectively reintroduce themselves outside of the confines of officialdom. As MacInnes puts it in a very different novel, *All Day Saturday* (1966), set in 1920s Australia, '[a]t rare moments in history, by a series of accidents never to be repeated, there flower societies in which the cult of happiness is paramount: hedonistic, mindless, intent upon the glorious physical instant!' (MacInnes 1985: 54). To MacInnes's eyes, 1950s immigration to London afforded one such rare moment where new social possibilities were opened by the popular pursuit of pleasure.

On the other hand, MacInnes's representation of Johnny at this moment is problematic on three related counts. First there is his misogyny, as revealed in the contemptuous remarks about white female revellers. Second, MacInnes perhaps worryingly presumes that misogyny is somehow a constitutive aspect of black men and hence mobilizes a disappointing and imperious stereotype. Third, through Johnny's mouth MacInnes happily connects the Cosmopolitan's glad spectacle to 'the gaiety and happiness' of Lagos, and risks constructing a clichéd representation of colonial people and places. The dance hall's cosmopolitan hedonism is underwritten by an imagined 'African' authenticity that equates life in Nigeria with a highly sensual notion of joy. This questionable equation is part of MacInnes's problematic 'anthropological' association of black people with 'life'. Although MacInnes virulently opposed racism in London, at this moment he ultimately colludes in a racializing view of black men, as well as reproducing the stereotype of the black man in London as the predator of white women thoughtlessly described as 'female rubbish'. MacInnes's cosmopolitan visions in *City of Spades* frequently rest upon some highly questionable assumptions about cultural difference.

In his essay 'The New British' MacInnes wrote that in 'race hatred, there seems to be psychological security; in the lack of it, a freedom that terrifies most souls . . . [T]he choice is to be terrified and be; or cling to safe hatreds, and destroy ourselves as no bomb ever will' (1979: 100). Yet these public pronouncements against race were compromised by his fictional portrayal of black peoples as the bringers of 'life' and 'joy' to London. Montgomery Pew attends daily performances of a ballet dance featuring a black troupe led by Isabella Cornwallis. Brazilian by birth, Isabella 'choreographs a cosmopolitan style' (MacInnes 1993: 131), using Haitian drummers and black American dancers, and blending African, Afro-Cuban and classical influences. Montgomery is riveted by the spectacle this makes:

And as they danced, they were clothed in what seemed the antique innocence and wisdom of humanity before the Fall – the ancient, simple splendour of the millennially distant days before thought began, and civilisations . . . before the glories of conscious creation, and the horrors of conscious debasement, came into the world! In the theatre, they were *savages* again: but the savage is no barbarian – he is an entire man of a complete, forgotten world, intense and mindless, for which we, with all our conquests, must feel a disturbing, deep nostalgia. These immensely adult children, who'd carried into a later age a precious vestige of our former life, could throw off their twentieth-century garments, and all their ruthlessness and avarice and spleen, and radiate, on the stage, an atmosphere of goodness! of happiness! of love! And I thought I saw at last what was the mystery of the deep attraction to us of the Spades – the fact that they were still a mystery to themselves.

(177)

It is difficult to read this passage, with its references to prelapsarian, mindless and childlike savages whose ancient mystery contrasts with the modernity of the Western conquistador, without recalling similar sentiments voiced (however ironically) in Joseph Conrad's *Heart of Darkness* (1899). These are the attitudes not so much of the insider but of the voyeur, objectifying black peoples into mythic 'Spades'. The novel seems to collude in this view of black people by frequently depicting dance as the most significant and recurring aspect of black culture. Black people seem to do little else but dance – at the Cosmopolitan dance hall, the Moonbeam club, Mr Vial's party in Maida Vale and the Candy Bowl where Montgomery has the above vision. Dance is asserted as revealing the intimacy of black peoples with a kind of elemental 'joy' (76), while white Britain is contrastingly a place of insipid lacklustre and predictability, lacking spontaneity – as Tamberlaine puts it to Theodora, the English are 'always reliable for what no man could desire: like making sure he pays his income tax instalments highly punctually' (140). Music and dancing hold the key, it seems, to the creation of a new, cosmopolitan London injecting 'life' and 'joy' into a lacklustre city, yet these assumptions of vitality discovered in the mysterious 'Spades' remain highly questionable.

On one or two occasions MacInnes attempts to admit a self-critical discourse about this view of black peoples, as if the act of writing fiction enables MacInnes reluctantly to discover the problems at the root of his version of London's popular-cultural cosmopolitanism. In one important scene Montgomery and Theodora criticize each other's views of the 'Spades' as oppressive. Montgomery is accused of taking a 'vulgar irresponsible curiosity' in black Londoners which is 'simply another form of *nostalgie de la boue*' (174). He retorts by pointing to Theodora's 'animal attraction' (174) for Johnny – they have begun a sexual affair – as compromising her intellectual interest in London's black population. Karl Marx Bo and Tamberlaine also mock their perspectives. Bo suggests that Montgomery's and Theodora's benevolence makes them into 'what we despise even more than we do those who hate us – you are full-time professional admirers of the coloured peoples, who like us as you like pet animals' (80). Tamberlaine rejects Theodora's seeming liberalism as an imperious sham: 'We're not interested in what your kind ideas about us are, but chiefly in your personal behaviour. We even prefer the man who doesn't want to help us, but is nice and easy with us, to one who wants to lecture us for our benefit' (142).

Although few and far between, these moments admit an attempt on MacInnes's part to hold up his attitudes for questioning. It is also an attempt to acknowledge that there are ways of seeing beyond MacInnes's line of vision which he cannot articulate, and which problematically appear only as 'mystery'. Montgomery tells Theodora to remember that Africans such as Johnny 'have other spiritual ties, quite unknown to us, and are very different from our own, that are every bit as strong' (175). Theodora's last words in the novel, in a letter she sends Montgomery from the country after miscarrying the child she conceived with Johnny, mentions a look she has seen in many black people's eyes 'when they suddenly depart irrevocably within themselves far off towards some hidden, alien, secretive, quite untouchable horizon' (235). Combined with those critical encounters highlighted above, such moments both are a familiar racialization of black peoples and also mark a consciousness of the novel's limits of vision. It is as if MacInnes knows that the attitudes of Montgomery and Theodora are questionable, but he cannot relinquish his support for a new, joyful London which pivots upon their assumptions of race and sexuality; nor can he discover the means to represent the possibilities of London's popular cultural scene which eschew the rhetoric of race. The acknowledgement of ways of seeing beyond his own (the 'untouchable horizon' of Theodora's last words) is an attempt to avoid the imperiousness of white liberalism condemned by Tamberlaine, yet it cannot avoid adopting a racializing optic.

Hence the paradox at the heart of *City of Spades*: MacInnes can see immense possibilities in a youthful, transcultural London, yet those possibilities are ultimately thwarted by the divisiveness of race in which the novel colludes in its quest for 'joy'. MacInnes remains caught between two contradictory impulses: to assert and critique a regenerative vision of London which rests upon the 'overflowing joys' which black immigrants have allegedly brought to the city in the 1950s. Its contradictions are reflected in the divergent impulses identified with each of its first-person narrators: the benign yet problematic negrophilia and utopianism of Montgomery, and the unhappy fortunes of Johnny who never quite escapes the stereotype of imagined African male sexuality. For these reasons, *City of Spades* is an unsettled and unsettling novel despite the intentions of its author to embrace and explore with enthusiasm the new London spaces created in the 1950s.

In his next novel, *Absolute Beginners*, MacInnes comes to consider more critically the contradictions at the heart of his utopianism, as well as the difficulties in creating a new version of the city from the energies and enthusiasms of youth. *Absolute Beginners* encapsulates the collision between those who wish to make a new London from their pleasures and dreams, and the harsh realities of racial conflict (so unforgivable to MacInnes) which betray its possibilities. It is also one of the most important narratives of postcolonial London from the decade, as it is the only novelistic representation of the Notting Hill riots of August and September 1958 written in the immediate aftermath of events. Its vital closing sound, as in *The Lonely Londoners*, is laughter.

Writing in the wake of the riots for *Encounter* in December 1958, the British-based South African novelist Dan Jacobson described Notting Hill as 'grindingly dispirited and ugly, with an ugliness that too much of London shares for one to be shocked especially by it' (1958: 6). He noted that most of the immigrants had settled to the west of the area. This was Notting Dale, situated in the immediate vicinity of the Latimer Road railway station, which had enjoyed a particularly grim reputation for many years as a '"London Avernus", a hell on earth' (White 2001: 119). In the mid-nineteenth century it was the insalubrious home to local pig keepers with one of the highest mortality rates in London. A quarter of its inhabitants were Irish, and it also boasted a significant gypsy population. As Edward Pilkington explains, 'Notting Dale had always been a working-class area with houses to match . . . Until most of the area was knocked down in the late 1960s it was one of the most derelict pockets in London' (1988: 78). According to Mike and Trevor Phillips, by the late 1950s it was home to

> a large population of internal migrants, gypsies and Irish, many of them transient single men, packed into a honeycomb of rooms with communal kitchens, toilets and no bathrooms. It had depressed English families who had lived through the war years then watched the rush to the suburbs pass them by while they were trapped in low income jobs and rotten housing. It had a raft of dodgy pubs and poor street lighting. It had gang fighting, illegal drinking clubs, gambling and prostitution.
>
> (1998: 171)

Many newcomers ended up in and around Notting Hill as it was one of the few areas where rooms could be rented, although at highly inflated prices. The notorious slum landlord Peter Rachman became a millionaire by acquiring 147 properties in the area and leasing them at extortionate prices to black arrivants, who were intimidated if they complained to the rent tribunal or were late with payments. Gradually as the 1950s wore on the area became a site of activity for a number of racist right-wing agitators as well as home to 'a higher proportion than any other district of bold, reckless young black men who lived their lives out in public and would not cross the road for anyone' (Phillips and Phillips 1998: 173). Tensions gradually mounted. On Saturday 30 August 1958, one week after violence in St Ann's, Nottingham, trouble flared in Notting Dale with local properties attacked and black people assaulted by gangs of white youths and 'Teddy boys'. The violence spread from Notting Dale throughout Notting Hill and Shepherds Bush, with black people forced to defend themselves against a growing number of white rioters. By Wednesday 3 September the worst was over. Many were injured but, amazingly perhaps, no one was killed.

MacInnes was already writing *Absolute Beginners* when the riots occurred, and events came to preoccupy his fiction and political activities. The documentary aspect of *Absolute Beginners* is certainly a major part of its value and it is often either regarded as a reliable account of events or read transparently as the 'authentic' voice of MacInnes. However, the relationship between MacInnes and his unnamed teenage narrator is more complicated than is often assumed. The narrator is far from simply a mouthpiece for the forty-four-year-old MacInnes, and is presented until the novel's conclusion as a problematic and blinkered figure. MacInnes creates a narrator who enshrines his optimistic and progressive vision of youthful London, but for the primary purpose of critique. In looking at London through his narrator's eyes, MacInnes attempts not only to explore critically the political shortcomings of new forms of popular culture nurtured by young people at the time, but also to examine at arm's length his idealistic and problematic visions of London which the riots had dramatically threatened.

In contrast to *City of Spades*, *Absolute Beginners* is set almost wholly in West London. For much of the novel we are with a predominantly white assemblage of local hustlers, media types and partygoers. Apart from one visit south of the Thames to the Elephant and Castle and a scene near Windsor Castle, the novel's action occurs in a cluster of locations which include Belgravia, Soho, Pimlico, Shepherds Bush, White City, Paddington, Notting Hill and Notting Dale. Significantly, the narrator renames Notting Dale as 'Napoli'. Napoli is best considered an hallucinatory location, a fictional projection that shapes space in terms of the narrator's personality and prejudices. The riots are so devastating not simply because of the violence and destruction they bring, but also because they threaten to destroy his fanciful spatial creation with the riotous realities of prejudice and hostility.

As we shall see on many occasions in *Postcolonial London*, the ruined and neglected parts of the city are frequently those where London's new communities take root, transforming these sites into new spaces of social and cultural creativity. In explaining why he lives in Napoli, the narrator argues that the possibilities of the region far outweigh its insalubrious qualities. Despite the 'broken milk bottles *everywhere* scattering the cracked asphalt roads like snow, and cars parked in the streets looking if they're stolen or abandoned . . . and diarrhoea-coloured street lighting' (MacInnes

1992: 47) which contribute to its 'radically *wrong*' (47) atmosphere, Napoli is lauded as an important site where difference and deviance can be accommodated beyond the confines of the social mores of the adult world:

> however horrible the area is, you're *free* there! No one, I repeat it, no one, has ever asked me there what I am, or what I do, or where I came from, or what my social group is, or whether I'm educated or not, and if there's one thing I cannot tolerate in this world, it's nosey questions.
> (48)

This illusion of freedom converts the 'residential doss-house of our city' (47) into a significant site of cultural and social creativity. The house in which the narrator lives symbolises the social admixture of Napoli in a tempting vision of tolerance. It is owned by Omar, a Pakistani. The narrator occupies the top floor of the building, while below him reside The Fabulous Hoplite, formerly a 'male whore's maid' (49), Mr Cool, born in London to black and white parents, and big Jill described as a 'Les. ponce' (50). Although some of the narrator's descriptions of his fellow residents can at times tend towards stereotype, the overriding impression is of a place devoid of racial and sexual barriers – the characters are frequently in and out of each other's rooms. The spatial dynamics of the house come to stand for the potential of Napoli as a whole, and the narrator presents himself as our guide to this chameleon locale in a telling reference to Rudyard Kipling's *Kim* (1901) as 'pal of the whole wide world' (MacInnes 1992: 55). Just as the youthful Kim's Grand Trunk Road becomes a vibrant and colourful junction of manifold cultures, colours and creeds, so too is Napoli presented as a creative crossroads, in this instance forged by those formerly deemed socially and sexually deviant on a derelict and neglected site.

The perceived social and sexual freedoms of Napoli are connected to two forms of popular cultural expression. The first is the creation of the teenager and the teenage scene. As MacInnes reflected in his essay 'Pop Songs and Teenagers' (1958), popular culture in the 1950s had been affected by two related phenomena: the relative affluence of postwar youth and the new enthusiasm for American pop music by such figures as Bill Haley. Teenagers were consequently more classless than in previous decades and more 'internationally-minded' (1966: 59) in their outlook. MacInnes was clearly excited by the postwar teenage revolution and valued the popular music it created, but he came to criticize its shortcomings from an enthusiast's point of view. In his study of late nineteenth- and early twentieth-century music hall (MacInnes's passion) he argued that its popular songs could 'both reveal and teach' (1967: 148) by creating 'a kind of epitome of what you had vaguely felt hitherto' (148) and by delivering a message to think about. Modern pop songs, however, were often deficient in this regard: they could 'certainly encourage you to feel, but not much to think about why you feel what you do' (148). In *Absolute Beginners* the narrator praises the songwriter Zesty-Boy Sift for penning songs concerned with teenage London which 'all referred to places and to persons which the kids could actually identify round the purlieus of the city' (MacInnes 1992: 102). But he is the exception, and much of the novel is concerned with criticizing the adult world's utilization of teenage pop for the purposes of mass-produced (and lucrative) entertainment – indeed, it begins with the narrator discussing with his friend the Wiz the exploitation of the fourteen-year-old singer Laurie London by the 'tax-payers' (11). Pop music promises but fails to establish an autonomous space beyond the realm of adult control – a site of absolute beginning, free from the influence of others – from the very first page. Indeed, in the first line of the novel we learn that 'the whole teenage epic was tottering to doom' (11). Rather than enthusiastically endorse the world of pop songs and teenagers, *Absolute Beginners* is decidedly ambivalent about their counter-cultural credentials.

With the integrity of pop music under threat, the narrator turns unexpectedly to the jazz scene to secure and protect a form of cultural creativity where the freedoms of Napoli's youthful social admixture find expression. Here MacInnes perhaps shows his age in preferring jazz before rock and roll, while also revealing the influence of Soho's cultural scene in which he moved during the late 1950s, where jazz was both influential and popular. Jazz is lauded by the narrator almost as the anthem of Napoli's alleged social freedoms. In the jazz world

> no one, not a soul, cares what your class is, or what your race is, or what your income, or if you're boy, or girl, or bent, or versatile, or what you are – so long as you dig the scene and can behave yourself, and have left *all that crap* behind you, too, when you come in the jazz club door. The result of this is that, in the jazz world, you meet all kinds of cats, on absolutely equal terms, who can clue you up in all kinds of directions – in social directions, in culture directions, in sexual directions, and in racial directions . . . in fact almost anywhere, really, you want to go to learn.
>
> (61, emphasis added)

This utopian vision is another version of the progressive possibilities mooted in both the Cosmopolitan Club and the ballet dance which feature in *City of Spades*, although now the racializing rhetoric of the previous novel is significantly much less visible. The description of the jazz club is particularly explicit in making a link between popular cultural activity and its social consequences, and as a learning environment and place of equality its value seems immeasurable as a point of departure: one can go 'almost anywhere'. In the narrator's ideal world, Napoli's present should be London's future. But this space only functions if preconceptions of race, class, gender and sexuality – 'all that crap' – are left outside. This is a revealing moment as it hints at the narrator's struggle throughout the novel to stop social divisions from impinging upon his vision of Napoli. In plotting this struggle which becomes increasingly desperate as the narrative proceeds, MacInnes expresses his disillusionment with the creative social potential of postwar London's popular culture by holding his narrator up for question as short-sighted and naïve. In this novel, at least until its final paragraph, youth culture has failed spectacularly in its quest to create something autonomous and progressive.

Nowhere is this more discernible than in the persona of the narrator and the narrative he tries to tell. It is strange that *Absolute Beginners* is so frequently read as providing the authentic voice of the teenager or a celebration of youthful popular culture when MacInnes makes it clear from the opening that the narrator's ability to look at London is limited and selective. The first scene is set at the top of a department store in Chelsea which affords a panoramic view over London. The narrator describes the view while turning on his bar stool, and thrills in particular to the image of the Thames and its busy port life. Revealingly, he notes that '[l]ooking north you don't see much, it's true, and westward the view's entirely blocked up by the building you're inside' (11). Ironically, Napoli is located to the west of the building. The scene emphasizes the incompleteness of the narrator's vision of London and warns that throughout the novel his view of Napoli will be blocked, limited by the position he adopts. In addition, the narrator makes his living as a photographer, which suggests that he is in the business of producing reliable representations. Yet his pictures are often pornographic and require the stylization of the body and the deliberate posing of models (such as his friend Dean Swift). If pornography presents arousing air-brushed images of a sexual nature which often have very little to do with the often prosaic experience of sexual activities themselves, then so too do the narrator's idealized and chic representations of Napoli fail to approximate to its realities. Indeed, one might go so far as to say that as a counter-cultural space Napoli is more pornographic than geographic: a stylized, postured environment, one that attempts to satisfy the desire for a certain kind of city in tune with the narrator's excited adolescent imagination.

The substance of Napoli's problems soon challenges the narrator's idealistic vision of its possibilities. On being confronted with less appetizing perspectives he adopts an idealistic rhetoric which is made to appear

inadequate and redundant. In the second part of the novel he is visited by
Ed the Ted who tells him that the local Teddy boys have demanded that
Mr Cool must leave the area on account of his race. The incident forces
the narrator to acknowledge that Napoli is not the tolerant cosmopolitan
confection he presumes. Later, when confronted by Mr Cool, his idealistic
vision crumbles when faced with evidence of racialized social conflict:

> I couldn't take all this nightmare. I cried out, 'Cool, this is London,
> not some hick city in the provinces! This is London, man, a capital, a
> great big city where every kind of race has lived ever since the
> Romans!'
> Cool said, 'Oh, yeah. I believe you.'
> 'They'd never allow it!' I exclaimed.
> 'Who wouldn't?'
> 'The adults! The men! The women! All the authorities! Law and
> order is the one great English thing!'
>
> (136)

The 'nightmare' of racial violence punctures the narrator's dream-vision of
London, while Mr Cool's sarcastic retort to the narrator's depiction of
London's supposed long history of tolerance directly challenges its idyllic
cosmopolitanism. It is revealing to note that as soon as the narrator is
forced to see Napoli through another pair of eyes he resorts immediately to
the authority of the adults and their system of law and order – precisely the
primary targets of teenage rebellion. London's teenage 'revolution' has
failed to facilitate any meaningful, responsible or progressive political
response to the decade's social conflicts. The narrator's inadequate reaction
to the news of trouble ahead warns that teenage style has little political
substance, and serves to question the extent to which cultural creativity in
the capital has facilitated any meaningful social effects as he refuses to look
when presented with evidence that the issue of racial prejudice is present
in Napoli. In this contest of perspectives, Mr Cool's warning suggests that
it is not at all easy to leave 'all that crap' behind.

The riot in Napoli dominates the novel's final part, 'In September',
which reflects three conflicting impulses on the part of MacInnes: to make
a record of the violence; to depict the dangers of teenage political vacuity;
but also to uphold the integrity, perhaps the necessity, of the narrator's
utopian vision of London. This makes the novel's final chapter a disjointed
affair, with the narrator dashing anxiously from scene to scene. The riots
invite him to look and think again about London; significantly he decides
against carrying his Rolleiflex camera with which he had previously taken
his pornographic pictures 'because it didn't seem useful any longer' (189).

Outraged by events and their reporting in the media, he tours the area on his Vespa scooter keen to make an alternative record of events – 'Picture this!' (178) he demands – and to help black Londoners under attack. Eventually he stumbles into a rally held by the White Protection League where he encounters his friend Mr Wiz joining in the cry of 'Keep England white!' (191). Mr Wiz's actions bankrupt the vision that London's teenagers have facilitated a substantial new political and social climate beyond 'all that crap' of class, race, gender and sexuality, as well as questioning the progressive internationalism of 1950s youth. As MacInnes remarked in 'Pop Songs and Teenagers', published before the riots in Notting Hill, it was possible to see 'in the teenage neutralism and indifference to politics, and self-sufficiency, and instinct for enjoyment – in short, in their kind of happy mindlessness – the raw material for crypto-fascisms of the worst kind' (1966: 61). The riots seemed to prove MacInnes's worst fears about the vacuity of teenage rebellion.

The riots predicate a crisis for the narrator's sanitized vision of Napoli. The racism at large in the city exposes the extent to which London's youth-cultural scene can slide easily into complicity with divisive and unpalatable attitudes, as well as its inability to create a resistant and transformative social space. However, whereas MacInnes problematically attempted to maintain his utopian vision of London in *City of Spades* by imperfectly ironizing the racializing rhetoric upon which its model of cosmopolitanism rested, *Absolute Beginners* achieves much more than the previous novel in attempting to deliver up the narrator to a position of responsible political self-consciousness. The actions of youth appal and depress MacInnes; but his faith in their subversive and creative potential remains. In the novel's final pages, MacInnes exposes his narrator to the responsibilities of political agency and conscience and suggests a possible redemption for the generation in which he placed so much conviction prior to the riots.

The riots herald a moment of important maturation for the narrator: their occasion coincides with his nineteenth birthday, the consummation of his relationship with Suzette (a moment of masculinist sexual maturity), and the death of his father. His father has been writing a *History of Pimlico* and is particularly interested in the unhappy conditions of the 1930s, especially for the young. At his death the narrator inherits the manuscript of his father's book, and a sum of money which he splits with his half-brother Vern. The narrator's father represents the knowledge of history and politics, precisely the things which the narrator has chosen to neglect for much of the novel in his attempt to be a postwar 'absolute beginner', making a fresh start. In having his narrator inherit his father's manuscript, MacInnes suggests that any radical movement with youth at its heart requires a political conscience and an historical understanding of the conditions of its own possibility as a protection against the 'happy mindless-ness' that leads to complicity with racism. Importantly, at the novel's close the narrator's idealism is symbolically conjoined to a new, informed knowl-edge of London's social conditions shorn of glib abstractions.

This is powerfully evoked in the novel's closing scene at London airport. The narrator has used his inheritance money to secure a flight to Brazil (and, when this falls through, to Oslo) as he has 'often heard from seamen Spades that they were nice to them up there' (MacInnes 1992: 201). This decision is part of the narrator's inner turmoil when faced by the riots and represents a characteristic attempt to evade reality and live in a place which he merely imagines is devoid of problems. It is as if he has learned nothing and remains to mature. Yet, and crucially, he does not take the flight, and his closing actions hint at the beginnings of a process of political self-consciousness and informed commitment to making concrete his ideal of London's progressive cosmopolitanism. At the airport he watches a plane arrive from Africa through a torrential downpour, from which a number of newcomers disembark:

> they came down grinning and chattering, and they all looked so dam pleased to be in England at the end of their long journey, that I was heartbroken at all the disappointments that were in store for them. And I ran up to them through the water, and shouted out above the engines, 'Welcome to London! Greetings from England! Meet your first teenager! We're all going up to Napoli to have a ball!' And I flung my arms round the first of them, who was a stout old number with a beard and a brief-case and a little bonnet, and they all paused and stared at me in amazement, until the old boy looked me in the face and said to me, 'Greetings!' and he took me by the shoulder, and sud-denly they all burst out laughing in the storm.
>
> (203)

Napoli no longer means what it used to mean for the narrator; but he does not desert either its possibilities or its problems in the novel's closing scene. His embrace is an act of deliberate defiance towards the violence and hos-tility visited upon newcomers in Napoli, one which attempts to keep possible the new relations nurtured in his West London enclave. At this moment, perhaps, he has just become the 'first teenager' – rather than the starry-eyed 'absolute beginner' of the previous 202 pages – in so far as he represents the potent and as-yet-unrealized potential of youthful subversion merging with a politicizing sense of heartbreaking realism attuned to London's racializing 'disappointments'. This is a possibility far more radical and responsible than anything countenanced in *City of Spades*.

The storm that rages in this scene symbolizes the storm of racial violence in Napoli, as well as the stormy welcome which no doubt will await many newcomers in London. Yet, as in *The Lonely Londoners*, the final sound is laughter, the value of which should not be underestimated. It preserves the promise which the narrator invested in Napoli, if not the 'overflowing joys' which MacInnes prized so highly as engendering a new London. But whereas the laughter at the end of Selvon's novel falls 'softly', the laughter which closes *Absolute Beginners* seems almost manic, hinting at the disturbing events of Napoli which represent a kind of insanity. The laughter marks both the possibilities and the problems of Napoli, while the narrator's decision to return there with the African newcomers 'to have a ball' is perhaps his first politically committed act. Resourced by his father's *History of Pimlico* and all that it symbolizes, the novel ends with the narrator at the beginning of a process of commitment and determination. For these reasons, Steven Connor's argument that the narrator 'remains impervious to and untransformed by the telling' (1996: 90) of his tale to the end seems difficult to warrant. I would suggest that the novel closes with a moment of profound transformation for both the narrator and his creator. In his critique of London's youth-cultural scene which is also an exploration of his own convictions, MacInnes maps out the kinds of political challenges which the latest generation of Londoners must meet if they are to bring into existence the optimistic, cosmopolitan city which their cultural life envisions but has yet to inaugurate or make concrete.

For Selvon and MacInnes the burgeoning popular entertainments of London fuelled by postwar migration and which revolved around song and dance suggest different kinds of social blueprints for a new city, one where the popular creative energies they prized offered strategies of both survival and transformation. Lord Kitchener's dance epitomizes a process of spatial creolization in the city as London is rewritten according to the rhythm and score of Trinidadian music. The creative possibilities of this process, found at the heart of postcolonial London writing in the 1950s, must not be forgotten not least because they function as ground-breaking and transformative declarations of tenure – in spite of the racism of landlords and lovers, London is determinedly remapped and revisioned as 'the place for me'. To be sure, these are specifically masculinist visions in which the particular experiences and fortunes of women make little impact, and where women are frequently figured in terms of heterosexual desire as erotic objects. This fact must qualify the progressive character of such work, as well as any enthusiasm we have for it. But we must also not forget that although Selvon and MacInnes were forced to contemplate bleakly the unhappy social relations which structured the lives of African and

Caribbean newcomers in 1950s London, their creative investment in the social possibilities of London's multicultural youth ultimately contradicted the efforts of those who wished to erase such newcomers, and the new London spaces they helped create, from the city entirely.

2 London, England
V. S. Naipaul, Doris Lessing and Janet Frame

Dan Jacobson arrived in London from South Africa in 1954, with ambitions to become a writer. On disembarking at Dover, his first action was to buy copies of *The Times* and *New Statesman*. Years later he remembers feeling

> with gratification, after years of handling only the overseas editions, the thickness of the paper between my fingers; with the same gratification I saw the dateline on the papers to be the actual date, not that of two or three weeks before. So I was in England, truly in England at last.
> (1986: 75)

Being in London afforded him the opportunity to encounter the substance of English life which he had only previously encountered imaginatively through his reading of literature. As the narrator of his novel *The Evidence of Love* (1959) puts it, for many South Africans London existed in 'books; in the pictures that were on the walls of their rooms, their schools, their galleries; in films; on the radio; through the mouths of their teachers and the memories of parents; in the letters of those who preceded them here' (1962: 120). So although Jacobson had never visited before, he arrived in a country and a culture which he had so long revered from afar, and which London promised to deliver. '[T]his city offered me a continuity between past and present, between words and things, which I had hardly known I was seeking until it was offered to me' (1986: 83), he remarks. London, England, civilization, continuity, culture, order – each seemed seamlessly allied with each other, creating an impression of substance conjured vividly in the image of the thick newspaper pages which thrilled and gratified Jacobson at Dover, and which contrasted to the slenderness of the out-of-date overseas editions.

Not long after arriving in London, Jacobson attempted to locate the house in Tavistock Square where Virginia Woolf once lived. From this address she had composed a series of letters to Logan Pearsall Smith, which

Jacobson had read on his journey to England. When he sought out the address he found instead a bomb-site where the house should have been:

> Part of what they [the writers] had meant by Bloomsbury I saw to be these trees and houses, the glimpses above them of some of the buildings of London University, the traffic of Southampton Row. Was there nothing else? With the disappointment that the house should have been scooped out of the square another began to grow. So this was it. I had seen it. True, I had not seen, and thought it unlikely I would ever see, any of the people who had made up the Bloomsbury society; but the physical Bloomsbury was about me. The disappointment was not with its appearance, which was black enough, and severe enough, and imposing enough; it arose from the very fact of my having seen it. The half-conscious, always-unfinished guesswork which had been so inextricably an aspect of my reading, throughout my childhood and adolescence in South Africa, the dreamlike otherness or remoteness in the books I had read, which I had valued more than I had supposed, were being taken from me, bit by bit. Here was one bit of it gone. I would never again be able to visit a Bloomsbury of my own imagination – a district vaguer and therefore more glamorous than the reality; one less hard and angular and self-defining.
>
> (1986: 79)

Rather than affording Jacobson the opportunity to indulge in his imaginative relationship with English culture, the visit robs Bloomsbury of its auratic substance. Tavistock Square is ruinous, voided of its significance, delivering only 'disappointment'. It is a disequilibriating moment, where the alliance of London, England, order and culture comes apart in the derelict and ruined spaces of postwar London. Rather than encountering the substance of English culture in the trees and houses of Bloomsbury, Jacobson discovers its opposite. The disappointing hole in the ground challenges his previous flights of fancy, while the 'hard' and 'angular' character of the concrete environment assaults the insubstantial 'dreamlike otherness' of the London he cherished from afar.

Jacobson's revealing memories of arriving in London stage a particular kind of troublesome encounter with England and English culture which, as we shall see, was by no means uncommon in the 1950s and 1960s. Many budding writers from colonized countries who came to London suffered similarly dislocating experiences. Coming to London was a vital and inevitable part of their attempts to develop their careers. As Gail Low has expertly shown in her account of the publishing of Commonwealth writing in London in the immediate postwar decades, the editors of a number of new publishing houses and literary journals, excited by writing in English from the colonies, were directly responsible for putting into print the work of a variety of up-and-coming writers – with the consequence that London's presence as the centre of English literary publishing and culture was strengthened. Importantly, such writing was considered by several influential editors in London to be the infant additions to the English literary family. 'The insistence on the centrality of English', Low writes, 'seen in the tropic emphasis on English literature's origin, parent or root status, becomes a metaphoric way of containing centrifugal forces in anglophone writing. All innovations must return to and strengthen the parent literary culture. London, of course, retains its centrality in the newly re-configured global cultural map' (2002: 26). Through the publishing of such writing in postwar London both the culture industry and the imperious evaluative criteria of English literature often worked together, buttressing the supremacy of each while tethering the 'infant' texts from non-native writers to the mother country.

For writers such as Jacobson, to live and write in London was not just to participate in the day-to-day activities of the city, but to be at the heart of a wider English cultural milieu which was familiar to millions. In the words of George Lamming, many in the Caribbean, if not throughout the colonized world, were subservient to a myth of England which began 'with the fact of England's supremacy in taste and judgement . . . for all the books they had read, their whole introduction to something called culture, all of it, in the form of words, came from outside: Dickens, Jane Austen, Kipling and that sacred gang' (1960: 27). For some budding writers, a trip to the motherland was a glorious opportunity to indulge in the high cultural reveries associated with the 'sacred gang' of English letters. In his memoir of coming to England from India in 1955, *A Passage to England* (1959), Nirad C. Chaudhuri confessed that his view of England had long been based upon 'an enormous load of book-derived notions . . . acquired from literature, history and geography' (1966: 3–4). Interspersed with loving quotations from English Romantic poets, his reflections are generally celebratory of the perfect balance between man and nature visible in the English countryside, and he seems delighted to confirm at every opportunity his friends' view that he suffers from 'chronic Anglomania' (201).

Yet, as the example of Jacobson proves – and as we shall see in the work of V. S. Naipaul, Doris Lessing and Janet Frame – other writers struggled to discover in London the England of their (literary) dreams. Instead, they encountered a city substantially ruined by the ravages of war and inhabited by a diverse and transitory population with competing and conflicting loyalties to divergent class, cultural and national affiliations. Refugees from Europe, Irish migrants, Commonwealth arrivants, American soldiers, demobbed service personnel, working-class women – these and others made up a heterogeneous urban populace and contributed to making a city that did not necessarily square with received notions of England and English culture perpetuated overseas. For these reasons, many newcomers encountered a city which – in its novelty, confusion and ruined condition – seemed disconcertingly lacking in substance to colonial eyes. But whereas V. S. Naipaul was upset by the transitional, disorderly London he witnessed as a younger man in which imperious notions of Englishness did not hold, Lessing and Frame seized upon London's ruined condition and transitory populace in order to contest notions of national belonging and cultural subservience to 'that sacred gang'. To live and write in London was not just to participate in English high culture; it was also to discover the means to disrupt and change it as part of a liberating and liberalizing postcolonial critique. In writing about London during this period, Naipaul, Lessing and Frame directly, if differently, reassessed their relationship with England and English culture. For each, London came to function imaginatively as a location where received imperious notions of culture are threatened with dissolution. As we shall see first with V. S. Naipaul, the social changes happening in London were by no means always welcome to one reluctant to revise his long-held image of the city as epitomizing the order, culture and civilization of England.

Naipaul arrived in London from Trinidad in 1950, prior to going up to Oxford. He too was disappointed. 'I had come to London as to a place I knew very well', recalls the semi-autobiographical narrator of his novel *The Enigma of Arrival* (1987). 'I found a city that was strange and unknown – in its style of houses, and even in the names of its districts . . . The disturbance in me, faced with this strangeness, was very great' (123). Naipaul's expectations of London were partly derived from the cinema, partly from reading English writers such as Dickens; so coming to London seemed paradoxically like 'entering the world of a novel, a book; entering the real world' (119). Viewed from a distance, that world seemed an image of perfection, 'the centre of things' which underlined the 'wrongness' of Trinidad and accentuated his troubled sense of existing 'far away' (120). But on arriving in London, he found that the city of his imagination was unavailable. 'I came to London', he recalled in *An Area of Darkness* (1964). 'It had become the centre of my world and I had worked hard to come to it. And I was lost. London was not the centre of my world. I had been misled; but there was nowhere else to go' (1968: 42).

Captivated by his cinema-going and reading of Dickens, it is no surprise that postwar London disappointed the young Naipaul. The meagre proportions of his boarding house, the bomb-sites, the empty chocolate vending machines at the Underground stations – each contributed to a sense of the city in decline and, as the narrator of *The Enigma of Arrival* remembers, exposed the erroneous foundations of his youthful fantasies: 'I grew to feel that the grandeur belonged to the past; that I had come to England at the wrong time; that I had come too late to find the England, the heart of empire, which (like a provincial, from a far corner of the empire) I had created in my fantasy' (1987: 120). According to Ian Baucom, this growing feeling of belatedness incubates over a significant length of time – there are almost forty years between Naipaul's moment of arrival and his novelistic account of its enigma – in which the initial sense of London's fraudulence, its existence as 'an imperfect imitation of itself' (1999: 180) that refuses to substantiate the impressions which Naipaul made of it in Trinidad, is transformed paradoxically into a recuperative encounter with loss. For Baucom, this is at the heart of Naipaul's negotiation with Englishness:

> Between the recognition of himself as a man who has been defrauded and the identification of himself as a latecomer, a crucial change has taken place: Naipaul has admitted his need to believe in the imperial fictions of Englishness, even while acknowledging the fantastic quality of those fictions, and has discovered a means of doing so. In the place of an England that survives as its own counterfeit, he will locate an England that fails to exist, not because it never was but because it has been lost. He will find that England in the very fact of his belatedness and in the resonant stones of ruin.
>
> (178)

Naipaul's sense of loss is stimulated by two historical phenomena. First, decolonization in Africa, Asia and the Caribbean, which gathers momentum during the early years of Naipaul's sojourn in London, condemns the Empire to terminal decline and robs the present of the grandeur and order of the past. Its effects can be keenly felt by migrants in the city, which seems to lose its substance as the Empire wanes. In *The Mimic Men* (1967), Ralph Singh considers London as the 'great city, the centre of the world' but finds solidity elusive: 'The factories and warehouses, whose exterior lights decorated the river, were empty and fraudulent . . . [I]n this solid city life was two-dimensional' (1969: 19). The second phenomenon, one which is rarely admitted in Naipaul's writing and which we will consider presently, is the transformation of postwar London by both its immigrant communities and its youth. Rob Nixon has accused Naipaul of quite deliberately failing to contextualize his arrival in London in terms of postwar immigration from the so-called Third World and carefully distancing himself from those new communities and subaltern city spaces subsequently created: 'The habit Naipaul exhibits of dissociating himself from surrounding society and being obsessed by his eccentric status induces him to play down his relation to the wider current of events of cultural mixing in London' (1992: 40).

However, Naipaul's alleged dissociation from surrounding society amounts to something more strategic than 'habit'. It is of a part with the loss he feels of the idealised, imagined London derived from literature and film. In his earliest reflections on the city he emphasized his sense of being continually excluded from the city's substance. London society was not easily penetrated, or comprehended. As he admitted in his 1958 essay 'London', his knowledge of the city, and of England, remained profoundly unsatisfactory despite his four years' residence. Naipaul confessed he held

> only a superficial knowledge of the country, and in order to write fiction it is necessary to know so much. We are not all brothers under the skin. It might have been possible for me, at the end of my first year here, to write about England. First impressions, reinforced by what one reads in the newspapers, are often enough to give an authenticity 'of a crudely naturalistic sort'. But now I feel I can never hope to know as much about people here as I do about Trinidad Indians, people I can place almost as soon as I see them.
>
> (1972: 14–15)

Naipaul's engagement with London often seems spoiled by his inability to penetrate beneath its surfaces and discover the substance of London life. In an early letter to his father dated 11 December 1950, he recalls his childhood Christmases in Trinidad as provoking 'a glorious feeling of fun we felt existed somewhere' (1999: 43), most probably Europe, from which the Naipauls were forever displaced. But in London at Christmas time he unhappily experiences the 'same feeling': 'The shops are bright, the streets are well lit and the streets are full of people. I walk through the streets, yet am so much alone, so much on the outside of this great festive feeling' (43). In his essay 'London' he laments that 'everything goes on behind closed doors' (1972: 14). He has met Londoners 'only in [their] official attitudes' and complains about 'the privacy of the big city' (14). He describes several nights out in London, at the theatre, nightclub and restaurant, which end with him lonely and looking for a bus, haunted by a sense of waste and disappointment. He concludes his essay by recording the barrenness of his life in the city and the impact it might have on his imaginative faculties: 'Unless I am able to refresh myself by travel – to Trinidad, to India – I fear that living here will eventually lead to my own sterility; and I may have to look for another job' (16).

Naipaul did indeed 'refresh' himself through travel: he visited a number of Caribbean and South American countries in 1961 which he wrote about in *The Middle Passage* (1962), and immediately afterwards spent a year in India. One of the products of Naipaul's Indian journey was his only novel set exclusively in England, *Mr Stone and the Knights Companion* (1963), which he wrote while staying at the Liward Hotel in Srinigar. In the novel the anxieties which arise from Naipaul's sense of being defrauded by and displaced from London's substance are decanted into the curious figure of Mr Stone, the sixty-three-year-old, unspectacular English central character who attempts to arrest his sense of decline, old age and belatedness by investing in a flight of fancy. In his depiction of Mr Stone and London, Naipaul registers his self-consciously peripheral engagement with the English in which images connected to weight play a significant role. Additionally, in presenting Mr Stone's unhappy fortunes in the novel as an index of the impossibility of recuperating a reassuring model of imperious and patriarchal English society and culture in contemporary London, Naipaul subtly makes London's youth and immigrant population culpable in the destruction of the England for which he yearned from afar.

In looking to London from 1960s India, and on the other side of an experience of living in the city, Naipaul no longer regarded it as an image of 'the perfect world'. It is interesting that *An Area of Darkness* concludes with him recounting a dream he experienced not long after his return to London from India in which he imagines a stiff piece of cloth that unravels with surreal consequences: 'the unravelling would spread from the cloth to the table to the house to all matter, *until the whole trick was undone*' (1968: 266). An analogous sense of London as a 'trick', the substantiality of which comes apart, also pervades *Mr Stone and the Knights Companion*. As Landeg White has argued, the novel marks the beginning of a process, also discernible in the story 'A Flag on the Island' (1967), by which Naipaul comes to qualify the closing sentiment of *A House for Mr Biswas* (1961) 'that England by contrast [to Trinidad] is a coherent place where everyone is born to a position and an identity' (1975: 127–8). A qualification, to be sure, but not a negation: in much of Naipaul's subsequent writing London is suspended between a dream of perfection and a knowledge of its fraudulence as the centre of the 'perfect world'. For example, Indar, an Indian-descended East African character in Naipaul's novel *A Bend in the River* (1979), recalls a moment of revelation while walking on the Embankment by the River Thames, when he first discovered that the lamp standards and pavement benches were decorated with dolphins and camels: 'I stopped, stepped back mentally, as it were, and all at once saw the beauty in which I had been walking – the beauty of the river and the sky, the soft colours of the clouds, the beauty of light on water, the beauty of the buildings, the care with which it had all been arranged . . . For someone like me there was only one civilization and one place – London, or a place like it' (1980: 157). Civilization, understood as a care for order, is expressed on the Embankment in the artistic patterning of space where nature and the built environment harmoniously blend into an inspiring spectacle. The dolphins and camels depicted on the lamps and benches establish London as at the heart of colonial conquest over both land and sea, the standard against which colonial locations (such as the novel's predominant setting at a bend in an African river) will always be measured. London, England, civilization: Naipaul's writing frequently calls attention to his characters' collusion in what is ultimately a colonial chimera. And although several novels written after *Mr Stone and the Knights Companion* brutally depict London's failure to live up to its promise – consider again Ralph Singh's unhappy experience of London in *The Mimic Men* – its existence as a trope of civilization is never fully ironized.

In *Mr Stone and the Knights Companion*, Naipaul's assumption of England's order and perfection encapsulated by London – 'this perfect world' – is both acknowledged and unravelled. London promises to be the location of England's recuperation but ends up acting as its site of disassembly. There is the unhappy recognition born from experience of the fraudulence and disorderliness of London. But there is also the indulgence – gently but not fully ironized – of the myth of the city's grandeur which is associated with the recent past of Empire. As we shall see, the novel's ambivalent response is best detected in the figure of Mr Stone, whose characterization, torn between substance and superficiality, reflects Naipaul's contrasting impulses to indulge in imperious myths of England while unhappily registering their deceit and decline.

Mr Stone and the Knights Companion is the story of its central character's attempt to bring to life a fantasy. Mr Stone works as chief librarian of Excal and is fast approaching retirement. In the autumn of his life, he becomes haunted by distressing sensations of insubstantiality. He senses that the enduring regularity and orderliness of 'all the motions of human existence' (Naipaul 1988: 42) in which he has invested so much comfort are ultimately fragile. This is expressed early in the novel in a fascinating and curious vision of London unravelled, its concrete surfaces undone:

> [Mr Stone] was assailed by a vision of the city stripped of stone and concrete and timber and metal, stripped of all buildings, with people suspended next to and above and below one another, going through all the motions of human existence. And he had a realisation, too upsetting to be more than momentarily examined, that all that was solid

and immutable and enduring about the world, all to which man linked himself . . . flattered only to deceive.

(42)

This 'upsetting' vision of London is part of Mr Stone's mounting obsession with age, decay and corruption. As a response to these increasing feelings of mutability and weightlessness, he devises a plan which will guarantee purpose for those like himself who consider their lives to be entering a period of decline. According to the plan, retired Excal employees (known as Knights Companion – the name is coined by Mr Stone's enthusiastic assistant Whymper) visit the pensioners of clients with a small gift from the firm. For Mr Stone, such noble endeavours rescue the old men from inactivity by giving them renewed comradeship and a sense of significance; for Excal, it is an exercise in public relations and a way of ensuring loyalty to the company that is enthusiastically endorsed by its head, Sir Harry.

The fantasy of the Knights Companion scheme comes to Mr Stone suitably at night, while he is away from London on holiday with his wife in Cornwall, and is brought into the city from afar. The description of Mr Stone contemplating his plan on the way back to London seems especially resonant when one recalls Naipaul's disappointment with his arrival in the city: 'All the way to London [Mr Stone] turned it over in his mind, adding nothing, experiencing only the anxious joy of someone who fears that his creation may yet in some way elude him' (57). Not surprisingly, then, the process of making concrete Mr Stone's fantasy serves ultimately to corrupt it: dream and reality do not readily synchronize. One Knights Companion uses the scheme as an excuse to embark on an expensive tour of Wales at Excal's expense; another exploits his visits to propagate the creed of Jehovah's Witnesses; a third claims expenses from Excal without visiting his allocated pensioners. Mr Stone's colleague, Whymper, exploits his role in the scheme's development to improve the quality of his professional and personal lives. Through his contact with Mr Stone he becomes engaged to Mr Stone's niece, Gwen, after she becomes pregnant, and he eventually secures a lucrative job as a publicity director at a rival firm having been solely credited with the creation and success of the Knights Companion scheme. The novel ends with Mr Stone learning this news before leaving his office to wander home through the chaos of the transport strike which disorganizes London, leaving 'the Embankment choked with unmoving cars and buses' (124), the 'hopeless queues' (124), the 'crowds of black and white' (125) through which Mr Stone wanders. His dream has been betrayed and a painful lesson learned: 'Nothing that came out of the heart, nothing that was pure ought to be exposed' (118).

In the creation of Mr Stone and his attempt to realise his vision, Naipaul confronts his conflicting perceptions of London: the fantasy of reassuring metropolitan purpose when seen from afar, and its betrayal both in and by the postwar city. London's purposefulness is suggested by investing illusion with weight, much as Dickens's fictional London came to acquire a certain solidity as representing the grand 'heart' of the Empire, for Naipaul in Trinidad. Mr Stone's name suggests bulk: of the physicality of stone (which is, as we have seen, envisioned as part of London's solidity alongside concrete, timber and metal), and of the grandeur of legend. Stone's surname joins a variety of references to the story of King Arthur and the Knights of the Round Table which include the names of his niece Gwen and his employer Excal (Batt 1999). He is a weighty figure, a 'big man, well-made', in his sixties yet seeming 'older than he was' (Naipaul 1988: 16). The orderliness of Mr Stone's life both is supported by and contributes to the stability of London. As John Thieme has argued, 'Naipaul primarily characterizes Mr Stone in terms of his obsession with order' (1987: 98) established through his habits – Mr Stone shaves the right side of his face first, buys two evening newspapers to read after dinner, and eats the same food 'as punctiliously as if it had been ordered by a trusted doctor' (Naipaul 1988: 16). He manages space with the same punctiliousness. Whereas the image of the house in A House For Mr Biswas is frequently used to convey the disorder, transience and haphazardness of Trinidad, Mr Stone's house is a much more substantial affair, a regulated space which happily records a long history of occupancy. The permanence of habitation is hallowed with age. Mr Stone takes pleasure 'in the slow decay of his own house, the time-created shabbiness of its interiors, the hard polish of old grime on the lower areas of the hall wallpaper, feeling it right that objects like houses should age with their owners and carry marks of their habitation' (18). Hence he derides his neighbour, 'The Male', a 'do it yourself' enthusiast who makes 'never-ending improvements to his nest' (36). Mr Stone's sister, Olive, has moved 'from Balham to Brixton to Croydon to Sutton to Banstead, each move taking her farther out of the city' owing to her fear of burglars: so 'her houses had an unfinished look, which Mr Stone could not help contrasting with the appearance of his own' (22). This peripatetic relationship with accommodation – changing houses, or perpetually altering the house – is anathema to Mr Stone's seemingly static, even, solid existence.

Mr Stone's regulated, stable life already seems anachronistic within the novel's 1960s setting, and he deliberately indulges in the myths of the past when he senses his orderly existence is being corrupted by the unsettling passage of time. His marriage to Mrs Springer – itself part of Mr Stone's attempt to address his 'upsetting' feelings of insubstantiality – affords him the opportunity to resurrect the trappings of yesteryear. On several occasions Mrs Springer is connected to the bygone world of colonial late-

Victorian society in India. When she moves into Mr Stone's house she brings with her 'a new and alien mustiness' (33) and a variety of posses- sions which speak of a past time, upon which their maid Miss Millington falls 'with a delight as of one rediscovering glories thought dead and gone' (33). One significant object is

> a tigerskin, which came out of store in excellent condition and which Margaret explained by producing a framed sepia photograph of a dead tiger on whose chest lay the highly polished boot of an English cavalry officer, moustached, sitting bolt upright in a heavy wooden armchair (brought from goodness knows where), fighting back a smile, one hand caressing a rifle laid neatly across his thighs, with three sorrow- ful, top-heavily turbanned Indians, beaters or bearers or whatever they were, behind him.
>
> (33)

In this colonial vision of English supremacy, the male sits triumphantly amongst the evidence of foreign conquest: of a dangerous landscape, as sug- gested by the tiger and the gun, and of a mysterious people, figured by the servile Indians whose ultimate purpose remains unknown. As the novel proceeds, Mr Stone's house comes increasingly to parody those of the British in India. Whereas Miss Millington was inefficient and decrepit, she now comes to be a precious part of the illusion, with her maid's uniform and habit of ringing a large gong in the hall to summon the Stones to dinner.

Mr Stone's attempt to fashion himself and his domestic environment through habit, and by mimicking a stylized depiction of the English in India, indexes one of Naipaul's impulses on being faced with the dis- appointment of living in London: the desire to indulge in relics from the past, reflected in Mr Stone's Arthurian name, in which substantial order is reiterated as a salve to the vicissitudes and fraudulence of the present. Mr Stone wants a clearly defined, predictable, authoritarian and weighty exis- tence and habitat which will safeguard him from the novelties of time and the feelings of belatedness.

Yet a contrary impulse is also registered in the characterization of Mr Stone, namely the revelation of that sense of fraudulence which has made such indulgence necessary. Naipaul never lets his reader forget the poten- tial hollowness of Mr Stone's seemingly weighty existence. He may appear to personify the solidity and order promised by London, but he is also a curiously weightless creation, an aggregate of insubstantial surfaces. One telling incident occurs early in the novel, when Mr Stone is shocked to see a young, apparently deformed boy standing on the library steps with 'fangs instead of teeth' (21):

Seconds later [Mr Stone] passed the well-known shop, its windows lighted and streaming. He stopped, breathed deeply, a theatrical gesture, and closed his eyes.

An old man, neat with overcoat, briefcase and hat, standing before the window of the joke-shop, seeming to smile at the imitation glasses of Guinness, the plastic faeces, the masks, the rubber spiders, the joke teeth.

(21)

The joke teeth and imitation glasses of Guinness mirror aspects of Mr Stone's own physical presence and daily routine: he too wears false teeth and each lunchtime drinks Guinness at a local pub. He is also a figure of levity. Indeed, the streaming window which seems to divide Mr Stone from the inauthentic objects on display might as well not exist. The overcoat, briefcase and hat, along with the Guinness and joke teeth, constitute the 'theatrical gesture' that *is* Mr Stone. Just as he comes to realize that the boy's fangs are an illusion, so are we invited to contemplate the plasticity of Mr Stone's characterization which undercuts his apparent 'weighty' substance with the joke-shop's flippancy. Hence, in seeking to avoid mistaking the superficial appearance of life in London for its substance, Naipaul creates a character caught between weightiness and inauthenticity. Like Mr Stone's 'upsetting' vision of a London stripped of stone, concrete, timber and metal, his immutability as a character flatters 'only to deceive'. Naipaul knows that the order and coherency epitomized by Mr Stone and his native city are no more substantial than the troubling image of the boy with the fake teeth. At this moment Naipaul's sense of being displaced from the English and defrauded by their appearance is perhaps most poignantly marked.

On more than one occasion Mr Stone indulges in fantasies of defying gravity: 'he flew from pavement to pavement over people and cars and buses (the people flown over looking up in wonder while he floated serenely past, indifferent to their stupefaction)' (8). The 'upsetting' vision of Mr Stone being suspended above the streets of London or flying over its inhabitants creates a recurring trope – central to the fantasy of London as epitomizing order and substance – of the refined individual life elevated from the haphazard, stupefied crowd. As I have suggested, Mr Stone's domestic transformation attempts to cement a particular colonial fantasy of Englishness – orderly, authoritative, immutable, patriarchal – which guarantees continuity between England's past and its present, its colonial possessions overseas and its metropolitan heart. But it is defeated in the novel's closing stages by new forces incubating in the postwar city which are epitomized by the crowd. London's crowds appear as the physical manifestation of the city's betrayal of the promise of English order. Part of Mr Stone's irritation with Christmas concerns the conditions it creates in London: the streets become 'impossible' (19), and the pub in which he has his daily lunchtime glass of Guinness is 'unbearably hot and overcrowded', full of a 'boisterous, beery crowd' (20). On several occasions in the novel similar disruptive spaces are glimpsed which threaten the neatness of Mr Stone's version of the city with the chaos and threat of the crowd. Consider the description of his journey to Mrs Springer's flat, 'a refuge of respectability and calm' (26):

> Mrs Springer lived in Earl's Court. A disreputable, over-crowded area Mr Stone had always thought it, and he thought no better of it now. The entrance to the Underground station was filthy; in a street across the road a meeting of the British National Party was in progress, a man shouting himself hoarse from the back of a van. Behind neon lights and streaming glass windows the new-style coffee houses were packed; and the streets were full of young people in art-student dress and foreigners of every colour.
>
> (26)

If the photograph of the cavalry officer, Indians and the dead tiger which Mrs Springer brings to Mr Stone's house represents a certain kind of colonial order, this depiction of the crowded, disorderly space of Earl's Court featuring 'foreigners of every colour' articulates the shattered colonial fantasy of decorum and the disturbing muddle of contemporary, cosmopolitan London – where the certainties of English place are challenged by the spontaneous and contingent transformations of subaltern renegotiations of space. The meeting of the British National Party and the youthful crowd 'packed' into the new-style coffee houses are contradictory aspects of essentially the same urban reality: a dangerous environment, chaotic and haphazard. In Naipaul's postcolonial London, the city and Englishness are worryingly at odds.

This dangerous enclave is distinctly Whymper's world. Just as Mr Stone's surname carries with it a significant literary resonance, there are apocalyptic overtones attached to Whymper's name which recalls the climax of T. S. Eliot's 'The Hollow Men' (1925). Employed to help Mr Stone realize his vision of the Knights Companion scheme, Whymper is quite carefully defined as 'a Londoner . . . a man without a family, someone who belonged only to the city' (86). Whymper's Englishness is also subtly questioned. Whereas Mr Stone carries a general dislike of foreignness, acquired during an unpleasant visit to France, Whymper's inconstant attitudes are wittily suggested when he invites the Stones to dinner and serves them (much to their disgust) a meal which features cold beef, raw garlic, olive oil and black bread washed down with retsina and Turkish coffee. Is Whymper descended from postwar refugees from Europe? Yet such cosmopolitan tastes are not matched by a liberal attitude to race: on one occasion while walking with Whymper in Central London Mr Stone notes that the sight of 'black men on the London streets drove [Whymper] to fury' (90).

Whymper's foreignness and illiberalism make him Naipaul's representative figure of the filthy, crowded, predominantly youthful London made up by those 'of every colour' which Naipaul regards as a significant threat to the city's bygone grandeur, the respectability and calm signified by Mrs Springer's abode. Although Naipaul hardly takes us into this London (the realm of Selvon and MacInnes, of course) it lurks menacingly at the margins of the novel as an affront to the orderliness of Mr Stone's weighty English existence hallowed by the trappings of age. Just as Whymper effectively gazumps Mr Stone in taking credit for the Knights Companion scheme for ambitious ends, so too does this dangerous, multicultural, overcrowded version of London seem to be displacing the colonial fantasy of England by the novel's conclusion. Indeed, in the final chapter Mr Stone leaves his office to wander amongst the chaos of the transport strike only minutes after learning that Whymper has taken the credit for the Knights Companion scheme. The chaotic city wins out over the orderly one, just as Whymper's exploitation corrupts the creative purity of Mr Stone's idea. In a journey which signifies the end of the reassuring fantasies associated with England, Mr Stone walks away from the 'warm, bright heart' of London through 'long, dull streets' (125) to his prosaic fate: a lonely man in an empty house. He no longer has a place in London. The result is social and psychological breakdown: the Embankment is 'choked' by the strike; Londoners stand in 'hopeless queues and fought to get seats in buses' (124). As Mr Stone walks away the vision of the city 'stripped . . . of all that was enduring' (125) returns to him. His attempt to keep insubstantiality at bay has failed. At the end of the novel Central London resembles the 'disreputable' enclave of Earl's Court, its streets overcrowded and chaotic. England seems elsewhere, lost and irrecoverable.

In charting the failure of Mr Stone's fantasy there remains more than a trace of Naipaul's youthful longing for the 'warm, bright heart' of London, and for the 'purity' of the ideals which, when seen from a distance, it seemed to promise. The novel affords Naipaul the opportunity to mark mournfully the passing of the England which Mr Stone represents – orderly, colonial, weighty. Paradoxically, for Naipaul it is a constructive act, one which facilitates the beginnings of a long process of reconcilement with change. To borrow the terms of Ian Baucom's reading of *The Enigma of Arrival*, Mr Stone's fate at the end of the novel as an anachronism is perhaps Naipaul's first and uncertain attempt to engage with Englishness as a form of belatedness, a lost order. In *The Enigma of Arrival* the predominant figure for a lost England is the ruin; Baucom points out how that book is full of passages where Naipaul dwells upon the ruinous structures he sees all around him in Salisbury. This is how Naipaul acknowledges 'the imperial past inevitably tending towards its diminishment and ruin and sees perfection in that moment of ruin, in that moment of postimperial arrival' (1999: 182). The ruin enables Naipaul to become reconciled to the process of imperial decline, the existence of which is proved by its passing: it accommodates the imperial past 'by signalling that past's terminus, by marking, in falling stones, its boundary. It is because the ruin of country-house England marks the closure of a narrative of British imperialism that the ruin, as the final page of a national epic, signifies perfection. It closes the book. It is the final utterance in an imperial discourse of cultural belonging' (183). Although *Mr Stone and the Knights Companion* does not offer the recuperative sense of irrevocability and perfection which Baucom suggests is the marrow of *The Enigma of Arrival*, the themes of diminishment and ruin are clearly articulated in Mr Stone's fortunes. Most curious of all is the final paragraph which depicts Mr Stone patiently waiting for Margaret to arrive home. 'He was no destroyer' (Naipaul 1988: 126), writes Naipaul. 'Once before the world had collapsed about him. But he had survived. And he had no doubt that in time calm would come to him again' (125). There is, of course, a name for things which both collapse and survive. Although Mr Stone, and Naipaul behind him, cannot succeed in shoring up an imperious England from the vicissitudes of postwar change made all too visible in London, in Mr Stone's survival as an anachronism of a collapsed world there are perhaps the seeds of a process of expiation which would only be realized years later in *The Enigma of Arrival*. To put it bluntly: Mr Stone is Naipaul's first English ruin.

Arriving not long before Naipaul, Doris Lessing took up residence in London in 1949, staying first in Bayswater before moving to Denbigh Road, W11, in Notting Hill. She arrived from Rhodesia, via South Africa, full of the ambition to be a writer. Amongst her belongings was the manuscript of her first novel *The Grass is Singing* (1950) which she soon placed with the publisher Michael Joseph. In the second volume of her autobiography *Walking in the Shade* (1997) Lessing recalls her thoughts while looking expectantly at London's Dockland as she stood with her son on the deck of the ship that brought them from South Africa: 'real London was still ahead, like the beginning of my real life, which would have happened years before if the war hadn't stopped me coming to London. A clean slate, a new page – everything still to come' (3). But what was to come at first unsettled Lessing and upset the fantasy of 'real life' she associated with the capital. She remembers looking at London during her first weeks in the city through child-like eyes, and with 'the grotesque vision of Dickens, on the verge of the surreal' (4). 'Real London' turned out to be an anticlimax, a ruined and decrepit city which disturbed and disappointed her:

> It was unpainted, buildings were stained and cracked and dull and grey; it was war-damaged, some areas all ruins, under them holes full of dirty water, once cellars, and it was subject to sudden dark fogs – that was before the Clean Air Act . . . No cafés. No good restaurants. Clothes were still 'austerity' from the war, dismal and ugly. Everyone was indoors by ten, and the streets were empty.
>
> (4–5)

Lessing's desire for cleanliness and newness seemed thwarted in London, while 'what was to come' was held back by the damage of war which remained in the austere and empty surroundings.

A few months later, in the summer of 1950, and with her novel accepted for publication, Lessing moved to Church Street, Kensington. A decade later she returned imaginatively to her sojourn in Denbigh Road and her initial mixed impressions of London in a work of non-fiction, *In Pursuit of the English* (1960). Subtitled 'A Documentary', the book describes the narrator's passage to London and initial lodging with a memorable working-class English family in ramshackle conditions. 'I arrived in England exhausted' (Lessing 1993: 28), the narrator, 'Doris', records. 'The white cliffs of Dover depressed me. They were too small. The Isle of Dogs discouraged me. The Thames looked ugly. I had better confess at once that for the whole of the first year, London seemed to me a city of such appalling ugliness that I wanted only to leave it' (28). With her son she takes up occupancy of a room in a lodging house owned by a married couple, Flo and Dan. Also resident are their daughter Aurora; Jack, Flo's son from a previous marriage; Mr and Mrs Skeffington (and their child) whose frequent rows are clearly heard throughout the house; a cantankerous aged couple whom Flo and Dan are desperate to evict; and Rose, engaged to Dan's brother, Dickie, who becomes a major influence upon Doris. The fortunes of the tenants, much more so than the experiences of the narrator, constitute the primary preoccupation of the text. Doris portrays the household's attitudes, language, domestic rituals, fights, love-affairs and – in one memorable comic scene – a court case in which Flo and Dan attempt to oust the two aged and seemingly unruly tenants. Her narrative ends on the eve of her departure from the house.

As Louise Yelin has argued, *In Pursuit of the English* draws upon a tradition of British documentary writing about the changing conditions of working-class life which includes George Orwell's *Down and Out in Paris and London* (1933) and *The Road to Wigan Pier* (1937) (Yelin 1998). It was also published at a time when several significant social documentaries concerned with immigrant life in London were being written and which testify to a variety of ideological positions – such as Ruth Glass's *Newcomers* (1960), Sheila Patterson's *Dark Strangers* (1965) and Elspeth Huxley's *Back Street New Worlds* (1964) – yet Lessing does not obviously deal with the issues raised by these texts. The changes wrought by immigration on working-class London became topical in the 1960s; yet, in Yelin's view, *In Pursuit of the English* largely ignores the history of race and immigration which was making London a dangerous place of arrival specifically for New Commonwealth immigrants in 1949 and which dominated debates about British citizenship and national identity throughout the 1950s. As we shall see, this is not strictly true: the text marks these arrivals and debates in a number of small but telling references, while Lessing's reasons for writing the book may have been influenced by the increasingly racially conflicted environment of 1950s London. But Yelin is correct to point out that *In Pursuit of the English* is not first and foremost a record of immigrant London. Nor is it overtly a newcomer's documentary of London: the narrator's impressions of the city are few and far between, deemed of lesser importance than the day-to-day tribulations of the English household which dominates the narrative. Despite this, I want to suggest that Lessing's documentary is centrally if subtly focused upon issues of English national identity and belonging, and offers reserved yet firm disapproval of the increasingly racialized rhetoric of the postwar years. In a similar fashion to Naipaul, Lessing represents London as a transitional location in which dominant models of national identity are being challenged by emergent alternatives that are by no means desirable. But in contrast she turns to London's ruins and urban dereliction not as signs of a lost and better English life, but as images which figure the potential for challenging exclusionary models of English identity, old and new. Although she might recall London's war-damaged buildings over forty years later as dull and dispiriting, in *In Pursuit of the English* they are linked to Lessing's desire for 'a clean slate, a new page' – for her, the city, and ultimately the nation to which she had migrated.

One of most striking features of *In Pursuit of the English* is its highly tenuous claim on the genre of documentary. In her autobiography Lessing describes the book as 'more like a novel; it has the shape and pace of one' (1997: 4). Oddly for a documentary, *In Pursuit of the English* refuses to specify the West London environment in which it is set, or give much detail of Doris's journeys through the city. No street names are recorded, few areas of London are clearly identified. This is one way in which Lessing reproduces

for the reader her disorientation and confusion of arriving in London: early
in the text Doris is confounded in her attempts to secure accommodation
by looking for a street which 'was not in my guidebook' (Lessing 1993: 34).
London appears as an indistinguishable maze: 'To my right and left stretched
that street which seemed exactly like all the main streets in London, the
same names recurring at regular intervals, the same patterns of brick and
plaster' (41). (The potentially disorientating anonymity of Lessing's depiction of London is suggested by the blurb on the reverse of the current UK
paperback edition which assumes that the book is set in the East End.)
London is a 'terrible, frightening city' (94), and Doris's disconcerted state
of mind is expressed, as it is for Naipaul's Mr Stone, as a vertiginous sense
of weightlessness:

> Sometimes I put my ear to the wall and heard how, as the trains went
> past and the buses rocked their weight along the street, shock after
> shock came up through brick and plaster, so that the solid wall had the
> fluidity of dancing atoms, and I felt the house, the street, the pave-
> ment, and all the miles and miles of houses and streets as a pattern of
> magical balances, a weightless structure, as if this city hung on water,
> or on sound.
>
> (78)

The 'shock' of London renders its reassuring solidity as precarious, fragile,
dangerous. Doris's response is interesting: she copies the strategies of survival used by her friend and co-tenant Rose. This is reflected in the form
and focus of the narrative, and explains the curiously anonymous and
claustrophobic depiction of London which results. Doris records that Rose's
London constitutes only 'the half-mile of streets where she had been born
and brought up, populated by people she trusted; the house where she now
lived, surrounded by *them* – mostly hostile people; and the West End' (94).
It amounts to 'a sort of tunnel, shored against danger by habit, known
buildings, and trusted people' (94). Similarly, Doris's London is constructed
through a kind of protective tunnel-vision. There are brief glimpses of the
bright lights and monumental attractions of Central London – a walk up
Regent Street with Rose, watching dusk fall while standing on the steps of
the National Gallery in Trafalgar Square with Miss Privet – but rarely does
the narrative dwell outside of the small, anonymous environment of Flo
and Dan's house. And although Yelin notes with perspicuity Lessing's
latent indebtedness to English writers such as Anthony Trollope and
George Eliot in her representation of English life – especially the ironic use
of the boarding house as an image of the nation – arguably the day-to-day
tactics of living in, surviving and cognitively mapping London as practised

by the working-class characters, especially Rose, primarily dictate the shape and focus of the narrative. If Lessing engages with English literary culture, she does so ironically and by refracting it through the experiences of working-class London life. This gives us a clue as to Lessing's disjunctive relationship with England and English culture which her representation of London also surreptitiously establishes.

A working-class Londoner who has hardly strayed from the streets where she was born, Rose is the central figure in Lessing's attempt to interrogate exclusionary definitions of the English. Through the character of Rose, dominant models of English identity collide with the disruptive, ruinous and resistant energies of London – an important conflict between city and nation is played out in her words and actions. Her name, of course, recalls a familiar cliché of English pastoral, yet her urban existence immediately renders ironic her potential role as an allegorical figure of the nation. She is a remarkably inconsistent and contradictory figure who struggles throughout the book when contemplating notions of cultural, racial and national difference. On several occasions Rose becomes muddled when pressed by Doris to account for those who can legitimately lay claim to be considered 'properly' English, and in her responses we can perceive received notions of English national identity conflicting with urban tactics of accommodating otherness. Her description of Flo while in conversation with Doris is one such occasion of confusion:

'. . . And not everyone's like Flo – I don't want you to be thinking that.' She added guiltily – 'It's because she's a foreigner, it's not her fault.'

'What kind of a foreigner?'

'I'm not saying anything against her; don't think it. She's English really. She was born here. But her grandmother was Italian, see? She comes from a restaurant family. So she behaves different. And then the trouble is, Dan, isn't a good influence – not that I'm saying a word against him.'

'Isn't he English?'

'Not really, he's from Newcastle. They're different from us, up in places like that. Oh no, he's not English, not *properly speaking.*'

'And you?'

She was confused at once. 'Me, dear? But I've lived in London all my life. Oh, I see what you mean – I wouldn't say I was English so much as a Londoner, see? It's different'.

'I see,' I said.

(56–7 – emphasis added)

In Rose's perplexity a number of different models of English identity collide, none of which is granted precedence. Flo's alleged foreign identity is built upon a myth of 'Italian blood' (64) that explains her behaviour and complicates the legitimacy of her claim to be English based upon her place of birth. The claim that Flo is 'English really' does not fully neutralize the foreignness of Flo's 'blood', which can be appropriated to explain her unconventionality. Here two conflicting models of national identity sit uncomfortably together: the first derived from one's place of birth (*jus soli*), the second predicated upon lineage and racializing notions of inheritance and blood-lines (*jus sanguinus*) – and the shift from the former to the latter will come to dominate British notions of national identity in subsequent decades (Cohen 1994; Baucom 1999). Dan's affiliations to Newcastle introduce further complications: differences between North and South England, and the capital and the provinces. But as a Londoner Rose is no more English than the provincial Dan, and the categories of Londoner and English do not tally. Later Rose adds another difference between city and country when she speaks of the conventional pastoral vision of the nation: 'When I talk of English, what I mean is, my grandad and my grandma. That's English. The country. They were quite different from us – I mean my mother and me' (106). As with Naipaul, a coherent sense of the English is surrendered to the past. According to Rose, then, no one qualifies as English, 'properly speaking'. The only category that can accommodate the comings and goings of the household is 'Londoner' – but Rose knows that this term is too inclusive and unstable to offer anything solid. In London differences are tolerated to a degree, but not eradicated; and significantly none of the characters we meet in the book is legitimately English. In journeying to London in pursuit of the English, Doris has come to the wrong place. London and Londoners do not square with England and the English.

Yet, it is precisely the untidy inclusiveness of 'Londoner' which Lessing comes to value. If Rose's 'tunnelling' strategy of surviving in London influences Lessing's anonymous and selective representation of the city which barely reaches beyond the enclave of Doris's lodgings, her inability to define the English satisfactorily amidst the diversity of the city thwarts the divisive rhetoric of native and foreigner, no matter how keen Rose might be to cling to it. As Lessing would have it, at the moment of the book's setting (1949–50) one cannot find in London a clear or dominant way of defining the English which might resolve Rose's confusion. I would hazard that, on reflecting upon this experience ten years later, Lessing seizes upon London's capacity to interfere with notions of national identity as she is concerned about the increasingly divisive and inflammatory role of race in the 1950s.

In *In Pursuit of the English*, new versions of older racist attitudes are seen to be forming, ones which would ultimately influence the violence of the late 1950s as in the Notting Hill riots. Lessing is careful to record racist representations of black newcomers in London, considered to be 'taking the bread out of our mouths' (212) by a white builder who mends Doris's war-damaged room. These function in a similar fashion to previous discriminatory attitudes to London's Jews as threatening foreign outsiders. The old lady whom Flo and Dan successfully evict pours scorn upon the court's proceedings with the words 'Lies! Lies! Lies! Justice, British justice, it's all Jews and foreigners, it's a plot, it's a conspiracy' (185). Significantly, Rose is complicit in and comfortable with racism and is described as anti-Semitic 'in a tired tolerant sort of way'; she can, when provoked, talk 'like a minor Goebbels' (137). Black newcomers in London appear to be assigned a position previously occupied primarily by Jews in a racializing narrative of national identity. 'We're not having blacks' (39), declares one prospective landlady to Doris. 'We don't take Jews either. Not that that's any protection' (38). The shifts that are occurring within ways of regarding those deemed racially different can be gauged by considering Dan's wartime anecdote of rescuing a sailor from drowning in the Thames: 'he was a Lascar . . . a black man if you like, but he was human, and I could have died' (173). The dignifying category of 'human' seems much less readily assigned to black newcomers in postwar London – ironically, Dan has become a slum landlord in Notting Hill by the close of the book.

Rose's racism, along with that of others, suggests the ways in which definitions of the English are being pursued after the war through the vocabulary of race that has shifted its primary focus to newcomers from New Commonwealth countries. And although such definitions might enable Doris paradoxically to join the ranks of the English as a white woman, Lessing's experiences of, and opposition to, racial discrimination in Rhodesia and South Africa make her very wary indeed of England's postwar racializing turn. In writing about the transitory condition of London in 1949–50, on the one hand Lessing quietly charts the early stages of a chilling racializing manoeuvre in postwar narratives of national belonging; while on the other hand she attempts to recover something of the muddled inclusiveness discovered in Rose's articulation of 'Londoner' precisely as a rejoinder to racism. Indeed, aspects of *In Pursuit of the English* seem deliberately designed to provoke and promote London's muddle, especially as regards identity. In contrast to Yelin, who argues that the book 'occludes an ongoing cultural and social debate' (1998: 61) about race at the time it was published, I would suggest that Lessing's portrayal of London during a period of instability and transition can be read as a guarded *response* to the ossification of the categories of white native and black foreigner effected in the 1950s.

The unstable and various identities of Lessing's Londoners are matched by the atmosphere of the city in its ruins and dereliction which capture something of the haphazardness and muddle which she values. Indeed, describing the war-damaged buildings, Lessing draws upon notions of reconstruction which reach far beyond the built environment. London's ruins, like its muddled Londoners, suggest exactly the kind of space where new inclusive ways of conceiving of identity might be built in which the relationship between so-called native and foreigner is recalibrated. The London landscape of *In Pursuit of the English* is figurative of the book's advocacy of the possibility of confusion and transience. Early in the text Rose and Doris walk past a 'couple of acres of rubble' (Lessing 1993: 47) created by wartime bombing:

> It was as if the houses had shaken themselves to the ground. Thin shells of wall stood brokenly among debris; and from this desolation I heard a sound which reminded me of a cricket chirping with quiet persistence from sun-warmed grasses in the veld. It was a typewriter; and peering over a bricky gulf I saw a man in his shirt-sleeves, which were held neatly above the elbow by expanding bands, sitting on a tidy pile of rubble, the typewriter on a broken girder, clean white paper fluttering from the rim of the machine.
>
> 'Who's he?' I asked.
>
> 'An optimist', said Rose grimly. 'Thinks he's going to be rebuilt, I shouldn't be surprised. Well, it takes all sorts, that's what I say.'
>
> (47)

Like the 'weightless structure' of London which Doris imagines early in the book, this scene importantly articulates a vision of the city as insubstantial and disassembled, flimsy and precarious. The image of the typist writing amongst ruins particularly emphasizes London as a space, and at a moment, of vital re-creation and reinscription. The debris which contributed to Lessing's (and Naipaul's) initial disappointment with postwar London as dismal and ugly is transfigured in this passage into an optimistic symbol of creativity and opportunity. The clean white paper which flutters from the rim of the typewriter recalls the hopes Lessing attached to London ('a clean slate, a new page – everything still to come'). The changes to postwar London have, at this moment in history, yet to be written, just as the rubble awaits clearing up and new buildings erected. Amongst the ruins, in the confusion of London's diverse population, creativity might be possible: something as yet indefinable remains to be written. The unexpected comparison between the bomb-site and the Rhodesian veld underwrites the inseparability of the imperial centre and its periphery. What is 'foreign' can manifest itself at the heart of the Empire, in London: the division cannot hold.

It is this vision of London as admitting both native and foreigner, and at a moment before the racism of the 1950s gathers momentum, which Lessing pits against the divisiveness of the decade. The London and Londoners she initially experienced hold out the promise of a way of thinking about belonging beyond received categories – 'I wouldn't say I was English so much as a Londoner' (57), says Rose. And those arriving from British colonies will reimagine the city and, of course, physically rebuild it through their labour. It will indeed require 'all sorts' to reconstruct London, with workers from colonized countries swelling a depleted postwar workforce. Yet in sorting out such newcomers into racialized camps, the inclusive potential of 'Londoner' will be thwarted by an incubating racism which realigns the muddle of English identity. Rose's cynicism towards rebuilding reminds us of the thwarting of these hopes. The blank page in the typewriter will soon be marked by the scripts of racialization as the 1950s unfold.

Looking back at 1949–50 from the moment of the text's publication, 1960, the optimism encountered in the scene and the transient moment of the text's setting perhaps constitute lost possibilities for Lessing, possibilities which may well require resurrecting. In these terms, Lessing's 'documentary' of the English can be considered as a plea to remember the instability and transience epitomized by London and Londoners which complicate exclusionary forms of national identification that dictate precisely who can be regarded as English, 'properly speaking'. The ugliness, confusion, disappointment and disorder of the London in which Lessing arrived may have disconcerted her at first and caused her to shudder when she recalled it in her autobiography forty years later. But in 1960, in the wake of a decade in which race rose to prominence as the key arbiter of identity and belonging, ruined London and its 'inauthentic' Londoners offered Lessing a way of thinking critically about exclusionary notions of English national identity.

Janet Frame also recalls London's ruins in her autobiographical text *The Envoy from Mirror City* (1985), which includes an account of coming to the city from New Zealand in August 1956. Working temporarily as a housemaid at Battersea Technical College, she had listened to her colleagues' stories of the Blitz and began to see London through their eyes: 'The relics [of the war] were evident: bombed sites not yet rebuilt, overgrown with grass and weeds and scattered with rubble; the former Underground station with its hundreds of entombed Londoners caught in an air raid; squares and streets where death and destruction had now been given a place and names' (1990: 309). Aged thirty-one, Frame had travelled across the Pacific Ocean

and through the Panama Canal to England. Apart from spending short
spells in Ibiza and Andorra, she lived in London until 1963, when she
returned to New Zealand prompted by the death of her father. Coming to
England afforded Frame the opportunity to encounter the landscape of so
much of the English poetry and fiction she admired, and had devoured
while growing up in Oamaru. 'I dreamed of seeing King's College Chapel,
Cambridge', she records in *An Angel at My Table* (1984). 'I wanted to roam
the countryside of the Scholar-Gypsy, and that of the Hardy novels; to see,
in Shakespeare country, the "bank whereon the wild thyme grows"; and
even to walk in Kew Gardens among the lilacs!' (1990: 272). Her fearful
visions of London were similarly fabricated from literature: 'when I tried to
imagine being in, say, London, I furnished my images with darkness and
poverty and wild-eyed medieval characters set against tall grey stone buildings' (272).

After her arrival, Frame also became disappointed with London. She felt
betrayed by places such as Crystal Palace, Ponders End, Shepherds Bush
and Swiss Cottage, whose haunting names masked a grim and unspectacular reality, existing often as 'a cluster of dreary-looking buildings set in a
waste of concrete and brick' (306). In her account of a visit to Hampstead
Heath to explore the neighbourhood where Keats once lived, she admits to
significant misgivings:

> Looking down at London I could sense the accumulation of artistic
> weavings, and feel that there could be a time when the carpet became
> a web or shroud and other times a warm blanket or shawl: the prospect
> for burial by entrapment or warmth was close. How different it
> appeared to be in New Zealand where the place names and the land-
> scape, the trees, the sea and the sky still echoed with their first voice
> while the earliest works of art uttered their first response, in a primary
> dialogue with the Gods.
>   On Hampstead Heath I did not know whether to thank or curse
> John Keats and others for having pledged their sedge, basil, woodbine
> and nodding violets, and arranged their perennial nightingales to sing
> in my mind.
>
> (307–8)

Whether it be the morbidity of the shroud or the solace of the shawl, the
disconcerting sensation of burial coupled with the image of weaving admits
to a contemplation of London's density against which the landscape of New
Zealand affords the artist the opportunity for almost preternatural, Adamic
creativity (although, perhaps, the alleged 'first voice' and 'primary dialogue'
between the New Zealand landscape and the writer problematically roman-

ticize and appropriate Maori voices which predate European settlement). Here the weight of English culture seems part of the smothering atmosphere of 'death and destruction' Frame experienced in 1950s London, and her 'burial by entrapment' curiously echoes the fortunes of wartime Londoners 'entombed' in the Underground stations sheltering from bombs.

In an excellent essay on Frame's London writing, Rod Edmond also detects a sense of density in the passage quoted above, which he describes as a moment where Frame 'is oppressed by the weight of English literary tradition' (1995: 166). The occasion becomes part of a necessary process of unburdening for Frame, prompted by the recognition that she must protect the 'Mirror City' of her imagination from becoming entombed in the English literary canon she has hitherto enjoyed. It should be no surprise, writes Edmond, that Frame acknowledges in *The Envoy from Mirror City* the influence of, and 'affinity with' (167), several migrant writers living and working in London at the time, especially those from the Caribbean, who were engaged in a process of taking imaginative possession of the countries from which they had travelled, or – as in the case of Sam Selvon, to whom Frame specifically refers in her autobiography – providing a 'morning vision of London and the United Kingdom' (Frame 1990: 308). For Frame, as for other writers of the period, living in London provoked unsettling feelings of disappointment. Yet these feelings fuelled a torrid yet ultimately liberating response to the city in which she searched for 'a freedom of the imagination' (415) unburdened of the weighty, deathly shroud of English literary culture. The contrast with Naipaul could not be more stark. As with Lessing, London's ruined condition, especially its perceived deathliness, affords Frame a vital imaginative opportunity.

The London remembered in *The Envoy from Mirror City* is a bewildering location, peopled in the main by other newcomers from once-colonized countries who are struggling to find a foothold in the city. Living at first at an address in Clapham Common, Frame encounters an Irishman, Patrick Reilly, with whom she develops an uncomfortable paternalist relationship. Their bond is cemented by the fact that, in Reilly's words, '[n]either of us was English . . . And as a colonial, he said, I would understand what the English had done to Ireland' (304). But Reilly's racism complicates the construction of a possible postcolonial camaraderie and bears further witness to the emergent centrality of race as an identitarian category in the postwar years. He warns Frame against 'the blacks in London' who are 'lower than us' and 'stealing all the work' (305) but does not consider the shared conditions of the Irish and New Commonwealth migrants in London which, only a moment earlier, he unwittingly implied in his description of the relations between the English and the Irish: 'They eat our pork and our butter and race our horses and we come here for jobs' (304).

Although the London Irish often found themselves discriminated against in the same terms as arrivants from Asia, Africa and the Caribbean – Frame records the prohibition of 'children, pets, coloured or Irish' (386) in many advertisements of accommodation – Reilly's behaviour suggests that the Irish could be complicit in the racially discriminatory and exploitative atmosphere of 1950s London predicated upon the presence of black peoples.

Unhappy with Reilly's racism, Frame also remembers an encounter with 'Nigel N.', a Nigerian, with whom she visits the cinema. Her trip is marred by her self-consciousness of racial difference. She at first feels smug at enjoying herself publicly with a black man, and thus thwarting the prevailing mood of racial prejudice, but soon comes to realize that these feelings are perhaps little more than an inversion of Reilly's 'open bigotry' (312). Later, while enjoying sandwiches and coffee with Nigel in a Lyons café, she is also conscious of their public spectacle, 'having read the London scandals about black women and white men and white women and black men, with the implication that the women were prostitutes, the black men pimps, the white men unfortunate victims: the newspapers explained it all so neatly' (312). To tackle these feelings she determinedly enjoys Nigel's company and discovers a shared colonial heritage: 'heavy doses of British Empire, English history, products, rivers, cities, kings – and literature' (312). Yet their companionship is ultimately sundered at the end of their day when Frame refuses Nigel's amorous invitation to join him in his room to dance. He responds with the words '[y]ou all need to dance and enjoy yourselves more. You English don't know how to enjoy yourselves' (313). The incident splits the couple, with their shared colonial heritage, along racialized lines. The fact that Frame's ancestors were 'placed among the good, the strong, the brave, the friendly' (312) comes to matter more than her New Zealand upbringing and, in Nigel's eyes, ultimately claims her as English. Yet Frame feels remote from the English people she has met, such as her fellow housemaids in the Battersea Technical College Hostel, and stifled by English literary culture. When she discusses the English with other New Zealanders and Australians they agree that the English are obsessed with old-fashioned hierarchies of class and belong more 'in the Middle Ages' (310). No wonder, then, that Frame admits to considering herself as 'a colonial New Zealander overseas without any real identity' (308). The necessity of disengaging from English identity and culture, figured in deathly images of burial and shroud, becomes acute.

Looking back across a period of more than twenty years since she left London, in *The Envoy from Mirror City* Frame recalls her conundrum of identity as part of a process of creative liberation. The lack of 'real identity' is both cadaverous and full of potential: a fatal voiding of self which none the less makes possible a 'first voice' no longer determined by the ancestral legacy of 'the good, the strong, the brave, the friendly' which binds her to England and defines her identity through the history of settlement. Her novel of 1962, *The Edge of the Alphabet*, also bears morbid witness to the opportunity which London affords Frame to unburden herself of her subservience to England as, variously, the source of meaning, identity and distant belonging. Yet in this text – written while Frame was resident in Camberwell – the difficulty, distress and turmoil involved are emphasized with an intensity and tumultuousness that contrast with the cooler, mature recollections of *The Envoy from Mirror City*. If Frame's autobiographical account of her London years offers a relatively controlled retrospective, her novel conveys a much more agitated and unsettled experience of London written at a time of transition for both the author and the city, one which seizes upon the deathliness and ruined condition of the city as she saw it in the 1960s. In *The Edge of the Alphabet*, the burdensome weight of England is frequently figured in the funereal terms of the 'shroud'. London is represented as a morbid, derelict hellish city – a 'London Avernus' the fatality of which marks the end, or the edge, of English authority portrayed in terminal decline. Rather than cast London as the stable centre or origin of identity, culture and civilization, Frame's fictional city is rewritten as a derelict and corrosive space significantly epitomized by the ruined surroundings of the house in which its narrator, Thora Pattern, writes her tale.

As Marc Delrez has warned, it is dangerous to read Frame's challenging fiction in terms of realist novelistic representations of lived experience or within the reassuring and stabilizing parameters of social allegory. In Delrez's words, 'verisimilitude may simply not be Frame's primary criterion of excellence in fiction, and . . . her determination to explore new imaginative depths in her novels involves moving beyond – or turning back from – the social-realist, descriptive urge which is often an aspect of her country's obsession with cultural self-definition' (2002: xxii). In *The Edge of the Alphabet* these imaginative depths make for an experimental and often unpredictable narrative. The narrator, Thora Pattern, is already dead before the story begins; a prefatory note explains that the manuscript was found among her papers and submitted for publication by one of the novel's minor characters, Peter Heron. The ensuing narrative is split into three sections and primarily concerns the fortunes of three characters – Toby Withers, Zoe Bryce and Pat Keenan – who meet aboard the *Matua*, a ship travelling from New Zealand to England. Toby is travelling to England for the first time; Zoe and Pat (English and Irish respectively), are returning after short spells in New Zealand. The narrative shifts unpredictably between first- and third-person narration, with the narrative 'I' at times passing from the narrator to her characters. Thora's prose intermittently gives way to lyric poetry; on other occasions grammatical precision is suspended by a narra- tive style closer to modernist experiments with streams of consciousness. Most remarkable perhaps are Frame's unanticipated similes and metaphors which make almost surrealist connections and juxtapositions: when Toby lands at Southampton the sky is described as 'crowding down close like grey pastry being pressed around a tenpenny steak and kidney pie that has been cooked once then warmed up, fouled by great black squawking birds with ragged wings that lean forward in the sky like clergymen striving for a pit- tance' (Frame 1962: 134). Consequently, the novel promotes a degree of randomness and disorientation and seems to place the reader at the mercy of the wanderings and flights of fancy of an unpredictable mind. This is mirrored in the depiction of London which dominates the novel's third part and is consequently irregular, filtered through the consciousnesses of the characters and ultimately Thora, whom we glimpse in her South London flat writing her book. We could not be further away perhaps from the documentary ambitions of Lessing's London writing or the orderliness of Naipaul's prose.

For these reasons, we must consider the possibility that *The Edge of the Alphabet* might not be at all concerned with London as a concrete location. 'London' is perhaps little more than the fantastical creation of the novel's narrator, characterized by her metaphorical flights of fancy, and ultimately more noumenal than actual. As Frame's writing generally reveals – consider, for example, the rendering of place in *Living in the Maniototo* (1979) – place is often highly provisional and unstable, mediated through the inventive novelty and imaginative freedoms of 'Mirror City' – to the extent that it is difficult to regard her work as offering a dependable or material engagement with place. None the less, although Delrez's warnings must be heeded, it remains fair to say that a 'descriptive urge' lies some- where near the heart of *The Edge of the Alphabet*, and questions of 'cultural self-definition' form a major part of its fictional enquiry. In my reading of the novel, then, I inevitably risk regarding Frame's representation of London as commensurate with the concrete location. Although one must beware reading it as an allegory of social relations, the novel certainly engages with the historical legacy and continued influence of England and the English, and representations of the ruined landscape of postwar London play an important role. The novel inscribes and contests England as an icon of aesthetic and ancestral authority in a deliberate attempt to termi- nate prevailing colonial relationships and free the imagination from the deathly shroud which weighs it down. Although Frame's London has none of the concrete certainty of Naipaul's or Lessing's rendering of the city, once again London is imagined as making possible the opportunity to interfere with and contest the culture and identity of England. City and nation remain counterpoised. As I shall suggest, *The Edge of the Alphabet* can be considered as an attempt to *execute* certain kinds of influence – in the double sense of 'performing' and 'putting to death' – as part of a post-colonial refusal of the ancestral authority of English culture.

In *The Edge of the Alphabet* the influence of English culture often appears through references to mothers, with London represented as a colonial matrix, the ultimate origin and source of writing and meaning. Yet rather than giving life, the novel's mothers – and London as mother – are, like Toby's mother, dead; although their webs of influence reach beyond the grave. When Toby first tells his father Bob of his desire to travel from New Zealand to England, and is belittled, he imagines his dead mother's response: 'You see. Toby's going to write a book. He was always good at English at school, top marks for his composition that time. And his great great grandmother wrote a book of poems, signed by the Archbishop of Canterbury' (Frame 1962: 18). Through the mouth of the dead mother, England is identified with legitimacy and writing. It is a weighty centre of composition epitomized by the book of poems signed by the patrician hand of the Archbishop, and has been passed down to Toby through the maternal line. This is an idealized view of colonial ancestry which Bob is right to mock: 'Don't mention the murderers and convicts. And don't mind me, my mother began work in the mills when she was ten' (18). But Toby rejects his father's cynicism, and the book he plans to write overseas, *The Lost Tribe*, will resurrect the maternal connections with England which his mother was so keen to emphasize when she was alive. She had urged Toby to visit the places of his ancestors, whose features could be detected in the design of her face, 'registered parcel of history delivered to the womb's door' (14). Toby's journey, then, takes him to the matrix, the origin and source of identity and culture. But it is as much a journey towards death as it is towards life: Toby is obeying a dead mother's wish and seeking meaning from his connections with dead ancestors. Indeed, while travelling aboard the *Matua* Toby is assigned the part of mythical Orpheus at a social get-together. The moniker is apt: like Orpheus' journey to the underworld in search of his lost Eurydice, Toby's trip to London is an attempt to connect with his dead English ancestors. As with Orpheus, Toby's creative endeavours will ultimately fail to bring the dead back to life.

Frame's London is a city of the dead. On his first day in the capital Toby walks amongst 'the blind city workers in their dark clothes, tapping and stabbing their way, with the aid of umbrellas, to an important funeral' (137). When it rains the umbrellas which open on Oxford Street acquire a gleam which 'was like the soaking fur of the black cat that had strayed and died and been rained on and they found it under the holly tree with the water still pouring on it and its body stiff and arched and the flesh decayed already from around its mouth so that its teeth showed in a snarl' (139). As in *The Lonely Londoners*, the hellish and unhappy atmosphere of the city is epitomized by its winter weather:

> Winter. The curtains drawn completely in the sky and the smell of death on the hands of the people who touch each other in the night . . . [T]he West Indians, stricken with cold, shrunk in their cheap baggy suits, standing on the grille above the Underground, warming their feet; below, the harpy scream and hiss of warm air, the whine, the hurtle of trains through the tiled catacombs, past the cave-paintings of corsets, milk drinks, cough cures; the winter need to go home towards the light . . . the dead sliding by in tall cars manned by rosy-faced attendants; the wet clay heaped like a new grave around the filled entrance to the old bomb shelters.
>
> (155)

The fetid, morbid atmosphere of the city, emphasized above in the several references to death, renders 'composition' impossible. Instead, and punningly, London decomposes: writing is impossible. The narrator provides a memorable image of Londoners mummified by wet newspapers, 'who do not struggle except to jag holes for eyes and peer out through a face of headlines' (133). Shreds of newspapers clog the streets; Toby shares his accommodation with Mike and John, street-sweepers who shuffle 'leaves and newspapers along behind a wide wet broom, scooping the muck into their small cart' (143). These images of newspapers decomposing into wet muck or torn with holes accentuate the sense of the disintegration and insubstantiality of language in London. As a schoolboy Toby had found writing an arduous and expressly physical task. Sometimes 'he felt the words moving in his arms, down his arm into his hand, wriggling like silkworms awaiting their third change of skin before their mouth begins to drop golden silk' (63). But in London writing is arrested, and he develops a festering sore on his arm which stops him working. *The Lost Tribe* is never written.

The narrator tells us that Toby sometimes sits alone in his room in Kentish Town and gains comfort from tracing 'the map of London, journeying his finger many times over every street' (159), perhaps as an attempt to achieve a modicum of control over a disorientating city which does not square with its representation. But in London images lie; they have no depth and cannot be relied upon. Recalling my reading of *Mr Stone and the Knights Companion*, it is interesting that almost immediately on arriving in London Toby stumbles across a joke-shop full of 'disguises and tricks – false noses, wigs, beards, rubber food, stink bombs, squeaking cushions' (139). The shop is a synecdoche of the city at large, which is similarly fraudulent and presents itself almost like a confidence trick to the newly arrived Toby (and, of course, to the novel's readers). He feels cheated when searching for Piccadilly Circus to find that the name does not refer to a travelling variety show. The name and purpose of the Wonderland cinema where he secures initial employment underlines the city as location of illusions that exist only as projections. And like the Palace Cinema where Zoe eventually works (its name another false promise of splendour), its fraudulent decorations contradict its luxury: 'the out-of-date faded plush curtains, the scratched gold-painted plaster pillars, the cherubs set in their bubble-blowing poses on the roof, the polythene ferns sprouting along the footlights' (174). Rather than securing an ancestral connection with the Lost Tribe either in his experience of London or through writing, Toby becomes part of the rotting detritus that clogs the city streets and fogs its atmosphere. Like the discarded objects he encounters at the '*Great Railway Sale*' (145), he is soon part of London's lost property, one of the 'derelict people' (154) struggling to make ends meet in a brutal and uncaring city.

Perhaps the greatest confidence trick of all which is uncovered in London is England. This is revealed by the depiction of Ma Crane, the Clapham-based landlady of Pat and Zoe, who functions as an ironic figure of England as bucolic confection and colonial motherland. Her house can be regarded as a projection of idealized, pastoral visions of England which ultimately lack substance and authority. Owing to the winter weather she uses an electric fire 'which has been manufactured to resemble heaps of coal burning like rose-buds' (170). These are a 'cover-up' (172) for the electricity. Surrounded by pictures of seascapes and rural landscapes, and yearning for the summer, at one point Ma Crane is depicted at the piano singing 'Jerusalem', one of the *ur*-texts of postwar English nationhood. Composed in 1916 by Charles H. H. Parry and featuring the opening sixteen lines from William Blake's *Milton* (1804), the song promotes a pastoral confection of England, its 'ancient times', 'mountains green' and 'green and pleasant land' (at odds with the tenor of Blake's poem, it must be said). The contrast between the summer setting of the song, Ma Crane's idyllic pictures, and the bleak winter conditions in a ruined and tomblike city underlines the ways in which the cultural clichés of England are suspended and ironized by the novel's deathly London setting.

As Spring approaches Ma Crane decorates her house as a confection of Englishness. Her bathroom and lavatory are painted 'in rose and green' (183), yet the impression is one of stylization and artifice. Convinced by a salesman, she buys matching toilet paper, 'what she calls (with prompting from the advertisements) "a treat"' (183). The rose paint, like the rose-buds of the electric fire, is cosmetic, while the pastoral green indicates an ideal-ized landscape perhaps similar to those pictures which hang from her walls. These contrast vividly with the prevailing yellowness of London which recalls the yellow fog of T. S. Eliot's poem 'The Love Song of J. Alfred Prufrock' (1917). Toby watches 'that yellow stuff running out of the sky' (141), while at Hyde Park one morning he sees '[a]n old man with a reap-hook . . . harvesting the fog, hacking at the stiff yellow bushes that tumbled around him showering him with smoky pollen' (158). The sterility and deathliness of Ma Crane's house and the 'green' England which it, and she, represent are emphasized by its setting for Zoe's suicide. When Ma Crane takes a holiday to the Lake District – home to pastoral visions of England's Romantic poets – to recover from the shock of Zoe's death she again per-forms 'Jerusalem' at the piano while looking out of the window 'at the shadow of the atom station' (205–6). The juxtaposition of the song's evoca-tion of 'England's mountains green' with the new nuclear power stations in the Lake District is striking, and serves to underline the artifice of Ma Crane's myths of England by recasting a pastoral vision of England in the sinister shadow of nuclear power and its associations with disease and Armageddon.

For Frame, the writer must reach beyond a subservience to any specific location – England or New Zealand – in order to arrive at an imaginative space which permits 'primary dialogue' unfettered from the obligations of either place or cultural tradition. In depicting London she attempts to write *through* the cultural and colonial authority of England in order to reach a new, enabling threshold at the edge of received vision, figured elsewhere as the 'Mirror City'. In *The Edge of the Alphabet*, the dereliction and fraudu-lence of London makes imaginatively possible a postcolonial process of cultural manumission where England no longer appears as a weighty shawl or shroud for the budding writer. The determining influence of English cul-ture, epitomized by the 'perennial nightingales' and 'sedge, basil, woodbine and nodding violets' which John Keats and others have implanted in Frame's mind, must be put to death if one is to be free from their burden.

'How I am haunted by death and the dead!' (223) declares Thora Pat-tern, with whose voice the novel concludes. London remains stuck in winter, and the frosts 'visit during the night and in the ceremony known as the laying-on of hands they touch the window-panes stark beneath the lace curtains' (219). In her 'last will and testament' she makes reference to the substance of her story and its setting in terms of ruin:

> I, Thora Pattern, have chosen Toby Withers, Zoe Bryce, Pat Keenan and all others whom I have known or dreamed of or constructed from tree-fern brains found on bombed sites and mountains of the interior,

as inheritors of my last will and testament, as if I bequeathed to them the parts of myself which I cannot invite as guests to this lonely house with its stoned-out windows and worm-eaten sashes and frames and its pile of sawdust which Time places in careful droppings (confectionery, icing-forced) in the corners of the rooms; and the ripped-up floor-boards revealing the treasure, the riddled earth, the casks of worms brewing the ferment of death.

Outside, all the buildings have toppled. Men in white suits, as if for tennis, prance about the debris in search of the last victims.

(208)

Whereas Lessing finds in London's bomb-sites an image for potential re-creation in which received notions of Englishness might be liberally rewritten, Frame appropriates images of urban ruin as part of an attempt to demolish the primacy of England as origin. Writing amongst ruins, Thora's narrative might be considered an English suicide note, a last-gasp attempt to make its colonial arrivants subservient to its design – our narrator is called Thora *Pattern*, after all – which serves only to render derelict and fraudulent its ancestral claims to meaning and authority. It is a required failure, a necessary death.

In Frame's presentation of London as the derelict graveyard in which England as a source of art, identity and authority is laid to rest, she achieves what might best be described as an act of cultural euthanasia, one which is part of a postcolonial refusal of and separation from the strictures of the mother country. As Howard McNaughton has argued in his reading of the novel, '[t]he project of post-colonial reclamation may thus appear self-voiding because it can articulate itself only in the alphabet of the parent culture' (1993: 137). Hence in the novel's closing pages we witness the destruction of metropolitan art: Peter Heron, a struggling artist, destroys his work, including a picture, titled *Tracing the Crime*, of a deserted city empty except for 'traces of humanity – newspapers, packets, cars, like the debris floating on the surface of the water after the flood and the wreck, or relics of memory rising to the surface of dreams' (Frame 1962: 210–11). Like the map of London which Toby comfortingly traces with his finger, the city's prevailing representations must be relinquished, their authority and status vacated – including, of course, Thora's narrative, which is discovered by Peter and submitted to the publishers perhaps as part of his 'clearing up', an activity which approximates to the white-suited men picking through the debris outside Thora's lonely, ruined house in South London.

Despite being the nation's capital city and often a key (if selective) location in representations of the nation, London can be regarded as a site which interferes with notions of national identity, culture and belonging.

In coming to London in the decades after the war, Naipaul, Lessing and Frame arrived in a city which paradoxically promised and withheld continuity with England and English culture, a transitional and conflicted environment where dominant models of national identity were being challenged both by those newly arriving in London and by some in the host community keen to redefine English identity and culture through the prism of race. Whereas Naipaul dwelled gloomily upon the loss of a certain version of England in postwar ruined London, and in many ways made the resulting disappointment the theme of his writing, Lessing and Frame find in the city's dereliction the figurative resources to challenge either rapidly ossifying racializing models of English identity (as in *In Pursuit of the English*) or the authoritative and suffocating burden of received English culture (as in *The Edge of the Alphabet*). As the texts explored in this chapter suggest in contrasting ways, London potentially interfered with the reception and perpetuation of images of England, English identities and national culture – ultimately making the city a dangerous and subversive location where revision, resistance and postcolonial critique could be purposefully entertained.

3 Living room
Buchi Emecheta, Joan Riley and Grace Nichols

During the 1960s, 1970s and 1980s several black communities in London formed a number of political organizations, some of them short-lived, which became active in resisting racial discrimination in housing and employment, and – most explosively – at the hands of the police on the streets, whose behaviour was deemed increasingly racist and hostile. These groups included the Campaign Against Racial Discrimination (CARD) established in 1965, Michael X's Racial Action Adjustment Society (RAAS) created in the same year, and the United Coloured People's Association (UCPA) formed in 1967 by Nigerian playwright Obi Egbuna under the influence of the Black Power movement in the United States. The 1970s heralded the formation of organizations such as the Black Unity and Freedom Party (BUFP). Coincident with these initiatives were organizations created by black women specifically about black women's experiences, condition and values. Although they worked alongside other black groups and feminist organizations, their existence was often a response to the chauvinism and insensitivity to gender allegedly discovered amongst black men, and the predominantly middle-class orientation of white British feminism which did not recognize racial discrimination as a priority or 'the boundaries of sisterhood in the overall struggle' (Ramdin 1999: 256). As regards London, these groups included Brixton's Black Women's Group (BWG) formed in 1973 (and which launched London's first Black Women's Centre in 1979), the Organisation of Women of Asian and African Descent (OWAAD) created in 1978, and the Southall Black Sisters set up by women of Asian descent in 1979 (Sivanandan 1982; Bryan, Dadzie and Scafe 1985; Ramdin 1999; Donnell 2002).

These groups were fundamentally important to the politicizing and organizing of black women in London, and their efforts were expended against both the discriminatory practices visited upon black communities and – especially as regards black women's movements – gendered inequalities within them. The Southall Black Sisters offered crucial support to those pursuing judicial proceedings against men accused of domestic violence against their wives. Several such organizations were short-lived: OWAAD lasted only five years. In accounting for the demise of such groups, reference is often made to the inability of the racializing rhetoric of blackness successfully to accommodate and unify the competing interests of different constituencies of black women. 'Black' could not function for long as an organizing category for those with links to Africa, Asia and the Caribbean whose priorities were not necessarily identical. In their appreciative review of Beverley Bryan, Stella Dadzie and Suzanne Scafe's book *The Heart of the Race: Black Women's Lives in Britain* (1985), the 'Sisters in Study' took issue with the lack of interest paid to Caribbean women of Asian descent, and criticized its inability to account adequately for the 'failure to bridge the differences between the different hues – both literally and in the political sense – of the Black women within it' (Grewal *et al.* 1988: 93) which, combined with debates concerning sexuality, split groups such as OWAAD. As demonstrated by the work of Heidi Safia Mirza, the fortunes of postwar black women's social and political activism are often narrated in terms virtually identical with black British politics and culture in general, as popularized by Stuart Hall in his influential essay 'New Ethnicities' – namely, that the 'first moment' of postwar black British organization and representation mobilized the unifying category of race to mount opposition to state and popular discrimination, but was challenged in the 1980s by a 'second moment' in which an awareness of sexual, cultural, ethnic and class differences effectively questioned the possibility and desirability of continuing to invest in a homogenizing notion of blackness (Mirza 1997). As Hall describes it, this shift can be considered 'a change from the struggle over the relations of representation to a politics of representation itself' (1996: 442). Although he is extremely careful to resist positing a mechanical account of this change – the two moments often overlap and are not easily separable – the evolution of postwar black British politics and culture is often understood as proceeding neatly from solidarity to diversity. As Mirza's account testifies, this potential metanarrative can be too easily imposed upon accounts of black feminist resistance too.

The texts I examine in this chapter offer another way of narrating black women's insurgency, not least because they articulate the spatial practices and subaltern resistance of women in London who neither necessarily had the option of organizing a black women's community of resistance nor could turn to a supportive network of black women in London for strength. What forms of resistance can be found beyond and before the ascendancy of mobilized social movements? The strategies of transformation we consider below date from the 1970s and engage with experiences across the 1960s to the 1980s, and suggest that – especially in the case of

Buchi Emecheta – the rejection of race as an emancipatory tactic for black women was neither a recent manoeuvre nor the exclusive discovery of the 1980s made in the light of the flawed mobilization of race by political organizations. The actions of the female figures in the work of Emecheta, Joan Riley and Grace Nichols suggest unpredictable moments and modes of radicalism which unsettle the dominant metanarrative of black British women's resistance and take us to communities of resistance far beyond the racialized and gendered imperatives of diaspora neighbourhoods such as those found in (as we shall see) Kentish Town and Brixton. In engaging with fictional representations of migrant female experiences in London, we encounter a horizon of experiences and crucially important forms of creative resistance which are not always admissible to postwar social and historical accounts of black female insurgency. The texts we encounter in this chapter reveal *ad hoc*, improvisatory ways of living and changing (in) the city which both predated and occurred beyond the theatre of organized formal political movements.

In understanding the shape and possibilities of these communities of resistance, created by but not necessarily exclusive to women, I want to maintain throughout this chapter a tension between filial obligation – an adherence to the social mores of a family or tribe – and affiliative encounters, where groups are formed and renegotiated across the boundaries of race, gender, nation or culture. To borrow a phrase used by Barbara Harlow, an affiliative space 'rewrites the social order to include a vision of new relational possibilities which transgress ethnic, class and racial divisions as well as family ties' (1987: 142). As we shall see, the 'new relational possibilities' discovered in women's representations of postcolonial London are often at the heart of their particularly hopeful models of a transformed city, where there is living room for all. Despite their often bleak depictions of the city, in the work of these writers London is forced to accommodate black women whose subaltern spatial practices evidence important modes of resistance and agency.

It is something of a myth in postwar accounts of migration to London, especially from Africa, the Caribbean and South Asia, that women arrived in the city out of filial obligation primarily to join husbands and families (Glass 1960). In recent years this presumption has been challenged in black feminist scholarship. In reviewing accounts of postwar immigration which ignore gender and 'collapse all of us into a single, and by implication recently arrived, generation', Amina Mama has pointed out that Caribbean female migrants in the 1950s were 'likely to have been single, and specifically recruited' (1997: 37) as workers by institutions such as the National Health Service, regardless of marital status. Beverley Bryan, Stella Dadzie and Suzanne Scafe have also recorded that '[a]lthough some

Black women came to Britain to join husbands who had come on ahead of them, many more came independently as recruits, or simply to seek employment' (1985: 25). The economic value of migrant female labour meant that black women played a pivotal role in Britain's postwar recovery, often carrying out some of the most arduous and unattractive work. These women were not a passive following of menfolk but an active and exploited presence in postwar Britain often to be found 'in the lower echelons of all the institutions where we are employed . . . where the work is physically heavy (in the factories and mills no less than in the caring professions), the pay is lowest, and the hours are longest and most anti-social' (Mama 1997: 37). As well as contributing importantly to the economic fortunes of the British state, Mama points out how these women also played a vital part in diaspora communities as 'Black women are also more likely to have unemployed menfolk, and when this is not the case, Black male wages are low. The Black woman's wage is therefore crucial to our communities' (40).

Yet, as bell hooks has argued in the context of African American communities, the role of black women as wage earners has been complicated by the politics of gender as both men and women in such communities sometimes regard this situation as improper: 'black women who enter the work force are encouraged to feel that they are taking jobs from black men or de-masculinizing them' (1982: 83). The economic contribution of black women to black communities in London has been similarly ambivalent: black female labour has often maintained the economic survival of black communities while destabilizing hierarchies of gender. As Bryan, Dadzie and Scafe have explained in their comments upon black men's experiences of racism, '[t]he domestic arena has become the only area in which Black men are able to conform to the dominant male role. Thus their attempts to subjugate Black women who are in a position of even less power must be seen as evidence of their alienation' (1985: 214). Although these remarks perhaps presume a homogeneity of male experience, domestic environment and sexual orientation, as well as a common response to the alienation created by racism, the creative works explored in this chapter are similarly sensitive to the racialized politics of gender which have contributed to the nervous condition of domestic life for some black families in London.

Buchi Emecheta's London writing of the 1970s exposes many of these predicaments. Emecheta arrived in London, via Liverpool, from Lagos, Nigeria, in the spring of 1962. Barely eighteen years old, she had come with her two children ostensibly out of filial obligation to join her husband, Sylvester Onwordi, who was studying in London. Her in-laws were against the trip; Emecheta was earning considerably more through her job at the American Embassy in Lagos than many Nigerians who had returned from Britain. Yet she was determined to go, partly out of her desire to escape the gendered condition of her life in Lagos (her economic affluence was not matched by independence, and she was unhappy at having to defer constantly to the authority of the family's senior males) and also because of the memory of her late father whose reverence for the United Kingdom inspired her to travel. Her impressions on disembarking at Liverpool quickly dispelled her father's mythical view, but not her determination to succeed in a new country. 'Pa, England is not the Kingdom of God you thought it was', she told herself on her first day in Britain; but 'I must make it here or perish' (1994c: 27). From the beginning of her adult life Emecheta was fiercely determined to make her way on her own terms and not sacrifice her ambitions on the altar of filial obligation.

Emecheta's first two novels *In the Ditch* (1972) and *Second-Class Citizen* (1974) are set primarily in the small enclave of North London which she made her home in the 1960s. It is an area whose borders can be drawn in the shape of a diamond, with the tube and railway stations of Kentish Town, Mornington Crescent, Chalk Farm and Camden Road marking respectively the points of north, south, east and west. At its heart is Queen's Crescent with its regular Saturday market which is an important location in Emecheta's early writing. Her novels offer fictional accounts of the people Emecheta encountered in this particular 1960s neighbourhood and the struggles she and other women faced in trying to survive London's racism, chauvinism and poverty.

The images of London which emerge from Emecheta's novels are quite different from those of the male figures whose work we explored in Chapter 1. To get a measure of these important differences, consider the following description of Queen's Crescent's Saturday market from the closing pages of *In the Ditch*:

> Saturday was always busy at the Crescent. There were many Indian shops selling African food, and this drew large numbers of Africans into the Crescent Market. The market was once in the centre of a poor working-class area. But modern housing estates had sprung up round it like mushrooms; people got mixed, the rich and the poor, and there was no knowing which was which.
>
> The noise, clatter and bustle was like that of birds in an aviary. People screamed and tumbled into each other, arguing and protesting over rising prices, filling the air with their shouted communications. Children with chocolatey mouths and fingers followed the trails of mums with shopping trolleys loaded to overflowing with 'bargain' foodstuffs. Africans, Pakistanis and West Indians shopped side by side

with the successful Jews, Americans and English from Highgate, Hampstead, Swiss Cottage and other equally expensive places.

(Emecheta 1994a: 131–2)

As we have seen, when Colin MacInnes looked upon the Sunday market in Petticoat Lane in 1962 with its Jewish, New Commonwealth and tourist clientele, he discovered a carnivalesque vision of the nation's 'happy mongrel breed' (1962: 23) cheerfully mixing amongst the merchandise. Emecheta affords her reader no such idealized indulgence. Caroline W. Sizemore reads the passage cited above as evidence of 'the variety of multi-cultural London' (1996: 374) in which Adah glories, and which permits her freedom. But this is hardly the case. In Queen's Crescent market it may be difficult to tell rich from poor, but like the new estates which have sprouted in the area there are important differences sustained between those who shop 'side by side'. The vibrant atmosphere, with people scream-ing and tumbling amongst the clatter and bustle, has a threatening edge. The purchase of bargain foodstuffs speaks to the unequal economic condi-tions between those living near the market and the affluent visitors from the 'expensive places'. Above all, it is a space where economic and gender inequalities reinforce each other. The narrator dwells particularly upon the 'mums with the shopping trolleys' who struggle to secure their bargains while coping with the responsibility of their small children. It is with the experiences of such Londoners – poor, female and often black – that Emecheta is concerned. Her representations of London are sensitive to the mechanics of class, gender and race that are missing from MacInnes's cos-mopolitan vision of Petticoat Lane (and ignored in Sizemore's criticism). In Queen's Crescent differences of class, race and gender are not simply erased by the multicultural gathering of Saturday morning shoppers.

The lines of division in Queen's Crescent market are made all the more visible by the fact that its description comes at the end of a novel which has bleakly explored the endurance of prejudice and oppression in 1960s London. *In the Ditch* takes as its subject the struggle for survival of a young Nigerian mother, Adah, and her five children at the Pussy Cat Mansions. From the beginning her lack of support from other Nigerians in London, especially men, is emphasized. Adah's husband is an absence throughout. The novel begins by depicting the activities of Adah's Yoruba landlord who, angered by her complaints about the filth and cockroaches in her room, attempts to evict Adah by dancing a juju masquerade outside her house. Adah is desperate: as a young black mother of five children she is aware that few landlords 'would dream of taking the like of her into their houses' (Emecheta 1994a: 2). She is relieved when she learns from the local council that she is to be rehoused in the Mansions. Conditions at the

Mansions are poor. The stairs leading to the top flats 'were always smelly with a thick lavatorial stink' (17) while the cupboards in Adah's flat are infested with mildew.

Although Emecheta takes care to document the degradation and poverty of life at the Mansions, she also suggests two important forms of support which assist Adah in her determined quest for survival: the welfare state and the community of working-class mothers at the Mansions. Adah's encounters with state officialdom are not altogether happy. After a visit by the local Family Advisor, Carol, who is concerned about the welfare of Adah's children, Adah is encouraged to give up her job at the British Museum and 'go on the dole', that is, claim a weekly subsistence payment from the local authority. Adah is at first ashamed – 'She had come to think of those on the dole as lazy, parasitic people who lived off Society' (33) – and she encounters several humiliations at the hands of state representatives. In one incident at the local Rent Office she nervously protests about the dog excrement which litters the Mansions and has her complaint recorded by an indifferent clerk who promises, falsely, that action will be taken. Throughout the novel the impression is given that welfare state institutions are staffed by middle-class clerks who fail to understand, or to care about, the conditions of those like Adah who are caught 'in the ditch' of poor housing, unemployment and poverty. When Adah is visited by two women from the council's Children's Department while she is ill, they make vague promises about securing home help while suggesting that she ask her children to do more housework in order to ease Adah's burden. They then leave, 'feeling very helpful and charitable' (87).

An exception of sorts is Carol, the Family Advisor who works at the Mansions. She is a link between state officialdom and the women who form an alternative affiliative community of resistance. Carol is looked upon with suspicion by many of the women, and in her first encounter with Adah she acts in a haughty and imperious fashion, presuming that Adah is Ghanaian; later, having learned her mistake, she attempts to befriend Adah by making some patronizing platitudes about the beauty of Lagos. None the less, Carol offers sound practical advice and works to assist Adah; she organizes baby-sitters to allow Adah to attend evening classes at college; when Adah returns home she 'could not help crying quietly' (29) on seeing that her children have been bathed and the flat cleaned. Carol's office sits in the middle of the Mansions central area, which Adah significantly calls a compound 'remembering Africa' (16), and it becomes an important subaltern space of support and resistance, where resources for surviving the sordid social conditions of London are mooted. Adah soon becomes part of a wider circle of women which includes Whoopey and Mrs Ashley (both English), Mrs O'Brien (a migrant from Ireland), Mrs Cook (a

Jamaican) and the Princess. To be sure, the compound is not an idealized or always happy space. Some of these women also display irritating assumptions about Adah's racial identity, such as Mrs O'Brien who tells Adah that she always liked 'your people' (46). 'Why', reflects Adah, 'was it that everybody would always judge one black person by the way another black person behaved?' (46). Yet, although such assumptions create barriers between the women who do not necessarily have the same backgrounds, their shared experiences enable them to bond temporarily and make of their squalid lived environment something new. On one sociable occasion Adah reflects upon the women finding 'joy in communal sorrow. Children ran between their legs, happy at the knowledge of the nearness of their mothers. Adah stopped being homesick. She was beginning to feel like a human being again' (61).

Such moments of joy rarely last, however, and for every incident of support amongst the women there seems to be one of conflict. The compound is a fragile, precarious and temporary space that struggles to make room for novel and sustained forms of identification and action. While cleaning her laundry one morning Adah is verbally abused by an old woman who asks her '[w]hy don't you go back to your own bleeding country' (110) – although some of the other women mock her racism by calling attention to the fact she is Greek. Even at the novel's close, Adah and her best friend, Whoopey, remain divided by race. When they encounter Mrs Cook at the Crescent market, a series of misapprehensions arise which emphasize the women's differences. Whoopey, unlike Adah, cannot understand why Mrs Cook is determined to save so much for the future (she intends to return to Jamaica). And when Whoopey talks enthusiastically about wanting to marry her new partner, a Nigerian man with whom she has become pregnant, Adah has not the heart to tell her friend that no Nigerian man would 'seriously consider marriage with a girl [already] with two children' (131) – although we might be a little concerned about the assumptions Adah makes here about a man she has never met. As the novel concludes, the future for the women does not seem especially bright and they each go their separate ways into the new accommodation they have secured, breaking the temporary supportive affiliative community they have built.

No doubt Emecheta's commitment to exposing the squalor, unhappiness and struggle of her Kentish Town neighbourhood overrides any optimistic or hopeful tone emerging from the novel, yet the affiliative community we glimpse – where Nigerians, English, Irish and Jamaicans meet in the humdrum concrete compound which recalls Africa – is crucial. Together, the women make room for themselves. Differences of race and culture mean that it is an uneasy space within which prejudices are momentarily suspended but never fully dismantled. But the women's shared experiences of adverse social conditions successfully create a space of solidarity even if such initiatives are complicated and fractured by prejudice. Crucially, it is not London's conflicted Nigerian community which provides support for Adah, as the eviction with which the novel opens emphasizes. Writing ten years before the alleged emergence of a 'second moment' in black British representations, in *In the Ditch* (and as with *Second-Class Citizen*) for Emecheta the possibility of a supportive community born from an allegedly shared black identity is seriously questioned.

Emecheta's desire to document the unhappy conditions of 1960s Kentish Town has earned her some curious critical remarks, often from those who praise her writing. In *Head Above Water* she has admitted her intention at the beginning of her career to write novels of social reality inspired by her reading of Nell Dunn and Monica Dickens. In endorsing the documentary aspects of her London fiction, some critics have felt it necessary to call attention to, and immediately forgive, Emecheta's perceived artlessness. Omar Sougou describes *Second-Class Citizen* as 'admittedly not exciting in terms of stylistic achievement' (1990: 511) while Olga Kenyon suggests that Emecheta 'is more interested in bearing witness than in creating rich discourse' (1991: 113). Lloyd W. Brown is particularly damning when commenting that the novels 'suffer from lapses into banal statement and into what is, quite simply, sloppy writing' (1981: 36), although he later suggests that *Second-Class Citizen* creates 'a relatively complex vision [which helps] to offset the thinness of style and occasional fuzziness' (43). Emecheta has acknowledged that her literary style is often 'plain' (1989: viii), while reminding readers that English is her fourth language, after Igbo, Yoruba and Agayin. But even so, such critical comments problematically equate documentary fiction with aesthetic poverty and cancel the consideration of the imaginative aspects of Emecheta's writing which are not simply issues of style. As I shall move now to argue, Emecheta's representation of London in *Second-Class Citizen* couples her documentary intentions with an imaginative projection of London in which the communal affiliations glimpsed at Pussy Cat Mansions are imagined to facilitate a resistant subaltern space discovered beyond the exclusionary realms of class, race and gender. It exists between the concrete and the invented, and is made possible through Adah's relationship with transcultural influences. It is manifested primarily at the Chalk Farm Library where Adah works, and acts as a hopeful alternative to those locations – primarily the family home and the squalid street – in which her second-class citizenship is created.

Second-Class Citizen tells the story of Adah Obi prior to the period of her life depicted in *In the Ditch*, from her childhood in Lagos to her early months in London, the breakdown of her marriage to her husband Francis, and her first attempts at writing. As in the previous novel, Adah is clearly a fictional surrogate for Emecheta, whose life often matches that of her central character, but is also part of an important strategy of distancing between author and character. This distancing makes possible the opportunity to regard Adah critically – one which the reader is at liberty to take even if the author seems to avoid direct critical comment. Certainly Adah's middle-class aspirations and youthful naivety can invite criticism, as there seems a short distance between her failings and those of her creator. However, on several occasions in the novel one wonders if Emecheta's London writing of the 1970s makes possible, albeit implicitly, the critical exploration both of her central character and, subsequently, Emecheta's younger self of the 1960s. Emecheta writes a documentary fiction which is rather more self-conscious and artful than her advocates and detractors presume.

Like Emecheta, Adah is drawn to England partly through the influence of her father whose reverence for the country makes the infant Adah imagine that it 'must be like heaven' (Emecheta 1994b: 2). But her arrival in Liverpool suggests the opposite, with the environment beyond the comfort of her cabin described as another hell: 'There were voices jabbering loudly, somebody laughed hysterically, and there were sounds of somebody running as if chased by demons' (32). She is appalled by the terraced house in Ashdown Street, in which Francis lives with other Nigerian migrants, for its lack of space. The family is to live in a 'half-room . . . with a single bed at one end and a new settee which Francis had bought with the money Adah sent him to buy her a top coat with' (35). Francis justifies the reason for their meagre habitat:

> You see, accommodation is very short in London, especially for black people with children. Everybody is coming to London, the West Indians, the Pakistanis and even the Indians, so that African students are usually grouped with them. We are all blacks, all coloureds, and the only houses we can get are horrors like these.
>
> (35)

Much of the novel depicts Adah's attempts to survive the 'horrors' of living in poor accommodation in London. Part of the responsibility for such conditions is laid at the door of racist landlords in the city; when Adah hunts for a new home she spots a card in the window of the Post Office on Queen's Crescent which reads 'Sorry, no coloureds' (74), and she later experiences a racist landlady in Hawley Street who denies that the rooms she has advertised are vacant the moment she realizes that Adah and her family are black. But from Adah's perspective, the bulk of the horrors of living are created by the Nigerians in the neighbourhood who demand that women live according to the gender restrictions which Adah has been keen to leave behind in Lagos. As the narrator reflects, after her first year in Britain 'Adah could not help wondering whether the real discrimination, if one could call it that, that she experienced was not more the work of her fellow-countrymen than of the whites' (70).

In particular, it is the family unit which preoccupies Emecheta as a force of discrimination. Filial relationships are rarely enabling in her writing. Francis expects Adah to accommodate his sexual desires for her, and other women, without question, while his beatings of her are so fierce that on one occasion the police have to be called. Families are rarely happy places in Emecheta's fiction, and the achievements of her heroines are often judged on the extent to which they leave the restricted enclaves of their families, which often means their home. It is significant that in *Second-Class Citizen*, prior to coming to London, Adah refuses to be photographed with Francis's family, and counts amongst her reasons for leaving the chance to escape filial obedience – in Lagos they 'had to bow down to their elders' (23). One of the greatest horrors for Adah on arriving is the realization that familial chains of obedience continue to function, with women presumed to be subservient to the decisions of their husbands and male elders.

The hypocrisies which characterize Adah's family are vividly drawn. As soon as she arrives in London Adah becomes the major wage earner in the family, working first at North Finchley Library. Her income supports Francis's studies to be an accountant which, it is clear, he is neglecting. When he fails his summer exams he blames Adah for burdening him with responsibility and disrupting his studies. He also pays little regard to his children, and leaves to Adah the responsibility of providing food and childcare. When he does take some responsibility for the provision for his children, the results are disastrous. He is very keen that Adah allows a local childminder, Trudy, to look after the children while Adah is at work, and an arrangement is struck. After becoming uneasy, Adah visits Trudy's house and discovers a 'slum': 'The backyard was filled with rubbish, broken furniture, and very near an uncovered dustbin was the toilet, the old type of toilet with faulty plumbing, smelly and damp' (49–50). Trudy is engaged in prostitution (indeed, it is hinted that Francis's enthusiasm for Trudy is based on their adulterous sexual encounters) and Adah's children have been left unattended amongst the waste: 'Vicky was busy pulling rubbish out of the bin and Titi was washing her hands and face with the water leaking from the toilet. When they saw [Adah], they ran to her, and Adah noticed that Vicky had no nappy on' (51). As a consequence of this neglectful environment, a few days later Vicky is rushed to hospital with viral meningitis and nearly dies. Such is the extent of Francis's attempts to organize childcare.

Adah's determination to raise and care for her children, rather then trust them to others, attracts hostility from both Francis and the other Nigerian families amongst whom they live. Things are complicated further by the fact that many of the families are Yorubas, whereas the Obis are Igbos. Francis acts as the interface between the immediate family and the Nigerian community at large, which functions in the same constricting way as the 'elders' in Lagos – on more than one occasion Adah 'could feel their neighbours speaking through Francis' (43) when he complains about Adah's refusal to conform to accepted behaviour. Adah's job in the library is the cause of local consternation as she refuses to work in a shirt factory where many of her neighbours are employed. There is general surprise that, unlike other Nigerian parents in London, Adah does not send her children away to be raised by white families – 'Most Nigerians with children sent their children away to foster-parents' (44) – and she receives little support in Ashdown Street for her decision not to accept the conditions in which they live:

> In fact, to most of her Nigerian neighbours, she was having her cake and eating it. She was in a white man's job, despite the fact that everybody had warned her against it, and looked as if she meant to keep it. She would not send her children away to be fostered like everybody else . . . To cap it all, they were Igbos, the hated people who always believe blindly in their ideologies.
>
> (69)

When Adah and Francis receive notice to quit their room in Ashdown Street the local women delight in Adah's misfortunes. They sing songs in her presence 'about the fact that she and her husband would soon have to make their home in the street' (72–3). 'It was all so Nigerian' (73), complains the narrator. 'It was all so typical' (73). Such comments reveal, on the one hand, the lack of a supportive migrant community for women like Adah whose behaviour refuses to conform to group norms. The community in which she lives is fractured by inequalities of gender and tribal rivalries obedient to other times and places and which work against the construction of the multiracial network of support mooted at the Pussy Cat Mansions. On the other hand, and worryingly perhaps, the narrator's comments also bear witness to a general antipathy towards Nigerians based on the particular circumstances of 1960s Kentish Town. As Susanne Pichler argues, 'Emecheta depicts the Nigerian community as a heartless agglomeration of egoists and as an obstruction to Adah's acculturation process' (2001: 104). For Emecheta, to be 'Nigerian' is to conform to, or be complicit with, modes of behaviour which oppress women.

Emecheta's representation of being 'Nigerian' is highly problematic. As well as potentially colluding in the othering of Nigerians in London via a depreciatory and generalizing rhetoric, her work too quickly forecloses the possibility of filial relations and resources in making new subaltern spaces of transformation (possibilities which, as we will soon see, are mooted in a different cultural context in the work of Joan Riley). Practically every Nigerian character in *Second-Class Citizen* (save Adah) is depicted pejoratively. One character, Mr Babalola, had previously arrived in London as a student on a rich scholarship but spent his money on entertainments and has long given up his studies. He befriended a white Londoner, sixteen-year-old Janet, whom he 'offered to any black man who wanted to know how a white woman looked undressed' (Emecheta 1994b: 48). Later, when Adah and her family move to Willes Road they lodge with Pa Noble, whose happiness to play the clown to white Londoners and his unflattering memories of Nigeria sicken Adah. Two chance encounters with Nigerian men similarly underline Adah's continuing predicament. In one incident, when Adah sits by herself in a park mulling over her unhappy life with Francis she is approached by Mr Okpara who recognizes her as an Igbo, guesses her unhappiness, presumes she has been fighting with Francis and suggests that they go together to beg her husband's forgiveness. 'Typical Igbo psychology', remarks the narrator; 'men never do wrong, only the women; they have to beg for forgiveness, because they are bought, paid for and must remain like that, silent, obedient slaves' (164). And at the novel's close, in a moment of bizarre coincidence when Adah has just left court at Clerkenwell having gained custody of her children, she is hailed by a childhood friend who, on spying her wedding ring, pays for her taxi home 'because he thought she was still with her husband' (186). Nigerians in London offer Adah not one ounce of support. Hence, *Second-Class Citizen* calls severely into question the effectiveness of London's diaspora community as a source of support and survival for women like Adah. Yet its stance is complicated by the blanket condemnation of Igbos and Nigerians (especially the men) as 'typically' unsupportive and chauvinist – which is perhaps not too remote from the processes of racialization which have declared Nigerians and others in London as inferior 'blacks'.

In Emecheta's London fiction the house is not a safe place. Violence, neglect, cruelty, disease and poverty are all to be found there. The same is true for London's streets through which – in contrast to Selvon's *The Lonely Londoners* – walking is not a sign of creativity but of a piece with the oppression experienced inside. Adah's attempts to find accommodation after the eviction from Ashdown Street take her and Francis into the insalubrious streets of Kentish Town and past a number of derelict houses and bomb-sites 'in different stages of demolition' (77). As in many of the texts explored in *Postcolonial London*, the bomb-site or derelict house offers an ambiguous place for London's newcomers as a location at once neglected and abandoned but also the area where the new communities which characterize postwar London take root and rebuild the city in new ways, irrevocably changing it. Adah's walking through the dereliction of Kentish Town has little of the creative optimism found in texts such as *In Pursuit of the English*, but rather emphasizes misery and homelessness. When they visit Pa Noble to seek lodging they walk through cold rain, 'their hearts . . . panicky and their steps uncertain' (89). Pa Noble's house, the oldest house in the street, sits in the gloomy part of Willes Road and appears 'neglected. The front garden contained piles of uncleared rubbish and the fence needed mending' (90). In *Second-Class Citizen* there is little of the figurative possibility of dereliction and ruin which we considered in the previous chapter, and walking through it is dispiriting. Similarly, one particularly bleak episode depicts Adah, heavily pregnant, struggling to a surgery in Queen's Crescent as she is concerned about the condition of the child she is carrying:

> Adah hurried, wobbling, to Dr Hudson's surgery at the Crescent. It was a horrid day, grey, with the sparse snow of the night before, clinging to the ground. It could not melt because the ghostly sun that shone from among the heavy clouds was hazy; too hazy to have any effect on the stubborn snow. It made it very dangerous for Adah to walk. But, anyhow, she padded on just like a duck, first to the right then to the left . . . Perhaps one or two people would have liked to ask her if she needed any help but got scared off by the determined look she gave them all. She walked on, and did not see the people.
>
> (105)

Wobbling like a duck down slippery streets that render progress slow and 'dangerous', Adah's walking strikes a vivid contrast with the motion of the men in Central London that we considered in Chapter 1. Walking in the city seems to offer little alternative to the oppressive conditions of Adah's existence. The meeting between Adah and Mr Okperi in the park also emphasizes this predicament. Hence, one is left to ask if London can ever facilitate a space where Adah can take control of her situation and fulfil her ambitions beyond the gendered and cultural restrictions she has experienced.

The novel's conclusion would tend to suggest, depressingly, that the answer to this question is in the negative. Emecheta chooses to conclude the novel not with Adah's successful court action against Francis forced by his violent behaviour, but with her childhood friend sending her home to her husband in a taxi. The friend calls to Adah by her childhood name,

'Nne nna' (185), using the same intonation as her father used to, which tends to suggest that even by the novel's close Adah remains subservient to the patriarchal definitions of Nigerian men. Certainly, as in *In the Ditch*, Emecheta refuses to provide a happy or conclusive ending. Adah's struggles against poverty, patriarchy and racism will continue beyond the limits of the narrative and continue to mould her experience of London presumably after Emecheta has finished telling Adah's story.

Yet, set against these dreary realities there is mooted an alternative, hopeful space which parallels some of the optimism and potential of Selvon's St Pancras Hall, MacInnes's Napoli and the derelict house with its typist described by Lessing – and recalls the affiliative compound described in *In the Ditch*. It is a space where the filial obligations of family, tribe and nation are confronted by the possibility of a supportive affiliative community which is exquisitely transcultural and liberatory. At its heart is language, especially the reading and writing of books. The possibilities of this utopian space are glimpsed in the events at Chalk Farm Library, to where Adah moves after a period of employment at North Finchley Library.

Throughout *Second-Class Citizen* libraries are represented as a salve to Adah's misfortunes. At a practical level they offer her work and money, but they are also places were Adah is free to explore imaginatively the world beyond the filiative constraints of her life in Kentish Town. When Adah takes a job at Chalk Farm Library she becomes part of an inclusive affiliative community and involved in important acts of reading and writing. As opposed to Adah's grim domestic environment, at the library the atmosphere is 'light-hearted' (161). Adah's new English boss is wittily called Mr Barking, and is thin and bad-tempered but 'without a touch of malice' (160). Her colleagues include Peggy, an Irish girl; Fay, described as 'a half-caste West Indian' (161); and Bill, a 'big handsome Canadian' (160). Each character has problems: Mr Barking's daughter is ill owing to her miserable marriage, Peggy's Italian sweetheart seems to have deserted her, Fay's self-consciousness regarding her race has led to an unhappy relationship with an English law student, while Bill's wife is expecting another baby and he is worried that their flat is too small to accommodate the family. Bill has an important influence on Adah. He encourages her to read the work of Nigerian writers such as Flora Nwapa and Chinua Achebe and teaches her about other black writers. Soon a community of readers is formed:

> During the staff break [Bill] would talk and expand on authors and their new books. He would then request [a book] and the Camden Borough would buy it, and he would read it first; then he would pass it on to Adah and she would pass it to Peggy. Peggy would pass it to any other members of the staff who were in the mood to read books. It was

through Bill that Adah knew of James Baldwin. She came to believe, through reading Baldwin, that black was beautiful.

(160–1)

The passage of the work of writers such as James Baldwin charted here bears witness to the affiliative and transcultural connections nurtured in the library: a London borough buys a book by an American writer at the request of a Canadian which is then passed between a Nigerian and an Irishwoman. In this way does the library make possible the crossing of borders of race, nationality and gender for the purposes of politicization. Through reading Baldwin Adah learns about black power and is further inspired to read the works of Karl Marx. Although Bill might appear to be another male authority figure, in truth his relationship with Adah is supportive and between equals. Bill 'is the first real friend she had had outside her family' and always in the mood for 'literary talk' (161). Adah's relationship with Bill holds forth the possibility that men and women can encounter each other fruitfully beyond the boundaries of patriarchal authority and racial, cultural and national differences. At the library Adah 'discovered a hidden talent which she did not know she had before – the uninhibited ability to make friends easily' (170). The value of this uninhibited location cannot be underestimated. In their staff breaks the employees collectively fashion an imaginative subaltern space of multicultural inclusiveness and equality that offers an alternative to the social divisions of the London beyond its doors. Susanne Pichler has remarked that although 'Emecheta's characters do interact across ethnic and racial boundaries . . . interaction is firmly restricted within the confines of minorities' (2001: 107). However, the resources which the affiliative community discover at the library offer the means by which, imaginatively at least, their restricted position can begin to be contested.

It is crucial to realize that although Adah engages with positive images of black identity through her reading, the subaltern space envisioned at Chalk Farm Library is not racially specific or exclusive but exists beyond the borders of racialized identity. In this way, it stands as a significant political and transcultural alternative to the political organizations of black British women such as OWAAD which, especially in the 1970s, attempted to unite around a common conception and experience of being black and female. In *Second-Class Citizen* the Nigerian community in London offers little hope of empowering women, while the possibility of a wider black community of African, Asian and Caribbean collective resistance is never entertained. The novel also suggests that the familiar narrative of postwar black British female dissidence – in which women initially mobilized using a common rhetoric of blackness that subsequently fragmented under the pressure of cultural difference – effectively ignores early alternative models of resistance formulated by black women *but not exclusive to them,* in which race did not function as a modality of militancy. Emecheta's work imagines novel forms of empowerment and transformation for black women in 1960s London which in many ways anticipate the 'second moment' of black representations normally attributed to the 1980s.

As with Selvon's St Pancras Hall, the fertility of the subaltern space of the Chalk Farm Library is undermined by its fragility; it is a space which remains more as a possibility than as a permanent achievement in London. Its fertility is emphasized by Adah's decision to write a book of her own, *The Bride Price,* after she leaves her post owing to the impending birth of her fourth child, Dada. Unlike her colleagues, Adah does not share her personal problems with others, but the writing of her novel allows her to vent her feelings. Her book contains 'everything that was lacking in her marriage' (175). Significantly, her first readers are Bill and Peggy at the library, and Bill in particular encourages her to publish her work, declaring it her 'brainchild' (176). These responses encourage Adah to consider herself as a writer, while the term 'brainchild' also suggests that Adah's creative potential need not be confined by her obligation as Francis's wife to provide (preferably male) children and administer their welfare. The equation of Adah's book with her children – whose survival she prizes above everything else – underlines the importance that Emecheta invests in the act of writing. Writing, like reading, is the means to agency, self-determination, politicization and the resistance of oppressive filiative obligations. Yet the fragility of the space nurtured in the library which has made possible the writing of Adah's book is underlined by its temporary existence. Francis's interventions attempt to close down the liberatory potential of Adah's reading and writing by declaring her incapable of producing a book and pronouncing upon the impropriety of a woman acting as a writer. 'You keep forgetting', he tells her, 'that you are a woman and that you are black. The white man can barely tolerate us men, to say nothing of brainless females like you who could think of nothing except how to breast-feed her baby' (178). His response to this 'brainless' woman's writing of a 'brainchild' is to burn it because 'my family would never be happy if a wife of mine was permitted to write a book like that' (181). The conflict between the filiative obligations of family and the affiliative networks which have inspired Adah's writing could not be more stark. The importance which Emecheta invests in the act of writing is underlined by the fact that it is the burning of Adah's book – not the beatings she has suffered, her husband's neglect of their children or his indolence – which finally prompts Adah to leave with the children and seek a legal ruling to stop Francis from threatening her with knives in her new flat.

So, mindful of Emecheta's investment in the act of writing as the discovery and performance of female self-determination in London, the writing of *In the Ditch* and *Second-Class Citizen* must be understood not simply as the social documentation of 1960s Kentish Town for which the perceived weaknesses of the author's style are patronizingly forgiven – but as fundamental acts of self-determination and agency on the part of a Nigerian woman in London who explores critically, and dares to project, the possibilities of subaltern communities of support. Certainly *Second-Class Citizen* is not immune from the utopian visioning to be found in many narratives of postcolonial London across the period considered in this book; but nor is it immune from making some prejudicial representations concerning Nigerians in London which perhaps limit the postcoloniality of its critique. Emecheta's London of the 1960s is violent, lonely, oppressive, bleak and injurious. Yet it is also a potentially transformative location where, in Homi K. Bhabha's phrase, '*something begins its presencing*' (1994: 5). The challenge which *Second-Class Citizen* presents to its 1970s readership is to find ways of protecting, nurturing and making concrete the liberatory space which it temporarily discovers, before it is destroyed by the coercive obligations of both the host and diaspora communities.

The significance and subversiveness of Emecheta's early fictions have been acknowledged by Joan Riley, who cites Emecheta in her essay 'Writing reality in a hostile environment' (1994) as importantly conveying the realities of black people in Britain from an insider position. 'The development of an indigenous literature based on the experience of black people in Britain is a relatively recent phenomena [*sic*]' (547), she claims. 'Although there are notable exceptions, i.e. Buchi Emecheta's *Second Class* [sic] *Citizen* and *In the Ditch*, the black experience in Britain was usually interpreted by "white" usually sociological parameters' (547). As her essay proceeds, it is clear that Riley considers her own fiction to share many of the concerns of Emecheta, specifically British racism, the patriarchal oppression of women within diaspora communities, and the experiences of 'women forced to strength through economic and social necessity' (548). The potentially burdensome obligations of community also weigh upon Riley's mind, especially as regards the role of the black writer in Britain. In a point which parallels Stuart Hall's identification of the 'first moment' in the cultural politics of black representation, she writes ambivalently of her position in relation to the people about whom she writes. In speaking of 'the responsibility for the collective consciousness of a community' (549) often loaded on to the shoulders of black writers in Britain, Riley points out that to reject this responsibility brings accusations of selling out one's roots from all sides – yet to accept it puts the writer 'in an unequally untenable position, where ownership of your own thought process is subject to community approval' (549). Significantly, as the essay reaches its conclusion, Riley represents the obligations of 'community approval' in terms of spatial restriction. Her determination to write about the ugly lives of 'women considered *losers*' (549), often suffering violence from husbands, fathers and siblings, invites complaints from those angered by her unflattering portrayal of black British life which, she feels, 'creates a difficult climate in certain situations for the writer to find manoeuvring space' (550). A few paragraphs later, she confesses that the hostility which her novels have provoked from some readers in the black community has influenced her ability to write: 'In my own creative process, there is an ongoing struggle to create a breathing space' (551). Riley's pitting of community against creativity, with the former threatening to paralyse the latter, recalls a similar tension explored in Emecheta's writing (epitomized by the burning of Adah's manuscript by Francis on the grounds of familial disapproval).

The need to discover and defend a space of agency where black women are neither paralysed nor smothered by the compulsion of others is at the heart of Riley's London fiction. Yet, in contrast to Emecheta's work, Riley offers few obvious resistant or transformative resources for her central characters, and their mercilessly bleak experiences of the city offer only shreds of hope. The dystopian thrust of her fiction is clearly part of an intention to ask uncomfortable questions of London's black diaspora communities, which she hopes 'raises the possibility of change' (552) – yet it is problematic that London's 'hostile environment' as Riley portrays it seems almost to neutralize the subversive and transformative elements of 'writing reality' (552). Jana Gohrisch has mounted a spirited defence of Riley's work as making possible social change 'because Riley's construction of reality includes all of its elements: gender, race and class. Thus, the reader is able to decode her stories and to draw her or his own conclusions in order to develop strategies for future intervention' (2001: 280–1). But as I hope to show in my reading of *Waiting in the Twilight*, Gohrisch's optimism (however much one wants to support it) is unwarranted. In Riley's novel 'the possibility of change' is almost thwarted by the representation of London as a place of repetition rather than a space of transformation, to the extent that strategies of intervention seem almost impossible to imagine, formulate and realize. That said, in the novel there *can* be discovered the faintest of traces of a transformative vision for black women in London which need to be teased out.

Riley's bleak, dispiriting and often upsetting representation of diasporic life in London perhaps owes something to its moment. Born in 1958 in St Mary, Jamaica, Riley came to Britain as a young woman. Her four novels to date – *The Unbelonging* (1985), *Waiting in the Twilight*, *Romance* (1988) and *A Kindness to the Children* (1992) – were written over twenty years after

Emecheta began to publish, and on the other side of a number of formative and unhappy events in postwar black British history (the impact of which we will consider more in the next chapter), such as the riots of 1976, 1981 and 1985, and the election of Margaret Thatcher's Conservative Government. Like *Second-Class Citizen*, *Waiting in the Twilight* explores the difficult conditions suffered by women living in London partly created by obligations of filial duty to both family and community (ever present in Adella's consciousness of 'respeck'). Yet in contrast to Emecheta, despite the overwhelmingly gloomy prospect of the novel's depiction of the city, Riley *can* envisage the (all-too-rare) loving aspects of filial relationships as helping to shape new progressive and resourceful social relations. Riley's subaltern communities of resistance have little of the transcultural inflection of Emecheta's hopeful convergences, while she is slightly but significantly more hopeful about the resourcefulness of filiative relationships in sustaining the fortunes of black women in London.

Narrated through a series of flashbacks, *Waiting in the Twilight* offers a sobering account of postcolonial London in which the hopes of the first postwar migrants to the city – of well-paid employment, jobs with prospects, decent accommodation – are taken away piece by piece. It does so from the perspective of a Jamaican migrant, Adella Johnson, whose struggle to survive in Brixton is compounded by the uncaring behaviour of her partner, her suffering a stroke which affects her ability to continue a career in embroidery, mounting poverty, an indifferent and often racist white population, and the social mores of the Caribbean diaspora in which she lives. Adella arrives in London having experienced the cruelty of both Jamaican society and men. As a young woman she worked as a seamstress in Kingston but lost many of her middle-class customers, as well as a place in her cousin's comfortable home, when she became pregnant to Beresford, a local policeman who was already married. Socially ostracized and condemned to a life in a Kingston yard, she begins to dream of travelling to England as a form of escape from poverty and social disapproval in Kingston, as she has heard that the 'country was so rich you could pick money off the street' (Riley 1987: 118). Her marriage to Stanton, at first so kind and considerate, promises to rescue her from an unhappy existence in the yard, and she follows him to London eighteen months after his departure. But Adella's life in London brings only more disappointment. Stanton's earnings on the buses are meagre, and he resents the fact that Adella has given birth only to daughters since her marriage as well as her determined attempts to buy a house for their family and leave their small, rented room. He begins regularly to 'hit and pound [Adella] as if she was to blame for all the things gone wrong with him since he had come to England' (90). When Adella falls ill after suffering a stroke and loses partial mobility of her body,

Stanton takes up with her cousin, Gladys. Regardless of her new immobility, Stanton beats and eventually leaves Adella to bring up their children on her own. Despite suffering years of abuse, as her death approaches Adella still waits for Stanton's return, dreaming of their reunion. Her last days are spent working as a cleaner in Brixton Town Hall and sitting quietly in her dark living room, smoking cigarettes and watching John Wayne westerns on TV while brooding over her unhappy past.

As in Emecheta's writing, in *Waiting in the Twilight* the family unit and the domestic interior are dangerous places for women. In the London sections of the novel Adella battles hard to possess and control her family's accommodation, haunted no doubt by her unhappy experiences in Kingston. Her determination to find, possess and control space by buying a house with money from the 'pardner' system sparks the first conflict with Stanton. She dates the beginning of their difficulties to the day she suggested that they move out of their rented room (owned by a landlord who likes to take advantage of female tenants) to 'gwine fine space' (12) to raise their children, some of whom are still in Jamaica and will soon arrive. Against Stanton's wishes she buys a large house on Eldridge Road in a 'decaying part of Brixton' (14) and is delighted at last to have 'her own place' (24) despite the damp and mildew. She secures the family financially by letting some rooms to other Caribbeans in London. Yet Stanton's antipathetic behaviour, fuelled by his frustration in not fathering a son, severely curtails Adella's sense that she now has room in which to live and she comes to spend her evenings in a state of semi-paralysis as Stanton spends more and more time away from home:

> It was bad enough with him out all the time, working late or out with his friends. All those hours after the children were asleep. All that time, just sitting in the half-dark, waiting for him to come back. It seemed to her that all she had done since coming to England was have his children, work, and in the evenings sit in a chair or lie in her bed, waiting for the furtive sounds that told her he was back.
>
> (30)

This passage marks the different relationship with space frequently experienced by migrant men and women in postcolonial London. Stanton's enjoyment of outdoors is contrasted with Adella's stasis within the home, and also reveals the extent to which his freedom of movement beyond the home is enabled by Adella's labour within it – her cooking, cleaning, management of the house and care of the children. Rather than Adella discovering freedom of movement and some welcome room through the acquisition of the decrepit house, Stanton's behaviour threatens to make her living space analogous with her subservient life in the Kingston yard. This is one of several ways in which life in London threatens to repeat Adella's unhappy existence in Kingston, severely curtailing a sense of the city as a transformative space through the perpetuation of patriarchal and filial obligations.

The house becomes a site of paralysis rather than agency for Adella, as evidenced by her suffering a stroke at the age of thirty-four which is described in terms that have particular resonance in Riley's writing:

> [Adella] came awake slowly, a muffling, suffocating weight choking down on her. It was everywhere. In her throat, pressing on her lids, crushing her. Her chest hurt from the effort to breathe, lungs labouring loud and gasping in her ears . . . Feelings seemed to be leaving her body, leaking rapidly from the left-hand side. Her legs were like lead weights, resisting every attempt, every command to move, and the panic increased, causing the blood to pump loudly in her ears. She tried to calm her rapid breathing.
>
> (49)

The crippling effects of Adella's stroke are suggestive of her general experience of living in London, in which she is denied an emancipatory space of agency where (to recall Riley's comments in her essay) she can both manoeuvre and breathe. The stroke takes away her ability to move freely: she has slowly to learn to walk again and to write, 'holding the pen in her left hand, the feel unfamiliar, as she wrote wavering letters, then words' (56). On one occasion its effects are recalled as Stanton tries to suffocate her with a pillow after she complains about Gladys's continued presence in their house: 'The soft suffocating weight pressed down on her, and she thrashed about in panic, her breathing loud and muffled in her ears' (63). Owing to her partial paralysis Adella loses her embroidery job and takes up lower-paid work as a cleaner. When Stanton finally leaves to settle with Gladys in Battersea, Adella's financial hardship forces her to accept favours from men in exchange for their sexual pleasure (recalling her dependence on Beresford). The increasing dereliction of her house drives away her tenants, and it is eventually repossessed. This, it seems, is the biggest blow to Adella in London: 'They had pulled the heart out of her when they took her house' (13). Adella is relocated nearby and suffers 'the shame of living in a government house' (127) in which there is 'less room to stretch herself out' (126). After suffering another stroke, she approaches death in the anonymous environment of the hospital as the staff, with cruel irony, try and fail to find a bed in a ward to accommodate her.

The gradual loss of living room for Adella in London is the measure of her decline and failure to find the space to manoeuvre and breathe. There is nowhere for her to reside in the city, and her death gloomily underlines her unsuccessful attempt to build for herself a better life away from Jamaica. In London she lives in a succession of 'waiting rooms', dependent on others and increasingly devoid of the ability and the room to move as the twilight of her life approaches. Even to leave 'the reluctant grip of the spongy chair' (44) in front of the television is a trial and requires the help of her daughter Carol: 'Adella stretched her limbs with relief, wincing as needles of cramp coursed through constricted limbs, mingling with the aching in her bones' (44).

Throughout her time in the city Adella has nowhere she can go for support, and there seems to be little chance of significant assistance in Brixton's Caribbean neighbourhood. Although churches provided black women with one of their main sources of support and sustenance in post-war Britain, Adella suffers only pain and humiliation at church where, during one service also attended by Stanton and Gladys, Stanton's adultery is publicly denounced by Pastor Douglas. Her rejection by her husband and the behaviour of her cousin suggest that the family is also a source of pain, while it is worth noting that Adella's relationship with her children is unhappy. Only her youngest daughter, Carol, seems to offer regular care and, with the exception of another daughter, Audrey, the other children are virtually absent. Adella's view that the children in general 'had got infected with white people's ideas' (133) suggests a generational tension between children and parents, and Carol makes reference to a conversation amongst her children about 'getting together and sending you back to Jamaica so you can live with Aunt Claudia' (9). Jana Gohrisch argues that Adella's daughters, whose lives are only glimpsed in the novel, offer positive role models in their rejection of Adella's values, language and adherence to 'respect' in order to embrace the 'liberal set-up of urban Britain' when compared to Kingston (2001: 285). Yet Adella's experiences of church and family in London question the extent to which London has proved to be more liberal than Kingston, while Gohrisch's argument seems to disqualify any transformative potential assigned to Adella and contradict her assertion that Riley 'celebrates the courage and stamina of black women of Adella's generation' (284).

The Caribbean community in Brixton, especially the behaviour of women, is a particular source of coercion and enmity which contributes to Adella's unhappy experience of the neighbourhood's public spaces. She perceives the neighbourhood at large as a demanding community obsessed with appearance and scandals of social impropriety; yet she conforms to its regulations. When her daughter Audrey drives her through Loughborough Road to a hospital appointment, Adella gets her 'to blow the car horn, feeling important as [people] looked up, startled. By the time she finished she knew that the whole neighbourhood would have heard how she went out with her daughter' (Riley 1987: 70). Yet the social masquerade of Adella as a good mother, lovingly looked after by her respectful children, is buckled by the memory of her daughters Dolores and Eena who, like Adella, become pregnant outside of wedlock, and whom we never see in the novel (not even at Adella's deathbed). Adella's life in the neighbourhood has been a painful process of keeping up the appearance of respectability in the face of the 'shameful' behaviour of her family.

The neighbourhood seizes with delight upon any story of social scandal. Despite the fact that Stanton is exposed as an adulterer in church, Adella is mortified: 'it was her they would talk about at the market. Already she had seen it: the sudden silences, the furtive looks' (11). As with the Queen's Crescent Saturday market in *In the Ditch*, Riley portrays Brixton market as a divisive and by no means liberating location. Adella is upset by the gossip about Stanton and Gladys she encounters 'on the street, in the market' (90), and her children also suffer during their visits after Stanton moves to Battersea: 'Often the children would come back from the market . . . angry and embarrassed. The other black women from the street had stopped them in the market, talked about their father and how well he was doing. They would always pity them, tell them what a shame he didn't care about them' (133–4). The market is a centre of gossip and conflict, the most important location in the community – 'Everything happened there' (140) – which seems unhappily to replicate the intolerant social mores of Kingston.

The most important form of speech valued in this community is scandalous gossip, in which Adella tries her best to participate. As a younger woman she spent much time 'trapped inside' (70) her Brixton home anxiously watching the neighbourhood from her window, as it 'would never do to have someone telling her what was happening on her street, and she not knowing enough to join the conversation' (70). According to this novel, women do not in general support each other in the neighbourhood but instead add to the sense of isolation and subservience to social coercion. Despite suffering many times the disapproving judgements of others which cause her feelings of intense shame, Adella continues to stick strictly to the principles of her upbringing, especially the importance of family. She scolds her children for speaking disrespectfully about Stanton – 'You pickney jus doan have no respeck' (139) – and clings to the dream that he will one day return to his place at her side as her husband. She fails to see that her uncritical 'respeck' for familial and social propriety makes her complicit with the very hypocritical and judgemental attitudes which fuel scandalous gossip and which were behind her eviction from her cousin's house in Kingston (and, after her marriage, her subsequent social acceptability). It is chilling that Riley makes 'respeck' Adella's dying word. Hence, Adella also falls under Riley's critical gaze – it is part of Riley's commitment to subjecting black lives to frank examination that she offers a 'portrayal of weakness' (1994: 549) in the character of Adella which makes her more than a stereotypical passive victim.

Riley suggests that London temporarily had a supportive, accommodating diaspora community, but it has gradually disintegrated and also come under threat from white racism. This is revealed in the brief juxtaposition made between Adella's early years in Loughborough Road surrounded by other Caribbean families, and the building of the Stockwell Park housing estate. In the novel's present, Loughborough Road 'was almost empty of houses now, full of the sprawling tangled yellow brick of Stockwell Park estate' (Riley 1987: 70) and, like the community it temporarily accommodated, is in ruins. The dangers of walking these streets are emphasized one evening when Adella walks down nearby Mostyn Road:

> She had turned down the unlit street, past the church where both Eena and Dolores got married after their disgrace. It was silent now, the brown long door painted a garish blue. The stained-glass windows had gaping holes or wire mesh across them. It looked empty and derelict – not well kept like it had been when the street had been the heart of the community, bristling with sounds and full of life. She knew that the council had decided to pull it down and put up flats like the ones that stood where tall houses once joined together. A woman had been found murdered in the car-park underneath those flats and a boy just turned eighteen had been given life imprisonment. It was from that time that her daughters had started worrying about her walking up the dark and empty street alone.
>
> (75)

Silence, emptiness, dereliction, the loss of old houses, violence against women – the fortunes of the neighbourhood seem to mirror those of Adella's life. As she walks down Mostyn Road she is mugged near a rubbish tip by two white youths who steal her bag and leave her bruised and shaken. On returning home her daughter Carol demands that she calls the police, much to Adella's annoyance: 'She had been wary of them since the riot when they had broken down her friend's door and beaten up her disabled husband just because he was black' (77). The police seem no different than Stanton in visiting violence on the disabled, and they appear indifferent to Adella's plight. They presume that Adella's attackers are black as it is 'unusual to hear of white youths engaged in mugging activity' (79). Brixton's public spaces and forms of authority replicate the violence of Adella's domestic life. Both the diaspora neighbourhood and the police offer little protection or support. The price, as ever, is the room to move freely: Adella's daughters demand that she no longer walks in such derelict areas.

For these reasons, *Waiting in the Twilight* is in many ways a pessimistic and unrelentingly bleak book which annuls virtually every act of subaltern resistance, empowerment and transformation in postwar London. Families are coercive, the streets are unsafe, the neighbourhood is a ferment of hypocrisy and scandal, the police are racist, and men and women seem perpetually locked in unhappy marriages or adulterous affairs. In contrast to the creation of Adah's brainchild in *Second-Class Citizen*, Riley's novel is pervaded by an atmosphere of waste and death, from the opening description Adella as a 'mobile rubbish tip' (1) as she cleans the Town Hall to her final depiction dying on a hospital trolley.

In her attempt to depict the 'hostile environment' of Brixton, Riley perhaps too quickly writes out the realities of female agency, survival, innovation, creativity and community formation in London. In so doing she is in danger of perpetuating the power of the very forces which she critiques: patriarchy and male chauvinism, claustrophobic families, the city's racism. The possibility of change in London seems remote. But there is, perhaps, something transformative suggested in the character of Adella's friend, Lisa, and the relationship she builds with Adella. They had first met on the boat which took them from the Caribbean to Britain, and throughout the novel Lisa strikes a marked contrast with Adella. If Adella's story recalls those women from the Caribbean who arrived in London at the behest of their husbands, Lisa's fortunes bear witness to the lives of migrant women who arrived and survived on their own. It is clear that Riley considers the independent circumstances of these women as the key to empowerment and transformation in London.

Throughout *Waiting in the Twilight* Lisa is a constant source of strength and uncompromising resourcefulness. She manages to convert Stanton's 'anger into resignation' (5) when she explains to him Adella's pregnancy as a result of an encounter she has on the boat coming over; she looks after Adella's children when Adella suffers her first stroke and is confined to hospital; and throughout their friendship she offers practical advice when Adella loses her embroidery job and encourages her to take a stand against Gladys's tenancy in Adella's home. She is a determined and proactive character, possessing a 'deep full laugh, vital, full of zest for life' (23). Despite being the same age as Adella, '[t]he bounce still in [Lisa's] feet, her shoulders still unbowed' (46). She sends regular money home to her family, including her husband and two children. She tolerates neither racism nor male authority: she gives up her training as a nurse when she realizes that the 'long hours and the rudeness of the white patients were not for her' (23) and demands that Adella confront Stanton over his affair. Significantly, although she indulges in local gossip with her friend, there is a mutual respect of privacy between them: 'It was alright to gossip about everyone else, to talk about the way they ran their lives, and all the things they did wrong; but that was not the way of friends. What Lisa wanted to know she told her, and everything else was not her business' (24). The affiliative relationship between two friends respectful of each other's privacy seems the only productive relationship in the novel, more so than Adella's relationship with her daughter Carol, with Lisa's determination to take control of her life a source of support and example for Adella. Lisa's characterization approaches idealization, perhaps, yet there is also a sense of her struggle and sacrifice which the novel does not show. On one occasion when they reflect on the past, Lisa praises Adella's decision to buy her house in Loughborough Road and contrasts it favourably with her decision to send her savings to her family in the Caribbean: 'Adella looked at [Lisa] in surprise. She had never thought of what Lisa had gone through. To her the other woman always seemed so carefree, so full of life' (128). Lisa's 'carefree' existence has come at the cost of her separation from her children and a life spent living alone; there is another story behind her happy existence which is not told. And although Lisa seems to possess more agency than Adella, she too is not free from the obligations of family as demonstrated by her regular remittances which stop her from buying a house in London. None the less, Lisa's presence in the novel hints at the possibility of relations which conflict with the scandalized imperiousness of the neighbourhood in which privacy is never respected and perceived acts of social impropriety are condemned.

Importantly, Lisa's input into Adella's well-being recalls the only act of kindness which Adella experienced in Kingston. When she had lived in disgrace in the yard she received important support from Granny Dee, who travelled from her village of Beaumont to take charge of Adella's situation. She was kind and forgiving: 'A was young once Adella. A didn't mek de same mistake, but what's to sey a wouldn't do it if a did get de chance?' (115). The suggestion is, it seems, that the loving support of figures like Granny Dee – by no means typical of the attitude taken towards Adella by members of her family – is required in London if women are to survive. If the novel has a utopian vision, it is that 'the possibility of change' can only occur if the filial love epitomized by Granny Dee informs Brixton's affiliative alliances – singularly lacking in the unhappy encounters at Brixton market, but importantly figured in the relationship between Adella and Lisa. It is a glimmer of possibility in a dark novel, to be sure, but its illuminating presence requires recognition even if very little happens in Brixton's market, churches and streets to establish permanently both community and change based upon this model. Although Riley's desire to write about the reality experienced by women like Adella almost ignores the ways in which women are not fully determined by London's hostile environment, ironically her discovery of meaningful, supportive and transformative practices in the positive and loving synthesis of the filial with the affiliative seems more generous than Emecheta's dismissive attitude to most things Nigerian.

I want to conclude this chapter by turning finally to the lyric poetry of Grace Nichols, in particular her second collection *The Fat Black Woman's Poems* (1984), in which a dynamic and confident sense of London as a resistant space for black women is created through the *ad hoc*, unpredictable and seemingly innocuous tactics of everyday life. Once again, the focus is upon a female figure who exists at a remove from a supportive diaspora neighbourhood, and whose relations with space are inflected with the discourses of racism and chauvinism. Born in Georgetown, Guyana, in 1950, Grace Nichols was educated at the University of Guyana and worked as a teacher and a journalist, before coming to Britain in 1977. In her poetry of the 1980s we discover an uncompromising and determined attitude towards change in London for black women. In particular, Nichols rewrites the domestic scene as a site of female empowerment and stresses that the resources gathered can be brought to bear on the discriminatory character of the city's public spaces. Notably, the advocacy of female solidarity, black consciousness or coordinated communities of resistance are just as absent from Nichols's work as they are from Emecheta's and Riley's. In contrast, however, the poetry's tone is significantly and strategically light. The women who appear in Nichols's work refuse to be vanquished by the circumstances of city life, often by challenging their burden of oppression with small-scale yet far-reaching acts of transformative levity.

Dennis Walder has described Nichols's poetic manner as 'sly, brash, exuberant, laid-back and wonderfully economic, refusing cliché while drawing on the myths of old and new worlds to articulate a complex, fluid vision' (1998: 148). Nichols's poems are frequently brief lyrics, occasionally organized into sequences, as in her first collection *i is a long memoried women* (1983). The London poems found in *The Fat Black Woman's Poems* evidence the ways in which Nichols's engagement with 'old and new worlds' in the city both reveals and confronts a racialized mapping of urban place. In the collection's second section, 'In Spite of Ourselves', several poems propose a vista of London in which their central figures struggle to bridge their Caribbean past and current sojourn in the city. An instructive poem is 'Like a Beacon', in which the speaker's craving for her mother's food causes her to 'leave art galleries / in search of plantains / saltfish / sweet potatoes' (1984: 27). The poem admits the possibility of finding 'mother's food' in London's markets and hence acknowledges a comforting Caribbean presence in the city. Yet the juxtaposition between the high cultural environment of the art gallery and the 'touch / of home' (27) to be searched out beyond it makes a comment about the cultural life of postcolonial London: in this instance, Caribbeans have brought a touch of home to the city in certain environments (especially markets) but not others (art galleries). Rather than envisioning London as a hybridizing location, Nichols's poem points to a city suffering from social and cultural division. The linking of 'old and new worlds', in Walder's phrase, which Nichols imaginatively forges is facilitated against by the city at large, creating a tension between text and city. In these terms, her use of the lyric genre can be considered as analogous to the presence of the migrant in the art gallery: a learned genre of English poetry is forced to admit the 'nation language' (11) of popular Caribbean consciousness and experience in London, just as London must be forced to make room for those like the speaker of 'Like a Beacon'. In its very form Nichols's poetry challenges the cultural cleavages of the city which keep separate the realms of officious and subaltern cultures.

A sense of London as a divisive social location is emphasized in two other poems, 'Island Man' and 'Fear'. In the former, a Caribbean island man in London awakes to the sounds of blue surf 'breaking and wombing' (29) and the seabirds and fisherman which recall his 'small emerald island' (29), only for these to change into the 'dull North Circular roar' (29) as he regains consciousness. The reassuring sounds of the Caribbean island jar with the surge of wheels that heralds 'Another London day' (29). The motion of the wheels and the orbital route of London's North Circular highway (which, with the South Circular highway, forms one of London's major ring roads) are of a piece with the repetitive monotony of 'another' day in the city. And in 'Fear', the speaker talks of further divisions when she remarks how 'Our culture rub skin / against your own / bruising awkward as plums' (28). Although 'black music enrich / food spice up' the host community, other kinds of presence (the black woman in the art gallery, perhaps) create awkwardness and, more sinisterly, 'bruising'.

These are not just circumstances affecting women, of course, but the particular challenges women face in such a hostile environment are especially addressed in the seventeen poems which constitute the opening section of the collection, also entitled 'The Fat Black Woman's Poems'. Their central figure, the Fat Black Woman, is neither the traditional singular consciousness of the English lyric genre nor simply a homogenizing cliché for fat black women everywhere. Rather, she exists between these two positions, appropriating the lyric 'I' while calling to mind different kinds of stereotypes of fat black women. These include Saartje Baartman, the 'Hottentot Venus', a Southern African bushwoman who was brought to London in 1810 and exhibited at 226 Piccadilly to an audience fasci-nated by her large body and prominent buttocks (Fryer 1984; Sandhu 2003); the 'mammy' figure or 'jovial Jemima' of American culture witnessed in such films as *Gone with the Wind* (1939) (Roberts 1994; Manring 1998); and the objectified, sexualized body such as that 'celebrated' in the Hep-tones' song 'Fatty Fatty' (1976). Nichols's Fat Black Woman 'remembers her Mama / and them days of playing / the Jovial Jemima' (1984: 9) while acknowledging the unhappy 'heritage / of my behind' (13). Importantly, Nichols juxtaposes images of the Fat Black Woman as a creature of beauty and sensuality. The opening poem of the sequence, 'Beauty', presents her 'walking the fields' while the sun 'lights up / her feet', and 'riding the waves / drifting in happy oblivion' (7). The final poem, 'Afterword', depicts her emerging from a forest 'flaunting waterpearls / in the bush of her thighs' and looking forward to 'when the winds pushes back the last curtain / of male white blindness' (24). A key element of each depiction is her ability to move: as she puts it in 'Invitation', 'when I move I'm target light' (12).

In the poems which depict the Fat Black Woman living in London she exists somewhere between these poles – the objectifying and weighty her-itage of the past and the beautific possibilities of the future which are gathered in the multiple meanings of the word 'light': clarity of vision, ease of movement, and frivolity or levity. The former tends to be experienced out of doors, while the latter is discovered inside the house. The Fat Black Woman's experience of London's public spaces makes her conscious of her perceived race, gender and size. In 'The Fat Black Woman Goes Shop-ping', she wanders unhappily through the cold of a London winter looking for clothes to fit her body. The 'frozen thin mannequins' (11) and the sales staff exchanging 'slimming glances' (11) fix her size as excessive and a prob-lem, as she acknowledges in the poem's conclusion. Yet its tone suggests agency and cunning:

> The fat black woman could only conclude
> that when it come to fashion
> the choice is lean
> > Nothing much beyond size 14
>
> > (11)

As well as rewriting the fashion world as lacking and impoverished by countering the 'slimming glances' with 'the choice is lean', the final line of the poem (which stands on the page slightly to one side of what has gone on above it) functions almost like a 'punch-line', making light of the unhappy 'journeying' it otherwise records. The rhyming of 'lean' with '14' creates a comic concluding couplet that challenges the arrested smiles of the thin mannequins 'fixing her with grin' (11). This momentary yet momentous act of levity, which refuses the paralysing propensity of the store to fix the Fat Black Woman's public persona as an aberration not easily accommodated, packs a subversive punch. In countering with witticisms her objectification in the store (which stores up unaccommodating prejudices and ways of seeing, not just ill-fitting clothes), the Fat Black Woman arguably mobilizes in a public space some of the resources she has made for herself at home.

Rather than envisaging the domestic environment as an arrested location in which women are trapped, abused or abandoned, Nichols presents it as a space where the Fat Black Woman discovers and discharges her subversive agency. She is, significantly, a solitary figure – the fourth poem in the sequence, 'Alone', depicts her sitting separately 'gathering // silence' (10) – yet her solitude is not necessarily a sign of her wretchedness, as it appears to be for Riley's Adella. Rather, it seems more of a piece with the single-minded determination and fortitude associated with Emecheta's Adah or Riley's Lisa. In 'Thoughts drifting through the fat black woman's head while having a full bubble bath', the motion of 'drifting' which featured in the poem 'Beauty' becomes a vital means of critique. The Fat Black Woman's wandering thoughts seize upon the dramatic situation of her bathing body and use its images to challenge the discourses of objectification and oppression. While happily bathing she at first trifles with the word 'steatopygous' – a term coined in the nineteenth century to describe the buttocks of 'Hottentot' women – before her attention wanders to the weighty matters of anthropology, history, theology and the slimming industry. She toys with each: she longs 'to swig my breasts / in the face of history' and 'scrub my back / with the dogma of theology' (15). These unaccommodating discourses are effectively cut down to size by her wayward thoughts during the seemingly innocuous act of taking a bath. Her body becomes scripted as a site of oppression *and* the means of imagining resistance; yet the tone throughout is as light as the bubbles in her bath in which, like her thoughts, she happily floats. The witty use of images of cleaning (scrubbing, soaping) emphasizes her inventiveness while underlining the importance of being able to 'drift'.

Similarly, 'The Fat Black Woman's Motto on Her Bedroom Door' consists of two lines which pit the flesh of hope against the slimness of despair, while in 'Looking at Miss World' the Fat Black Woman watches in vain for an entrant who looks like her. Disappointed, she 'gets up / and pours some gin / toasting herself as a likely win' (20). Once again, the witty rhyming couplet brings the poem to a frivolous conclusion at the same time as it records a moment of vital self-assertion and advocacy of her beauty. In 'The Fat Black Woman Versus Politics' she challenges those 'stalking the corridors of power' (22) with her own 'manifesto of lard' (22). These comical acts of subversion are epitomized in 'Small Questions Asked by the Fat Black Woman': in their frivolity, lightness, mobility and optimism, Nichols asks small questions of larger structures of division and oppression. Indeed, the fact that *The Fat Black Woman's Poems* is such a slim volume of poetry (sixty-four pages in total) is part of Nichols's general playfulness with scale and one aspect of her strategically light-hearted approach to conventionally weighty matters.

Nichols's Fat Black Woman is a restlessly subversive and disruptive presence whose imaginative flights of fancy make possible momentous acts of resistance. In focusing attention upon the agency and opportunities which exist at the level of the quotidian, Nichols unlocks the remarkable transformative potential of black women at large in London and suggests the ways in which they may make room on their own terms and in opposition to the determinants of racial, chauvinist and other discourses which attempt to keep such women in their perceived place – dutifully attending to negligent and violent men, struggling through the city's dangerous and violent streets, or taking low-paid and menial employment just to support themselves and their children. For Nichols, black women never fail to have promise and subversive potential in London, as emphasized in 'Waiting for Thelma's Laughter'. Dedicated to Nichols's West Indian born Afro-American neighbour, the speaker declares: 'You wanna take the world / in hand / and fix-it-up / the way you fix your living room' (36). In a different manner from the work of Emecheta and Riley, but in common with them too, Nichols's poetry suggests how black women might make 'living room' for themselves, both within the house and beyond its walls, where neither the racist heritage of the past nor the burdensome conflicts of the present may fully arrest their agency – and in a city which, both culturally and socially, is far from accommodating, hybrid or cosmopolitan.

The work of Emecheta, Riley and Nichols serves a number of important functions in our understanding of postcolonial London. Their images of women trying to settle in the city call attention to a gendered experience of London which impacts upon the agency to move at large. The seemingly supportive diaspora neighbourhoods are exposed as presenting not filial support but obligation, and for these writers prove to be unhappy places of compulsion which offer little respite from the racist and sexist city beyond. In seeking ways of resisting such adverse conditions, Emecheta and Riley question the efficacy of forms of neighbourhood support structured by the supposed similarities of race, nation or gender. Emecheta's writing is forthright in rejecting filiative forms of community and entertains instead the resistant possibilities resulting from, on the one hand, affiliative forms of practical support as depicted in *In the Ditch* and, on the other, the transcultural negotiation of imaginative resources which emerge briefly at the Chalk Farm Library in *Second-Class Citizen*. Riley's novel depicts a relentlessly unhappy portrait of female life in the city in the character of Adella, yet does not fully annihilate the possibility of support and agency born from the affiliative friendships struck in Brixton which echo and admit the possibility of filiative relations between women. Nichols's poetry is much more confident and determined in discovering, exploring and celebrating female resourcefulness in London where the domestic environment is rewritten as a significant site where tactics of resistance can be negotiated and deployed. Above all, the various kinds of subaltern transformative resources discovered in reading their work suggest that black female insurgency in London occurred before and beyond the activities of the important black women's groups of the 1970s and 1980s, and must not be forgotten when the history of formal social protest is narrated.

4   Babylon's burning

Linton Kwesi Johnson, Hanif Kureishi and Salman Rushdie

In the winter of 1987, the Jamaican-born novelist Ferdinand Dennis made several visits to Brixton as part of his journey around 'Afro-Britain'. He described the Brixton neighbourhood as a 'Jamaica Abroad', an ebullient and dynamic neighbourhood epitomized by the 'highly charged atmosphere' (1988: 188) of Brixton market on a Saturday morning. 'Even some of the street names suggest energy', he wrote: 'Electric Avenue, Coldharbour Lane' (188). Yet the exuberance of 1980s Brixton could not mask reminders of more sober and bleak times. Opposite Lambeth Town Hall stood the Tate Library, named after 'the sugar company which for centuries ran sugar plantations in the Caribbean' (188) and was implicated in Caribbean slavery. On taking a walk along Railton Road, known locally as the 'frontline' (198), Dennis surveyed the 'numerous shabby shop-fronts' (197) and recalled the days when '[t]he road used to fork, and in the triangle formed were buildings which had become a market for ganga' (197). Although the Frontline had recently changed, it was hard to forget recent events in which Brixton had been brought to the attention of the nation.

Further along Railton Road Dennis discovered a mural which captured and connected the pain of Atlantic slavery with the events of London's recent past:

> Titled 'The Dream, the Rumour and the Poet's Song', it was painted by two artists, South African born Gavin Jantes and Dominican Tom Joseph. It is a sort of homage to events in Brixton and the Brixton-based, Jamaican-born poet Linton Kwesi Johnson – note the Ghanaian day name. The mural tells a story. It starts with pictures of people migrating, followed by pictures of children caught in a terrible fire. It ends with the poet reading his works under a spotlight. The migration is easy to understand. The children and the fire less so. It is based on an incident which became known as the New Cross Massacre. In January '81, thirteen young Afro-Britons died in a fire

in New Cross, an area not far from Brixton. The cause of the fire
remains a mystery.

(199)

On public display, the mural records the transcultural travails at the heart
of London's history as well as the intolerant response towards those who
have settled and raised families in recent years. The 'terrible fire' of the
New Cross Massacre, possibly one of the most shameful events in postwar
British history, occurred on 18 January 1981. The community's dissatisfac-
tion with the response of the police and the Government to the tragedy led
to a day of action on 2 March which featured a march through Central
London, culminating in Hyde Park, while in the following month riots
exploded in Brixton. As Ron Ramdin puts it:

> the New Cross tragedy struck deep responses within the black commu-
> nities, where there was enough tinder needing only a spark, which was
> lit (after a long period of intense police harassment) in Brixton on
> Friday, 10 April 1981. This area of postwar settlement was ablaze . . .
> Youths (blacks, Asians and whites) responded to their perceived
> neglect to their lives and, between April and July 1981, they rioted in
> as many as 29 cities and towns across Britain in an unforgettable
> summer of crowd violence.
>
> (1999: 300)

Conjoined to this riotous response to social conditions was a significant
cultural response, epitomized in the Brixton mural by the figure of Linton
Kwesi Johnson, Brixton's foremost poet and chronicler of the neighbourhood's fortunes, captured at a moment of public recitation. Like Johnson's
dub poetry, the mural offers a record of significant social events which
locates them in the longer history of black migration and diaspora. In
depicting fire, it also mobilizes a recurring image in the work of three figures
whose representations of 1980s London and its violence preoccupy us in
this chapter – Linton Kwesi Johnson, Hanif Kureishi and Salman Rushdie.

In his account of the urban riots of the 1980s, Michael Keith has
pointed out that the flaring of violence did not happen randomly but was
in part produced by a long history of vexed social relations between
London's black communities and the police. 'The spaces in which police
and Black communities have clashed', he suggests, 'are not just a container
of these conflicts, they are a constitutive part of them. If we want to understand how conflict has evolved, we have to understand how histories are
written and geographies imagined on both sides of the divide' (1993: v). In
the 1970s and 1980s, London witnessed violent clashes often between the

police and young black Londoners in a number of neighbourhoods with histories of migration and settlement. Such locations included the Notting Hill Carnival celebrations of 1975 and, most dramatically, 1976; the Brixton riots of April 1981; the 1985 riots on the Broadwater Farm estate in Tottenham; and further disturbances at the close of the Notting Hill Carnival in 1987. Specific streets such as Railton Road in Brixton and All Saints Road in Notting Hill became contested spaces in the cognitive mapping of London as, from one perspective, centres of black criminality and lawlessness; or, from the other, political resistance and insurrection. The different and contested meanings of Brixton's Frontline are instructive. Keith cites an interview with Courtney Laws of the Brixton Neighbourhood Community Association who claims partial responsibility for the term, for whom the 'Frontline' denoted a space 'where people from the Caribbean normally gather, meet and talk and very often start up socializing groups and functions. It is very peaceful and quiet' (26). Yet this view was contradicted by a local policeman, Chief Superintendent Plowman, who claimed that the Frontline was named after its significance as 'the front line of confrontation between Black and White' (27).

Representations of postcolonial London join the contest of spatial meaning in their references, either direct or allusive, to such signs of history as 'Notting Hill 1976', 'Brixton 1981' or 'Tottenham 1985'. Many texts take issue with the pejorative representations of the riots as the crazed and spontaneous actions of an unruly mob running out of control, and of the rioter as a delinquent, destructive and mindless criminal. According to Lord Scarman's report on events in Brixton in April 1981, nothing could 'justify [or] excuse the disorders or the terrifying lawlessness of the crowds' (1982: 119). For Scarman, the seeming instantaneous chaos of riot in no way could be deemed to possess the purpose and coherency of a burgeoning social revolt. The texts we explore in this chapter question to different degrees such officious assumptions of the 'terrifying lawlessness' of London's riots – although as we shall see especially in the work of Kureishi and Rushdie, such representations are not immune from a number of anxieties which arise in connection to the incendiary activities of the rioters.

According to most commentators, London's history of inner-city rioting bears witness to the ongoing conflict between the city's Afro-Caribbean and Asian diaspora communities and the Metropolitan Police which progressively worsened during the 1970s and 1980s. Yasmin Alibhai-Brown records the words of a police officer working in London during the 1980s who clearly felt that his racist actions were sanctioned by the state: 'Thatcher let it be known to us, the police, that we could do anything to keep in control the enemy within . . . I know that when I was on duty in Notting Hill Gate, I would go for the blacks more than I should have done, but you get into a kind of state, like you are in the army and the enemy is the enemy. No wonder the blacks never trusted us' (2001: 81). The identification by members of the police of black peoples as the 'enemy within' is commensurate with the ideological manoeuvres of figures such as the Conservative politician Enoch Powell in the 1960s and 1970s, and Prime Minister Margaret Thatcher – described by Alibhai-Brown as the ideological 'daughter of Powell' (78) – who gained office in May 1979 and would centrally influence racialized definitions of British national identity in the 1980s. As Anna Marie Smith describes it, Thatcherism (as it came to be known) was an ideological project of the political right indebted to Enoch Powell's populist notions of race and immigration voiced from the late 1960s which attempted to redefine Britain as an all-white nation whose soul was deemed under attack from sinister and 'alien' diaspora communities (Smith 1994). Powell is often remembered for his apocalyptic 'Rivers of Blood' speech delivered at the West Midlands Conservative Political Centre, Birmingham, on 20 April 1968. Declaring immigration to Britain a madness, Powell apocalyptically declared that

> [a]s I look ahead, I am filled with foreboding. Like the Roman, I seem to see 'the River Tiber foaming with much blood'. That tragic and intractable phenomenon which we watch with horror on the other side of the Atlantic but which there is interwoven with the history and existence of the States itself, is coming upon us here by our own volition and our own neglect.
>
> (1969: 289)

Even though his speech immediately cost him his place in Edward Heath's Shadow Cabinet, Powell's declarations of race and nation sadly granted political respectability to racism and attracted instant popular support, the effects of which were immediately felt on London's streets (and elsewhere). More than 2000 workers in London's Tilbury and St Katharine's Docks walked out in support of his speech three days later. Hanif Kureishi remembers that after Powell's speeches were reported

> graffiti in support of him appeared in the London streets. Racists gained confidence. People insulted me in the street. Someone in a café refused to eat at the same table as me. The parents of a girl I was in love with told her she'd get a bad reputation by going out with darkies.
>
> (2002: 28)

Keen to frighten his white British audiences into a sense of apocalyptic doom, Powell was not immune from deploying incendiary images in his proleptic vision of a Britain destroyed by immigration. 'It is', he said, 'like watching a nation busily engaged in heaping up its own funeral pyre' (1969: 283).

By the 1970s racist attitudes were at the heart of authoritarian forms of state control and clearly animating the discourses of nation, citizenship and law and order which impacted readily in London and elsewhere. As Paul Gilroy has shown, although 'the identification of law with national interests, and of criminality with un-English qualities' (1991: 77) has a long history, in the postwar decades black Britons became increasingly portrayed 'as law-breakers and criminals, as a dangerous class and underclass' (75). Policing in the 1970s was often influenced by racist notions of black criminality which also functioned to legitimate heavy-handed police tactics. These included the notorious 'sus' law, Section 4 of the 1824 Vagrancy Act resurrected by the police to allow the lawful arrest of someone suspected of an intent to commit a criminal offence. In addition, and long before the worst riots erupted, in 1970 the police created Special Patrol Groups (SPGs) trained in riot control techniques (officers from the SPG are alleged to have killed the white anti-National Front demonstrator Blair Peach, during an anti-racist protest in Southall in April 1979). In the spring of 1981 the SPG embarked upon an operation in Lambeth, Swamp '81, which was 'characterised by road blocks, early morning raids and random street checks directed at four housing estates, all with predominantly black populations' (Ramdin 1999: 254). Subjected to repeated police harassment, institutionalized racism and discrimination in jobs and housing, and living in some of the most neglected areas of London, many in the black communities organized themselves politically and began forcefully to resist the behaviour of the police who had come to resemble, in A. Sivanandan's stark phrase, 'an army of occupation' (1982: 49). In short, they fought back.

In Ferdinand Dennis's view, Linton Kwesi Johnson's work 'sums up the radical political mood in Afro-Britain throughout the Seventies, culminating in the '81 riots' (1988: 200). Aged thirteen, Johnson came to London from Jamaica in November 1963. He lived in Brixton and went to Tulse Hill Comprehensive School. Although technically a migrant to the city like each of the other cultural figures we have considered in detail so far, his arrival as a child makes him distinctive. Johnson's life and work forms a bridge between the postwar generation of migrants to London, especially those from the Caribbean, and their children's generation – the so-called 'second generation' of British-born black Britons who reached young adulthood in the 1970s and 1980s. He too arrived with illusions that 'the streets of London were paved with gold', only to discover a city that 'was grey and cold and horrible' (Johnson 1999: 53). His experiences as a schoolboy were often shaped by racism from pupils and teachers alike. Verbal abuse from his peers was a daily reality, and despite being a bright student in Jamaica he was put in the lowest ability group with '95% of all the other black kids' (53). He also came across the racism of the police early in life. He recalls one youthful incident when he attempted to intervene in the arrest of a man in Brixton, only to find himself arrested along with three others and beaten up in a police van before being charged with assault.

In the early 1970s he met John La Rose, a major figure in the Caribbean Artists Movement (CAM), who introduced him to the works of Aimé Cesaire, Gwendolyn Brooks and other black writers, as well as important figures in CAM such as Andrew Salkey. These encounters gave Johnson both the inspiration and the means to write; he remembers being asked to participate in CAM events at Islington's Keskidee Centre (where he later worked briefly as the Library Resources and Education Officer). He was also drawn to the Black Panther Youth Movement, a significant militant presence in London in the late 1960s and early 1970s influenced by black resistance in the United States. A Black Panther group was set up in Shakespeare Road, Brixton, in 1968. Through his participation with the Panthers, which he joined in 1970, Johnson encountered the writings of C. L. R. James, Eric Williams and W. E. B. Du Bois. The Panthers also trained him to respond to racial harassment. When he was arrested, beaten and charged by the police, he advised his co-accused to ask to see a doctor and say nothing to the police until a lawyer arrived; the case against them was eventually dropped and the police officers involved were transferred. Of equal importance were the influences and energies of the streets – especially the social events, parties, sound-systems, reggae records, toasters and DJs beloved of Brixton's young people. Their cultural initiatives represented an alternative and youthful aspect of Caribbean-influenced creativity in London which contrasted with the work of Caribbean-born writers such as John La Rose who knew little of the key figures prized by this generation (Johnson 1999).

Johnson's dub poetry owes much to these influences: the exploration of Caribbean cultural forms by members of CAM, the political militancy of the Panthers, and the creative culture of Brixton's youth. It was forged in the oppressive and hostile cauldron of 1960s and 1970s Brixton and, as we shall see, bears witness to the explosive encounter between police harassment and black resistance. Unlike those figures associated with CAM, Johnson's work was not primarily concerned with Caribbean history, politics and culture, although these things are important to it. Rather, it captures something of the 'different hunger' (Sivanandan 1982: 49) of black youth in 1970s and 1980s London who had grown up knowing the city as their only home. Drawing upon the practices of toasters and DJs who add their own verbal commentaries ('talkovers') while playing records, dub poetry combines the spoken word with the rhythms of reggae music. The musical aspect of the genre, either provided by a band or in the shape of a recording with which the dub poet performs, is much more than 'accompaniment': it is integral to the dub poetry text and emphasizes the significance of the genre as a form of public performance and communication. It is worth remembering that live performances, studio recordings and publications of the textual element of dub poetry are essentially different things. Yet in all of its versions, dub poetry is 'the poetic articulation of a political discourse . . . Dub poets lend their voice to sufferers who have no say and no voice. The art form thus becomes an integral, ideologically committed and hortatory part of the political struggle it reflects' (Habekost 1993: 115).

As with Emecheta's fiction, it is tempting to read Johnson's dub poetry primarily for its documentary and political value, and as the informative voice of London's black youth which offers a view of their struggle in the inner city from within (and on behalf of) its oppressed communities. In my response to Johnson's work of the 1970s and early 1980s I want to consider the forms and functions of its aesthetic concerns, especially the recurring apocalyptic imagery and its vision of a community united in resistance to the machinations of 'Babylon'. Johnson offers a creative yet strategic mediation of the inner-city tensions of the period that makes his work more than a documentary or social record of the period.

As we have seen, to many migrants of the 1950s and 1960s, London's fabulous enchantment when seen from afar is often rendered through the loving incantation of place-names, as evidenced by the ways in which Lord Kitchener and Selvon's Sir Galahad are thrilled by the names of Shaftesbury Avenue, Waterloo Bridge and Charing Cross. Johnson's work offers an alternative inventory of place-names wholly devoid of mythical charm and rewrites the map of London to reflect a sombre geography of the city's realities that is grounded in the experiences of British-born or -raised black youth. In 'Inglan is a Bitch' he adopts the persona of an adult migrant who has 'jus come to Landan toun' (2002: 39). The migrant's optimism and hope is communicated through the music which adopts a spirited reggae rhythm punctuated by the horn section, and is written in a cheerful and uplifting major key. After a series of jobs working for the London Underground, washing dishes in a hotel, digging ditches and packing crockery, the narrator gloomily realizes that the metropolis is not the land of opportunity it seemed, and that 'dere's no escaping it' (39). The poem cancels entirely the mythical London prized by the generation to whom Johnson's parents belonged, and which is rendered by the totalizing and abstract term 'Landan toun'. Whereas figures from the previous generation (as we have seen) attempted either to keep faith with London's utopian potential or discover new and optimistic modes of self- and social transformation, Johnson's response is much more antagonistic and defiant. The verbal aspect of 'Inglan is a Bitch' ends with the line, 'is whe wi a goh dhu bout it?' (41). It is given dramatic effect in the Island Records studio recording: Johnson recites the line accompanied only by bass and drums while the words 'bout it?' are made to echo. At this moment, the voice of Brixton's youth arguably breaks into the migrant persona to demand a defiant and unbending response to the city's discriminatory conditions. And in a manoeuvre only visible to the reader of the textual version of the poem, Johnson welds together the individual voice and that of the community in his spelling of the pronoun 'wi' which captures both the plural 'we' and the singular 'I' (and also recalls the Rastafarian invocation of 'I and I'). Here the singular voice of the suffering migrant segues into a youthful narrative 'wi' which is both singular and communal, and which defiantly contests the unacceptable circumstances of the city by adopting a confrontational tone that attempts to rally the community into action.

In place of the migrant's mythical 'Landan toun', then, Johnson offers insight into 'di age af reality' (35) as perceived by Brixton's youth. His poetry is full of important references to significant sites for Brixton's youth. In early works such as 'Yout Scene', 'Double Skank', 'Five Nights of Bleeding' and 'Bass Culture', he makes reference to a number of people and places significant primarily to Brixton's black population. These include the Hip City record shop on Brixton's Atlantic Road; the Frontline on which could be found Shepherd's, a local name for the Railton Road Youth and Community Centre of the Methodist Church; and reggae rappers and DJs such as I-Roy and Big Yout. This strategy is discernible as dub poetry's 'inner discourse which discloses itself only to readers who can perceive and decipher patterns of allusion' (Habekost 1993: 9). In addressing a specific audience with the intimacy of a toaster in a dance hall, Johnson positions himself squarely in the locations and language of the local community – it is another aspect of his attempt to forge solidarity, conjured by the pronoun 'wi', from the singular 'I' and the communal 'we'. These references to location also make possible an alternative mapping of Brixton which is partly a rehearsal of tenure and a defiant celebration of the rooting of black peoples in the neighbourhood. In some of his later poems such as 'Di Great Insohrekshan', this tendency to make an inventory of people and places important to black communities in London (and occasionally elsewhere) comes to function as a determined act of 'Mekin Histri', through which Johnson records the names of those murdered by racists or deemed guilty of racism, and celebrates those communities (and their supporters) who defiantly resisted state-endorsed violence and 'chace di babylan away'

(2002: 65). Johnson's dub poetry makes a fundamentally important mapping of the city which rewrites it in terms of the places, people and events of its black communities.

Yet the claim to represent 'reality' at the heart of Johnson's work requires further comment. In dub poems such as 'Mekin Histri', which describes the Brixton riots of 1981, the impression is given of Brixton's youth uniting as one against the behaviour of the police and joining with other oppressed groups in a common insurrection – Johnson also makes reference to the 1979 uprising of London's Asians in Southhall that demonstrated 'plenty zeal' (64). Yet, as Michael Keith has argued, '[t]he disorders in London in the summer of 1981 did not involve a multi-racial alliance in insurrection and they were not attributable to any neatly defined demographic group that could be described as "Black youth"' (1993: 97). My point is not that Johnson misrepresents the 'reality' of the riots of 1981 – Keith's view does not necessarily represent the truth of what happened either – but that in writing about the riots Johnson imaginatively forges important communal bonds and claims a common political consciousness to events. The riots may not have facilitated communal spirit and political solidarity; but this *is* the purpose of Johnson's dub poem. In what he makes of the history of 1981, Johnson attempts to create a robust and coordinated image of communal action which resources its identity and celebrates its agency. It is not necessarily what occurred during the riot, but for Johnson it is what he wants strategically to *make* of it. Hence, in Johnson's representation of Brixton 1981 the inevitable 'mistri' (2002: 65) of precisely what really happened, common to all historical events, is firmly erased by the community's 'mekin [of] histri' (65) which is confidently asserted. It is not so much reality as a version of reality which Johnson wishes to promote for important political and strategic reasons (which, one might add, are by no means compromised as a consequence of their fictive characteristics).

Johnson bears witness to the joviality, determination and fortitude of the city's young blacks which spill over into reggae. The studio recording of 'Want fi Goh Rave' captures their mood in its upbeat, brisk and buoyant reggae beat, bright horn-section and restless percussion. Yet youth is constantly having to engage with a different kind of 'beat', namely the racist violence of the police who 'beat dem dung a grung' (3). In the studio recording of 'Sonny's Lettah (Anti-Sus Poem)' this is discernible in the section which describes the police's beating of 'likkle Jim' (27). In the lines 'dem tump him in him belly / an it turn to jelly / dem lick him pan him back / an him rib get pap' (28), the verbs and nouns gain an extra stress from occurring in-between the reggae off-beat ('tump, belly, turn, jelly, lick, back, rib, pap'). This helps to emphasize the violent impact of the repeated blows through the choice of verbs, while the nouns emphasize the pain suffered by Jim's body which we can almost hear being broken. The bodies of Brixton's black youth are constantly being pulled between two forces of animation: 'di bubble and di bouce' (14) of reggae rhythms, as it is described in 'Bass Culture', and the violence of the police which, as in 'Sonny's Lettah', arrests the motion of black youth and, in the word of the narrator, 'beat mi to di grung' (29).

The confluence of each force of animation in the word 'beat' reminds us that, like the violence of black youth, Johnson's dub poetry insists on making a resistant response to the social conditions of the inner city. If Johnson's work marks the violence of the police in its rhythms, it is also syncopated by violent acts of resistance in black communities. In 'Sonny's Lettah', Sonny attacks a police officer in an attempt to free Jim – 'mih jook one in him eye / and him started to cry' (29) – and, when the officer dies, is sentenced to life imprisonment in Brixton Prison for murder. The dark mood of the poem, at once melancholy and sinister, is emphasized by the minor key of the music and the mournful harmonica. It also paints a bleak picture of London: black youth is always in danger of attack while the police have at their disposal the 'sus' law (Sonny and Jim are simply waiting innocuously at a bus-stop when the police arrive). Above all, the poem demonstrates how the violence of black youth is not a sign of juvenile or racial delinquency but produced in response to the actions of state authority. The rebellious and determined response of youth to this state of affairs is conjured in Sonny's beating of the police and his declaration of action (which recalls the closing sentiment of 'Inglan is a Bitch'): 'I jus coudn stan-up deh / an noh dhu notn' (28). Time and time again Johnson celebrates those who stand up for their rights in London in the face of hostility and oppression. In 'All Wi Doin Is Defendin' the speaker warns the 'oppressin man' that 'wi will fite yu in di street wid we han' (11).

The violence to which black youth turns on London's streets is a recurring concern in Johnson's dub poetry. As well as suggesting it to be an entirely legitimate response to racism, it is crucial to understand that Johnson takes a great deal of care to differentiate it from the violence perpetrated by racists and the police. In 'Street 66', a poem which concerns a raid on a reggae party, one character, Western, invites the police to 'step rite in an tek some licks' (10). These 'licks' are not coincident with the beatings of racists and the police. Indeed, the fiery allusion in the term is part of a recurring register which Johnson uses to represent resistant violence as legitimate and righteous. Images of fire permeate many of his representations of London, which frequently appears as a fiery apocalyptic urbanscape where law and order do not function equitably, violence and death are rife, and the city is suffering social meltdown. Such infernal visions of the city bear particular witness to events such as those in Brixton in April 1981 (as in 'Di Great Insohrekshan') and the New Cross Massacre some weeks earlier. The latter event is captured in 'New Craas Massakah', one of Johnson's most moving poems. In the studio recording, the stanzas which deal with the 'rackin to di riddim' (54) of the jovial partygoers are recited to a swift reggae beat which captures the congenial atmosphere of the party that turns to chaos when the fire starts. The music stops dead when Johnson soliloquizes the terrible grief which bonded 'black Britn' (55) and records the failure of the police, the press and the Government to respond adequately to the massacre. Significantly, he records the black community's response as follows:

> yu noh remembah
> how di whole of black Britn did rack wid rage
> how di whole a black Britn tun a fiery red
> nat di callous red af di killah's eyes
> but red wid rage like the flames af di fyah

> (55–6)

The fires lit by London's racists which burn black peoples in their homes and streets cause unimaginable pain and ultimately prompt a similar *but not identical* fiery protest. It is crucial to realize that Johnson does *not* see the resistant rage of 'black Britn' as of a kind with the murderous violence of racism which is turned back upon London's racists. Johnson appropriates fire as an image of righteous rebellion which is different from the pathological hatred of 'di killah's eyes'. In this alternative sense of the fire as a red rage devoid of the killer's callousness, he captures both the pain of inner-city life and a legitimate angry response indebted to quite specific historical and cultural antecedents. In 'All We Doin is Defendin' the narrator warns that continued oppression will lead to a violent eruption. 'Black Britn' will sing 'songs of fire', for 'wi is fire!' and 'wi carry dandamite in wi teeth' (12). The 'dandamite in wi teeth' offers a novel way of understanding the verbal medium of Johnson's work as situated within the struggle of the community. Most importantly, the declaration that 'wi is fire' uses a vital image of resistant rebellion which is not equivalent to racist violence. If racists light fires out of a pathological hatred of those they deem to be different, the fires of resistance are inspired by song – or, more precisely, reggae.

For Johnson, reggae music has always made possible 'songs of fire'. In 'Reggae Sounds', reggae is considered to join the pain of oppressed black peoples throughout history with the pent-up passions of the present created by inner-city hostilities. In the pulse of reggae music and the passions it inflames, Johnson detects a means of connection with the history of slave rebellion in the Caribbean which (especially in Jamaica) frequently mobilized fire as a means of resistance. In a parallel fashion to Selvon's view of calypso as the popular creative mode of Trinidadians, Johnson regards reggae as the popular expression of the people's pain which both shapes and fuels their incendiary resistant rage, a cultural resource that both reflects and inspires social uprisings. In the poem the different elements of a reggae band – bass, drums, trumpet, organ, rhythm guitar – are connected to the natural elements of thunder and lightning, and the music they make is in harmony with the '[r]hythm of a tropical electrical storm' (17) that recalls the Caribbean landscape. This is, specifically, a 'flame-rhythm' appropriate for the 'time of turning / measuring the time for bombs and for burning' (17). Reggae is equipped to harness the red rage of the 'hurting black story' and 'shape it into violence for the people' who 'will know what to do, they will do it' (17). As in 'New Craas Massakah', this is a form of rebellion that is not the same as the callousness of the racist killer. The city's troubles are the latest chapter in the longer 'black story' that, as in the past, requires a 'time for turning'. A similar story is told in 'Bass Culture', which also contextualizes inner-city resistance in the history of plantation slaves 'burstin outta slave shackle' (15). In this poem the 'bubblin bass' (14) of reggae threatens racialized spatial boundaries 'pushin against di wall / whe bar black blood' (14). It is 'hattah than di hites of fire / livin heat doun volcano core' and 'is di cultural wave a dread people deal' (15). The reggae-fuelled rebelliousness resembles, but is not the same as, a form of madness. The oppressive conditions of Brixton and other such neighbourhoods may cause them to explode, but the fiery energies unleashed are not anarchic nor randomly murderous. Those energies take shape in reggae music and draw upon the example of a history of slave rebellion. So, in 'Di Great Insohrekshan' which records the 'truly histarical occayshan' (60) in April 1981 when 'wi run riat all owevah Brixtan' (61), the narrator acknowledges that 'wan an two innocent get mar' (61) yet makes it clear that the targets of the violence are structures of state authority rather than individuals. The poem records that the rioters burned down the George public house in Railton Road, a locally known racist locale, but spared the landlord; while their burning of police vans was an attempt to 'mash-up' the ideological forces it represented, namely 'do wicked wan plan' and 'Swamp Eighy Wan' – the latter a reference to a policing operation in the area in 1981 which targeted the black community.

Rather than consider fiery resistance as the racist violence of the state turned back anarchically against itself, Johnson suggests that the incendiary activities of black youth are of a different nature and originate from an alternative social and cultural history. If London is burning then those responsible are ultimately the agents of the state, such as the police, supported by a Government entirely unsympathetic to a particular constituency of the population. The fires lit as part of the uprising are not signs of anarchy or delinquency, but represent a coordinated and conscious social and cultural response indebted to the 'hurting black story' of previous centuries. Johnson's city, then, is a cauldron of domination and resistance, massacre and 'insohrekshan', in which black youth both demands and makes possible the extermination of the unacceptable conditions under which they live. Resourced by reggae, contextualized by a conscious history of protest against slavery, racism and oppression, they are hardly delinquent or criminal. In defiance of Lord Scarman's conclusion about the delinquent activities of black youth, in Johnson's poetry their endeavours are rewritten as a righteous revolt and not an anarchic riot.

As we saw in 'Reggae Sounds', the violence of fiery resistance is the possession of the 'people' who can be trusted to act appropriately: 'they will know what to do, they will do it' (17). It is a significant gesture of support for the integrity and purpose of popular revolt. In turning next to Hanif Kureishi's film *Sammy and Rosie Get Laid* (1988), directed by Stephen Frears, we encounter a different and less optimistic rendering of popular violence. Kureishi's approach questions the alleged righteousness of rioting and is less confident about its capacity to facilitate and constitute popular revolt. To a large extent the differences in attitudes between Johnson's dub poetry and Kureishi's film are both cultural and geographical. Whereas Johnson's teenage years in Brixton exposed him to the cruel realities of London's racism, Kureishi's suburban upbringing kept many of the problems of the city at bay. Oddly, despite being slightly younger than Johnson and born in London, Kureishi's visions of London seem more akin to those of the migrants of the 1950s rather than their children. His father was a migrant from Bombay whose family moved to Pakistan after the partition of the Indian subcontinent in August 1947, while his mother was British-born. Kureishi spent his childhood in Bromley, Kent, a suburb to the southeast of London, often experiencing discrimination and hostility as someone perceived to be of 'mixed race'. He did not grow up like Johnson as part of a wider black community radicalized by its experiences of racism.

Lonely in the suburbs and often discriminated against, Kureishi has remarked that his early life left him frustrated and stimulated the longing for the perceived excitements of Central London, marked by the threshold of the River Thames:

> for us the important place, really, was the river. And when you got on the train and you crossed the river, at that moment there was an incredible sense that you were entering another kind of world. And being in the suburbs, we could get to London quite easily on the train – about fifteen or twenty minutes – but it was a big jump . . .

And so, for me, London became a kind of inferno of pleasure and madness.

(MacCabe 1999: 37)

This 'inferno' is very different from the apocalyptic urbanscapes of Johnson's dub poetry. It is a visitor's view of London, part fantastical, part compensatory for the stasis and gloom of the suburbs. The popular creative endeavours of London's youth are imaged as the source of this enticing Promethean 'inferno of pleasure and madness'. As Karim Amir puts it in Kureishi's first novel, *The Buddha of Suburbia* (1990), which is significantly cleaved in two sections titled 'In the Suburbs' and 'In the City':

> There was a sound that London had. It was, I'm afraid, people in Hyde Park playing bongos with their hands; there was also the keyboard on the Doors's 'Light My Fire'. There were kids dressed in velvet cloaks who lived free lives; there were thousands of black people everywhere, so I wouldn't feel exposed; there were bookshops with racks of magazines printed without capital letters or bourgeois disturbance of full stops; there were shops selling all the records you could desire; there were parties where girls and boys you didn't know took you upstairs and fucked you; there were all the drugs you could use.
>
> (1990: 121)

The alleged freedom, multiracial tolerance, cultural novelty, sexual licence and narcotic adventurousness of the city find musical expression in the bongos of Hyde Park and, significantly, in the music of The Doors. Indeed, in citing their song, 'Light My Fire', the passage emphasizes London's popular-cultural Promethean possibilities in sexual terms as a form of 'longing'. This also reminds us that some of Kureishi's most important means for expressing the city's subversive agency include sexuality and youth, deemed key elements of that 'inferno of pleasure and madness'.

According to Ruvani Ranasinha, it is within the bohemian '"fringe world" of city culture that Kureishi's work is located, imbuing it with its distinctive metropolitan, hip quality' (2002: 15). Yet this assumption risks ignoring the profoundly dislocated relationship Kureishi has with this 'fringe world' which appears more often than not as a flimsy, imaginary location, much like MacInnes's Napoli in *Absolute Beginners*, that spectacularly fails to live up to expectations. Kureishi's work is actually concerned with exploring the disjunction between London's 'hip' utopian potential and its sobering realities. That said, he can never entirely relinquish his suburban utopian vision of London, and this complicates his depictions of the city, as *Sammy and Rosie Get Laid* readily evidences. Set in the 1980s, the film recalls the incendiary and riotous relations between the state, represented here by the Metropolitan police and Conservative politicians including Margaret Thatcher, and London's inner-city populations which are young and frequently black. It begins with the shooting by the police of an unnamed black woman, bringing to mind the shooting of Cherry Groce in her bed by police on the morning of 28 September 1985 (the police were looking for her son). This event sparked a riotous response in her Brixton neighbourhood in which one person died. Cherry Groce never walked again; the officer who shot her, PC Douglas Lovelock, was later cleared of all criminal charges and reinstated to his post. As the film proceeds, the action takes place against the backdrop of the neighbourhood's reaction to the killing where the two central protagonists, Sammy and Rosie, reside. An accountant and social worker respectively, Sammy (Ayub Khan Din) and Rosie (Frances Barber) are middle-class figures who enjoy a liberal marriage of 'freedom plus commitment' which, in theory at least, enables them guiltlessly to enjoy other lovers. The return to London of Sammy's Asian father, Rafi (Sashi Kapoor), a politician with a violent past whom Sammy hardly knows, adds complications to their relationship, as does the arrival on the scene of Danny (Roland Gift), also known as Victoria, who befriends Rafi and becomes Rosie's lover. Danny belongs to an alternative youthful community which lives on a makeshift caravan-site underneath a motorway that is threatened by the local property developer. The film heads towards its conclusion by pursuing the characters' numerous sexual relationships, portraying the eviction of Danny's community, and presenting Rafi's gradual decline and suicide.

In one of the opening scenes, Rafi looks out at London through his taxi window and tells the driver, 'for me England is hot buttered toast on a fork in front of an open fire. And cunty fingers.' As well as rendering England in smutty terms of (hetero)sexual longing, the sentiment also appropriates fire to depict an idealized vision of an orderly location. The 'open fire' which Rafi eulogizes provides a comforting, controlled and sustaining heat. It is of a part with his view of London as 'the centre of civilization – tolerant, intelligent and nowadays completely out of control'. Significantly, the city's breakdown of control is emphasized by other forms of fire which metaphorically challenge Rafi's dream of orderliness. Immediately before his sentiment about hot buttered toast, Rosie is depicted leaving a tenement building (she has just found the body of Mr Weaver) where there burns a large bonfire in the courtyard, on to which young people throw debris. This is a much more dangerous kind of 'open fire' which anticipates the night of burning and looting in Sammy and Rosie's (unnamed) South London neighbourhood, and which is also captured by the infernal inflection of Rafi's first words when he arrives there: 'what the hell is this?'

The juxtaposition between the two examples of 'open fire' suggests that the riotous protests depicted in the film are pitted against an imperious sense of civilization and nation. The latter is captured in Rafi's sentiments and echoed in the words of his white English lover Alice (Claire Bloom), whom he knew previously as a student in London. Raised in India and now living in the affluent enclave of Cockfosters, Alice condemns the incendiary activities of London's youth as disrespectful to 'this great land' and remarks to Rafi that 'being British has to mean an identification with other, similar people. If we're to survive, words like "unity" and "civilization" must be understood.' The concurrence of attitudes between Alice, the affluent colonial-born middle-class suburbanite, and Rafi, the Asian politician with a dubious political past, is important. As older characters, their imperial notion of civilization pitted against urban disorder offers a colonial context for the riots in London and the order they challenge. This perhaps recalls a strategy also found in Johnson's work: the representation of inner-city violence as the latest stage in a longer history of anti-colonial protest. When Rosie challenges Rafi one evening about the torturous activities of his government, his answer is forceful: 'I come from a land ground into the dust by 200 years of imperialism. We are still dominated by the West and you reproach us for the methods you taught us.' Rafi's response not only reveals that the violent history of colonialism and its aftermath has British roots, but also invites us daringly to consider the parallels between his autocracy and the rule of law in London's present. The film constructs a genealogical connection between centuries of British colonialist exploitation, Rafi's violent response to his unruly people in the recent past, and the actions of the police depicted in the film to which the rioters aggressively respond.

In responding violently to the police, the rioters are to an extent returning to the oppressors the subjugation they have suffered in a fashion which recalls anti-colonial insurgency. As Danny puts it, 'we have a kind of domestic colonialism to deal with here, because they don't allow us to run our own communities'. The film begins with a voiceover of Prime Minister Thatcher celebrating her third General Election victory in June 1987, which ends with the words 'we've got a big job to do in some of those inner cities'. This 'big job' requires state violence – if Rafi's neocolonial government shot their rioters dead in the street, London's police shoot people in their houses. In using the tyrannical regime of a violent government as a potential parallel for the activities of the British state in 1980s London, Kureishi makes a highly provocative condemnation of Thatcher's despotic approach to the 'big job' of dealing with the inner city. The complicity between a Tory MP and a property developer who are keen to evict the kids' community from the caravan-site – and, eventually, to develop Sammy and

Rosie's South London neighbourhood – as part of a lucrative plan of urban gentrification offers more evidence of Thatcher's utter disregard for London's inner-city population.

Whereas Johnson looked to slave rebellion as a source of inspiration for incendiary revolt, Kureishi's understanding of the fortunes of postcolonial South Asia – coupled with his suburban upbringing – makes his representation of violence particularly queasy. Rafi in particular suggests something of the corruption of power in once-colonized countries and the ways in which his nation-state has turned to torturous forms of coercion in its dealings with the people. The ease with which anti-colonial aggression can become the major mode of oppression in a newly independent nation is worrying, and suggests that for Kureishi the violent protest of London's rioters is at heart problematic. Throughout the film Rafi is pursued by Rosie's friends, Rani (Meera Syal) and Vivia (Suzette Llewellyn), keen to confront him with evidence of his human rights abuses. Near the conclusion he is confronted by the Ghost (Badl Uzzaman), representative of those physically abused by Rafi for the people's 'good', on whose wrecked body are attached electrodes and a headband used for the purpose of electrical torture (as if in a dream these are then placed on Rafi, who is made to suffer the burns). Rafi's crimes are a potent reminder of the ways in which violent protest and violent oppression are different in degree but not kind – or, to use the film's metaphorical register, they are essentially forged from the same fire. In a mode very different from Johnson, the film suggests that resistant hostility is little different from the carnage of despotism; fighting fire with fire brings no significant change.

Once again, it is Danny who raises these problems when conversing with Rafi about the nature of protest: 'But if full-scale civil war breaks out [in London] we can only lose. And what's going to happen to all that beauty? . . . [H]ow should we fight? That's what I want to know.' Not surprisingly then, the film presents the riotous activities of the protesters ambivalently. During the night-time scene when the neighbourhood is burned and the police come under attack, the rioters' activities bear witness to their frustration, pent-up anger and sense of injustice. The police are pelted with bricks; firemen are assaulted when they arrive to extinguish the blazing streets. In depicting these scenes, the film offers only a relatively sympathetic rendering of urban violence to its audience by probing its causes. As Kureishi records in his account of the making of the film, 'Some Time With Stephen', the film is intended to show 'how justifiable the riot is' (Kureishi 1988: 79) although he is also concerned that it may reinforce stereotypes of black youth. On the other hand, the violence engenders little, and increases friction and tensions within the community. During the night of trouble we see three men fighting over a stolen television set and a father battling to keep his son from leaving the house and joining in the neighbourhood's destruction. Danny insists to Rafi that the night's conflict constitutes a 'revolt' and not a 'riot', hence representing it as a form of social uprising. Yet the film is less certain. Indeed, in 'Some Time With Stephen' Kureishi is revealingly indecisive on this matter, referring to the scene with prevarication as 'the riot, or revolt' (79). *Sammy and Rose Get Laid* casts doubt on the extent to which an anarchic riot can become a collective revolt, not least because the community's revolutionary potential is compromised by the destructive propensity of rioting which mirrors the violence and divisiveness of the state. *Sammy and Rosie Get Laid* raises important questions about the extent to which the inner city's violence can be creative or progressive. It is on this point, perhaps, that Kureishi's suburban squeamishness concerning resistant violence can be detected, not least because that violence signals the death of his youthful dream of the city's essential tolerance and excitement.

The film explores critically two further modes of revolt against London's social divisions, the first of which is located amongst the middle-class community represented by Sammy and Rosie. Both characters are represented as having a degree of social conscience which is waning. When Sammy ventures into the riot with his father, he is happy to intellectualize the violence – 'the city is a mass of fascination', he says – and support its anti-authoritarian propensity, until he realises that his car has been vandalized. As an accountant he is part of the money-culture of the 1980s which prospered under Thatcherism, and he is perfectly happy to accept Rafi's gift of a large sum of money despite being aware of his father's corrupt past. There remains only the semblance of radicalism in Sammy and Rosie's shared interests: in one memorable scene, based on a similar moment from Woody Allen's *Annie Hall* (1977), Sammy tells Rafi of the pleasures of London he enjoys with his wife, which include attending the Royal Court Theatre (but only to see plays favourably reviewed by the *Guardian* newspaper), buying novels by women, attending an Alternative Cabaret in Earl's Court where the Government is abused and attending Colin MacCabe's lectures on semiotics at the Institute of Contemporary Arts. Yet these appear as the fashionable indulgences of the affluent middle class which postures liberalism and an openness to alternative politics and culture without becoming deeply involved in social struggles. Indeed, Sammy and Rosie perhaps represent the first stages in a process of gentrification represented in the film by the property developer – in 'Some Time With Stephen', Kureishi gloomily comments that 'the centre of the city is inhabited by the young rich and serviced by everyone else: now there is the re-establishment of firm class divisions; now the sixties and the ideals of that time seem like an impossible dream or naivety' (1988: 77). At one level, Sammy and Rosie represent London's emergent liberal middle class, born from (and nostalgic for) the 'pleasure and madness' of the sixties yet happily prospering in Thatcher's Britain to which they pose no significant threat.

Rosie seems to possess a more acute social conscience than Sammy, perhaps, as her position as a social worker suggests. As Gayatri Spivak wittily puts it, '[Rosie] loves all the right people' (1993: 245): she is happy with lesbianism, 'loves blacks' and is in an inter-racial marriage. Yet her responses to the inequalities of London tend towards solipsism rather than social conscience; after she finds Mr Weaver dead in his bath she tells Sammy and Rafi that 'you wonder what your own life means'. Although she opposes Rafi's offer of money and confronts him over his bloody past, her liberal version of social critique seems disconnected from the realities outside of her apartment. Her politics are increasingly gestural, and her interest in multiracial London and alternative forms of sexuality seems to be fuelled by the opportunities for new pleasurable experience they make possible, rather than their potential social radicalism. The article she is writing about 'snogging as a socio-economic, political psychological event sunk in a profound complex of determinations' seems politically vacant, a point emphasized when she uses a demonstration of her research to make her first advances to Danny. With London burning outside her window, the film suggests that both the sexual and intellectual predilections of the liberal middle class may well be remote from, and incapable of responding to, the social conflicts of 1980s London. In these terms, the scene of 'joyful love-making' at the film's heart shares a similar ambivalence to the actions of the rioters. Although the collage of couplings might be considered as an attempt to pit the pleasure-seeking of the 1960s against the authoritarianism of Thatcher's Britain and its support of 'Victorian' values, with the flames of passion analogous to the rioters' incendiary responses, it is just as likely that the characters' sexual intercourse is an attempt to evade the city's problems and has no meaningful political impact. If the city is, in Kureishi's phrase, 'an inferno of pleasure and madness', the pleasurable pursuits of Rosie and the others offer little means to challenge the apocalyptic madness which has engulfed their neighbourhood.

If Kureishi as a younger man projected London as a counter-cultural location of social and sexual revolution, *Sammy and Rosie Get Laid* records the collapse of this 'impossible dream' which has been fatally assaulted by the social realities of Thatcher's Britain. But as in MacInnes's *Absolute Beginners*, that dream of an alternative London, built upon the tolerant cosmopolitanism of youth, is not fully extinguished. Its potential lies with the occupants of the caravan-site – specifically referred to in the screenplay as 'kids' – and their straggly band who live under the motorway but whom we frequently see travelling through London. With their music and dancing, the kids epitomize a festive spirit that recalls the calypsonian and creolizing energies of Selvon's Londoners, although Kureishi's company is inclusive of men and women, as well as many different races. The kids often appear in spaces which emphasize mobility: immediately after the opening credits they are portrayed singing and dancing in a tube station, and when Sammy races home from Anna's house to greet his father's arrival they slow his passage by walking across the road in front of his car. Their mobile homes are parked below a flyover, the location of which might also be considered another of London's forgotten, derelict sites which – as we have seen throughout this book – play an important figurative role in the imagining of fledgling and alternative forms of community in London. The caravan-site is a creative space: the kids are depicted growing crops in the waste land and using a printing press to produce their own books. When Rafi visits Danny in his caravan a woman can be seen in the background playing music on a keyboard, while Danny has been using his typewriter. The coincidence of these two types of keyboard underlines the connections between popular music and creative writing which inform Kureishi's work, while the community in general suggests that the creative spirit which Kureishi so values in London's youth is at large in 1980s London. In contrast to Johnson, the city's popular music has little truck with riotous resistance and is presented as offering an alternative to, rather than inspiration for, incendiary acts of revolt.

Danny functions almost as a spokesperson for the community of kids, and he also provides a link to Sammy and Rosie's neighbourhood as he was raised by the black woman shot in the opening scene. His alternative name, Victoria, is taken from the Victoria Line on the London Underground which he regularly travels, and emphasizes once again the mobility associated with the kids – as well as wittily androgynizing the monarchical name which Thatcher used in her promotion of heterosexual and patriarchal families as a social ideal via the phrase 'Victorian values'. His supportive view of the rioters' activities is tempered by a critical approach to their methods, and he articulates a possible alternative to the social divisions of the neighbourhood (it is worth remembering that he cuts the tape which the police use to cordon off the street prior to the riot). He tells Rafi that he favours non-violence and applauds the Indians' defeat of colonialism via passive resistance (although he seems oblivious to Rafi's stone-throwing activities). Later he refers to his friends 'pulling whites out of cars and beating them in revenge. I didn't know if I should be doing it.' Danny draws attention to the destructiveness and divisiveness of violence and invites a contemplation of the riot as a travesty of subaltern resistance, rather than the righteous revolt of youth.

The kids amongst whom Danny lives present an alternative community of resistance – based on the principles of non-violence, tolerance and democracy – which is ambivalently represented in the film. When the community is evicted from the caravan-site the kids offer little resistance other than sitting down in front of the bulldozers' path, from which they are quickly removed. Danny does not have an effective answer to the eviction, and his parting words to Rosie, although spoken with a smile, are resigned: 'Looks like I'm on my way out!' The eviction is depressing evidence of the effectiveness of Thatcher's authoritarian approach to London's inner-city communities. The opening shot of the film dwells upon the vacated caravan-site as we listen to a voiceover of the jubilant Prime Minister – from the film's opening moments the kids' community is clearly doomed. During the eviction scene the soundtrack features a recording of the patriotic hymn 'I Vow to Thee, My Country' (which was played at the wedding of the Prince and Princess of Wales in 1981). It is followed by another voiceover of Prime Minister Thatcher, specifically her famous speech outside 10, Downing Street on 4 May 1979 which quoted from St Francis of Assisi. The clearing of London's fringe communities is firmly represented as part of an authoritarian attempt to cleanse the nation of its discord and construct harmony through the eradication of difference – or, as the jubilant property developer puts it, to make 'London a cleaner and safer place'.

However, the fact that the community moves on rather than breaks up suggests the inability of the state to remove permanently the alternative values it represents. Interestingly, in the final scene, just before Rafi is found hanging, Rosie's friends discuss the future of the kids' community. During the exchange, one character proposes that 'I expect they're heading towards Westminster'. 'The seat of our Parliament?' asks Alice. 'No' replies another: 'under the bridge'. The kids' community, mobile and animated by its straggly band, ideally contains the potential to disrupt the authority of those who occupy state power at Westminster. But as it was for MacInnes almost thirty years earlier, the challenge remains one of translating such subversive, subaltern potential into meaningful social change at large in the city, one which successfully and directly impacts upon the ideology and actions of those in Thatcher's Government. Ultimately, *Sammy and Rosie Gets Laid* keeps faith with the insurgent possibilities of urban youth and remains true to Kureishi's romantic view of London's fringe world nurtured from the wrong side of the river in the Bromley suburbs. Yet the film cannot discover the means by which these possibilities can be realized. Neither riotous nor non-violent protest has facilitated a successful revolt, while Sammy and Rosie's middle-class liberalism seems entirely impotent. Until the insurgent energies of the kids acquire meaningful agency, they always remain on the fringe, under the bridge. Their attempt to envisage a utopian communal space in London remains mobile, but their efficacy in challenging the city's divisive realities seems marginal, especially when contrasted with the direct action of Johnson's black youth. Hence, the overall impression of *Sammy and Rosie Get Laid* is one of reluctant defeat, if not exasperation. Kureishi cannot value the violent acts of resistance of London's youth as meaningfully different from the corrupt aggression of the state. Rather, he falls back upon ultimately mythical models of an alternative social milieu figured in the kids' community and the straggly band.

In moving finally to the work of Salman Rushdie, we encounter a writer and a book, *The Satanic Verses* (1988), which occupy a privileged place in postcolonial representations of London. Rushdie's novel has been considered the quintessential celebration of the city's migrant foundations and cosmopolitan melange, while his polyvocal fictional style – drawing upon Latin American magic realism, film and cartoons, Indian traditions of storytelling, postmodernist experimentation, Dickensian caricature and so much more – is often understood as capturing rhetorically the heterogeneity, diversity, bewildering change and rapid speed of city life. In defending his novel against those who deemed it to be blasphemous of Islam, Rushdie himself has described his novel as 'a love-song to our mongrel selves' which rejoices in the 'hybridity, impurity, intermingling, the transformation that comes of new and unexpected combinations of human beings, cultures, ideas, politics, movies, songs' (1991: 394). As Sushelia Nasta has convincingly argued, however, the critical reception of Rushdie's novel has tended to obscure writers such as Sam Selvon who had covered similar terrain in their writing and who helped clear the ground for the 'entrance and impact' (2002: 145) of Rushdie's work in the 1980s. Nasta also points out that Rushdie's position *vis-à-vis* the immigrant communities about which he writes is significantly dislocated, as a consequence of his 'classical and canonical "English"' (145) education at Rugby School and later Cambridge University. To read Rushdie as the literary spokesperson for immigrant London *par excellence* is to elide several significant social differences and ignore the potential tensions between London's diaspora communities and their fictional depiction by Rushdie. In a similar fashion to my reading of Kureishi's work, in what follows I want to consider closely Rushdie's representation of incendiary riotous violence in *The Satanic Verses*. It is my contention that the novel's seemingly celebratory narrative of London's 'mongrel self' breaks down significantly in Rushdie's uneasy depiction of popular uprising and threatens to call into question its migrant vision of London which has been so keenly celebrated by several of his critics.

Born in 1947 and raised in Bombay, Salman Rushdie migrated to Britain in 1961, aged fourteen, to attend the prestigious Rugby School, and later studied History at King's College, Cambridge. After graduating in 1968, he eventually settled in London after a brief spell in Pakistan with his family (they had moved from Bombay to Karachi). As his career progressed he became vocal about areas of London which had become significant sites of South Asian migration and settlement, such as the Bangladeshi community focused around Brick Lane in London's East End, and in several essays of the early 1980s he spoke out against the city's racism. One essay, 'An Unimportant Fire' (1984), records the death of Mrs Abdul Karim and her two children from suffocation in the London Borough of Camden, as Rushdie attacks the placing of black and Asian families by the local council in sub-standard temporary housing – 'disease-infested firetraps' (1991: 142) – rented from the private sector. Despite these efforts, it has become fashionable, especially in the light of Aijaz Ahmad's withering attack, to dismiss Rushdie's work as fatally flawed by its 'ideological moorings in the High Culture of the modern metropolitan bourgeoisie' (1992: 127) and barely interested in the conditions of those peoples who suffer the most from poverty, hardship and exploitation. Witness, for example, Gillian Gane's critique of the migrant community in *The Satanic Verses* as 'solidly middle-class' (2002: 38), in which women, children, the poor and the homeless are mostly invisible. Although these views are not without substance, they tend to elide Rushdie's political commitment to such people in the 1980s and forget his admirable attempts to represent London from something like their position in *The Satanic Verses*. But on the other hand, Rushdie's own defence of his novel during the so-called Rushdie Affair as 'an attempt to write about migration, its stresses and transformations, from the point of view of migrants from the Indian subcontinent to Britain' which expresses 'the immigrant culture of which *I am myself a member*' (Appignanesi and Maitland 1989: 75, emphasis added) similarly elides his dislocated relationship with migrant point-of-view and culture. These dislocations inflect his anxious representation of popular protest in 1980s London.

   The Satanic Verses is a multitudinous and polyvocal novel – part fantasy, part 'socio-political' (Rushdie 1988: 469) – that crosses time and space with bewildering and breathtaking speed. In Simon Gikandi words, the novel's complex and complicated rendering of issues familiar in postcolonial studies (such as hybridity, migrancy, home and exile) requires that it be read as 'a set of irresolvable oxymorons' (1996: 213) or antinomies. Beginning with the sabotage of an airliner over the English Channel – from which its chief protagonists, Saladin Chamcha and Gibreel Farishta, fall fantastically to earth – the novel moves from Bombay to London (and back again). Several of the London sections are set in the Bangladeshi community of Brickhall, a fictional location in East London which combines in its name Asian areas of settlement in Brick Lane and Southall. Into this tense location arrive

Saladin, transformed into a goatish figure complete with devilish horns, and Gibreel, sporting a halo and suffering from delusions of the divine (his dreams take the novel to other times and places, most notoriously to the moment of revelation of the Quran to the Prophet). Each character has already accrued a certain degree of cosmopolitan and media chic: Gibreel is a Bollywood film star, while Saladin, a life-long Anglophile, has forged a successful career in television as 'The Man of a Thousand Voices and a Voice' (Rushdie 1988: 60) and has settled in 'a five-storey mansion in Notting Hill' (59). After the fantastical metamorphoses each suffers on surviving the bombing of the aircraft, they make their separate ways to London. In particular, Saladin is forced to discover a hidden London, a city 'visible but unseen' (241) which conflicts with both his trendy Notting Hill neighbourhood but also his Anglophile migrant's dream of both city and nation which, in the words of his wife Pamela, consisted of '[c]ricket, the Houses of Parliament, the Queen. The place never stopped being a picture postcard to him. You couldn't get him to look at what was really real' (175). Instead of encountering and indulging in the homogenizing and abstracted vision of the city characterized by the auratic repetition of the proper name London so common in the representations of the 1950s and 1960s, Saladin is made starkly to confront 'Ellowen Deeowen' – a simultaneously humdrum and fantastical version of the city in which the melange and hybridity epitomized by Brickhall shred Saladin's comfortable Anglophone fiction, as signified by the spelling of the capital city's name which is shredded into capital letters (L-O-N-D-O-N).

As Rushdie told Sean French in an interview which appeared just after the novel's publication, '[t]he history of the London we live in is a composite history of all the peoples who are now here: Islamic history, Polish history, Caribbean history . . . I was writing about a sense of the city as an artificial, invented space which is constantly metamorphosing. It doesn't have roots, it has foundations' (Appignanesi and Maitland 1989: 9). In *The Satanic Verses*, the city's composite history is delightedly foregrounded. On one occasion Saladin attempts to conceive of the city's 'conglomerate nature' (Rushdie 1988: 398) as a mirror for the migrant self. London offers the migrant

> an imperfect welcome, true, one capable of bigotry, but a real thing, nonetheless, as was attested by the existence in a South London borough of a pub in which no language but Ukrainian could be heard, and by the annual reunion, in Wembley, a stone's throw from the great stadium surrounded by imperial echoes – Empire Way, the Empire Pool – of more than a hundred delegates, all tracing their ancestry back to a single, small Goan village . . . O Proper London! Dull would he truly

be of soul who did not prefer its faded splendours, its new hesitancies, to the hot certainties of that transatlantic New Rome with its Nazified architectural gigantism, which employed the oppressions of size to make its human occupants feel like worms.

(398–9)

Saladin's steadfast refusal to allow the 'imperfect welcome' of metropolitan bigotry to tarnish his dream is familiar to migrant visions of London in earlier decades, and in it we can detect Rushdie's attempt to celebrate the city's possibilities which, for all its attention to inner-city conflict, the novel, like Saladin, never fully relinquishes. In addition, it is important to note the contrast made here between London and the 'New Rome' of New York, and especially the reference to the 'hot certainties' of the latter. The equation made here between high temperature and possessing certainties is crucial to my reading of the novel, and I shall keep this phrase in the foreground as I pursue the novel's pattern of fiery or incendiary images.

The emphasis on London's migrant foundations, its manifold and ever-changing character, is emphasized when Saladin wakes up in the attic of the Shaandaar Café, having recently experienced an 'imperfect welcome' at the hands of the police and immigration services, and looks out of the window at an urban winter scene: 'Outside, in the treacherous city, a thaw had come, giving the streets the unreliable consistency of wet cardboard' (254). The image of wet cardboard neatly captures the permeability and pliability of the 'treacherous' city, shifting its shape and refusing to remain constant or solid. Although it is unwise to schematize *The Satanic Verses* – its endless mutations and manifold narrative threads make it dangerous to make tidy its superabundance – at its heart there seems a tension between two ways of conceptualizing London, each connected to differences in temperature. The first responds to the treachery of the city with the conviction of 'hot certainties', while the other treasures its 'unreliable consistency' captured by the more temperate climate that creates melting snow and wet cardboard, emphasizing a state of metamorphosis between solid and fluid states. These different conceptions of the city impact directly upon the representation of incendiary violence in Brickhall.

Changes in temperature frequently inflect the representation of London in *The Satanic Verses*. Most famously, while suffering from delusions that he is a divine being blessed with the power of creation, Gibreel attempts to 'tropicalize' (354) London. Defeated by the 'Pandemonium' (352) of the city that defies the cartographic certainty and manageability epitomized by the copy of the *London A–Z* which he carries in his pocket, his decision to replace the temperate English weather with the climate of a tropical city is a way of bringing a degree of certainty to London's treacherous 'soggy streets' (353) in which 'stark, imperative oppositions were drowned beneath an endless drizzle of greys' (354). It is an act of empowerment which contests the perceived 'moral fuzziness' (354) of the English with the extremities of truth. As he muses, 'truth is extreme, it is *so* and not *thus*, it is *him* and not *her*; a partisan matter, not a spectator sport. In brief, it is *heated*' (354). Gibreel's investment in the 'hot certainties' of truth recalls the figure of the Imam at the opening of the 'Ayesha' section, living in exile in a London flat with the central heating 'at full blast night and day' (208) in an attempt to simulate 'the dry heat of the Desh' (208). The exiled Imam's pious certainties, derived from a belief in the divine, are set against 'the greatest of lies – progress, science, rights' (210) which encapsulate the vicissitudes of a secular existence in which truth is deemed partial and plural while certainty is forever disabled by doubt. In tropicalizing London, then, Gibreel seems complicit in the exiled Imam's similar desire to challenge the satanic threat of unreliability epitomized by London's temperate and 'soggy streets'.

In terms of the novel's exploration of the conflict between sacred and secular models of creation, history and truth, it becomes difficult to read Gibreel's fantastical transformation of London's weather as a wholly progressive act. Yet curiously it is often regarded as such. In Homi Bhabha's view, Gibreel's actions mark the stubborn presence of the migrant in the metropolis who has 'come to change the history of the nation' (1994: 169–70) and renders the city as the space 'in which emergent identifications and new social movements of the people are played out' (170). In engaging with the English weather, Rushdie evokes 'the most changeable and immanent signs of national difference' (169) only for it to be menaced by its 'daemonic double . . . the tropical chaos that was deemed despotic and ungovernable and therefore worthy of the civilizing mission' (169). Bhabha reads the incident as a creative and politically enabling act, no doubt part of 'the vibrancy and insurgency of migrant life [which] result in a remarkable translation of the metropolis itself . . . Those who are excluded return to claim a place for themselves, to seize an alien time and make it their own and yours' (2000: 142). In a similar celebratory vein, Ian Baucom argues that 'Gibreel rewrites the cultural cartography of the city. He erases its boundaries and collapses the distinction between the here and the elsewhere. He opens London's gates to that most spectacular return of the repressed, in which the wilfully forgotten double appears not as an image of the *unheimlich* but as a coinhabitor of home' (1999: 212). It is my contention, however, that Rushdie is much more equivocal about Gibreel's tropicalization of London which may *not* be the translative act so cherished by Bhabha and Baucom.

Gibreel's actions might be regarded as a highly problematic response to

London's 'changeability'. He is driven crazy by his consciousness of the city as a site of mutation and transformation and wanders London's 'vague, amorphous' (Rushdie 1988: 459) streets convinced he is 'Archangel Gibreel, the angel of the Recitation' (461), haunted by the ghosts of the past that recall previous centuries of migration to London. Overloaded by the chaos of the city's manifold history and lost in 'Babylondon' (459), he attempts to impose a semblance of order by raising London's temperature and blows the trumpet he was given at John Maslama's shop 'Fair Winds'. Named '*Azraael, the Last Trump, Exterminator of Men!*' (448), the trumpet is an instrument of divine judgement, the blowing of which produces 'little buds of flame' (462). 'This is a city that has cleansed itself in flame', thinks Gibreel, '[and] purged itself by burning down to the ground' (461). Gibreel may well introduce the climate of England's overseas, uncivil colonies and remap the city anew, but his fiery activities directly contradict the migrant's vision of London which recasts the metropolis in terms of its inconstant foundations. It is precisely the superabundance of the city, its simultaneous hosting of 'several stories at once' (457), which Gibreel wishes to purge with retributive fire. Gibreel wants order and definition, not chaos and translation. The temperate changeable English weather is not so much a secure sign of national identity as it is a figure of secular inconstancy characterized by it disorienting 'fogs' (353), and which disconcerts both the exiled Imam and the crazed Gibreel, each of whom is linked by their penchant for high temperatures. As he tropicalizes London Gibreel is *not* acting as the secular translative migrant, but instead momentarily resembles the pious exiled Imam pining for 'hot certainties'.

Ian Baucom suggests that 'Gibreel's tropicalization of London [is] an act of riot in which the nation is redeemed by recalling its present to a past and an elsewhere' (1999: 216). In a similar vein, Baucom reads the Brickhall riot as a progressive act at the service of a migrant imaginary keen to reveal the 'city visible but unseen' at the heart of London. Yet this understanding of the novel's representation of the riot is also highly problematic. Baucom is correct in so far as he finds a connection between the tropical and riotous Londons in the novel; it is no coincidence that John Maslama, proprietor of 'Fair Winds', is also the owner of the Club Hot Wax located in Brickhall, an important subterranean site of local dissident energies in which wax effigies of black Britons since the eighteenth century stand alongside other figures, bathed in green light, such as Enoch Powell and Margaret Thatcher. These latter figures, hated amongst Brickhall's community for their racism, are ceremoniously melted down amidst 'the jouncing and bouncing of youth' (Rushdie 1988: 292). The spectacle is choreographed by Pinkwalla, described as a seven-feet-tall albino, an 'East-India-man from the West Indies' (292) and 'deejay nonpareil' (291). 'Now we really cookin', he cries as an effigy of Thatcher is burned; '[t]he fire this time' (293). This latter phrase recalls the title of James Baldwin's classic and influential meditation on racism in the United States, *The Fire Next Time* (1963), a central text in the Civil Rights movement during the 1960s. Significantly, Gibreel also quotes from an important figure in anti-racist and anti-colonial resistance, the Martinician writer Frantz Fanon, prior to his tropicalizing of London: 'Did they not think their history would return to haunt them? – "The native is an oppressed person whose perma-nent dream is to become the persecutor" (Fanon)' (353). In the English translation of Fanon's *The Wretched of the Earth* (1963), this quotation comes during Fanon's well-known discussion of anti-colonial violence. The recurring images of heat and fire assist in forging subtle but firm connec-tions between the exiled Imam, Gibreel, John Maslama and the Hot Wax Club; while the presence of references to Baldwin and Fanon implicate the subversive energies of the Hot Wax Club – if not violent resistance in gen-eral – with the problematic maintenance of Gibreel's 'hot certainties'. Gibreel singularly fails to regard London as a space of newness and consid-ers the conflicts on its streets in familiar Fanonian terms as 'that old dis-pute' between 'Native and settler' (353), rather than (in the lawyer Hanif Johnson's words) part of 'a process of change' (469). It is implied that Brickhall's youth's fiery opposition to racism is similarly locked in recursive dialectic which reaches for old certainties when fighting new battles: 'the fire this time'.

In his depiction of Brickhall's riot which flares up in the vicinity of the Hot Wax Club, Rushdie appears particularly anxious about the nature of popular protest in 1980s London. Are the riots another example of the inevitable combustion of incompatible realities which, when they meet, '[i]t's uranium and plutonium, each makes the other decompose, boom' (314)? Or might they be considered a regressive and worrying act that remains trapped inside an oppressive and Manichean mentality that, like the exiled Imam, is convinced of the purity and integrity of its 'hot certain-ties'? Some of the worries associated with the latter point of view emerge at a meeting in Brickhall which Saladin attends not long after lodging at the Shaandaar Café. A public meeting is called at the Brickhall Friends Meet-ing House in response to the arrest of Dr Uhuru Simba, a local activist, in connection with the 'Granny Ripper Murders' (411). The community detects a racial motive behind the arrest and is keen to mobilize in his defence. Sceptical of such actions, Saladin attends the meeting which, he is surprised to find, is 'packed wall-to-wall with every conceivable sort of person – old, wide women and uniformed schoolchildren, Rastas and restaurant workers, the staff of the small Chinese supermarket in Plassey Street, soberly dressed gents as well as wild boys, whites as well as blacks'

(413). The multiracial aspect of the crowd is important; like Pinkwalla, the East Indian albino from the Caribbean, it cannot be categorized easily with the divisive rhetoric of race. At the meeting Simba's mother, Antoinette, addresses the audience in a voice in which Saladin detects the tone of 'hellfire sermonizing' (414). When Saladin points out to his companion, Jumpy Joshi, that Simba was himself no angel – he has a history of violence against women – Jumpy defends him by saying that 'Simba's bull craziness is, you could say, a trouble in the family. What we have here is trouble with the Man' (415). Saladin's response is revealing:

> he didn't like the use of such American terms as 'the Man' in the very different British situation, where there was no history of slavery; it sounded like an attempt to borrow the glamour of other, more danger-ous struggles, a thing he also felt about the organizers' decision to punctuate the speeches with such meaning-loaded songs as *We Shall Overcome*, and even, for Pete's sake, *Nkosi Sikelel' iAfrika*. As if all causes were the same, all histories interchangeable.
>
> (415)

Clearly a racialized rhetoric of resistance sits uneasily among the multi-cultural gathering provoked by the arrest. Yet it is not clear why the orga-nizers' 'attempt to borrow' the strategies of analogous resistance initiatives is so quickly dismissed. It is more than a little peculiar that, as we have seen previously, Saladin can celebrate the migratory foundations of 'Proper London' yet cannot at this moment accept the presence in the city of other kinds of 'foreign' materials which, from another perspective, might be described as part of the transformative and translational tactics of the 'black Atlantic' (Gilroy 1993a). Saladin seems perfectly comfortable with the romantic reunion of Goan-descended Londoners a stone's throw away from Wembley Stadium but oddly disturbed by the presence in Brickhall of dissident thought associated with the United States and South Africa. In a novel which considers translation and metamorphosis the degree zero of migrant life in the metropolis, one might wonder why the transnational appropriation and popular recontextualization of the political resources from other causes is in this particular instance so problematic.

As Edward Said has written, 'the history of all cultures is the history of cultural borrowings' (1993: 261); but 'the attempt to borrow' which occurs at the Brickhall Friends Meeting House is presented as potentially illegiti-mate. Saladin is not a mouthpiece for Rushdie, of course, yet Saladin's view of the meeting is not effectively challenged. Here, perhaps, Rushdie's dislo-cated relationship with London's diaspora community can be glimpsed: it is permissible for a middle-class, Cambridge-educated intellectual to appropriate and mobilize a wealth of resources from the Quran to the Rolling Stones in portraying the world as it is seen by a 'translated man', but it is another thing entirely for those on the streets to make similar borrowings for the purposes of social action. Why are their acts of appropriation not considered part of the city's propensity for metamorphosis but deemed to be based on misguided notions of the interchangability of 'all histories'? Rushdie's squeamishness towards the rhetoric of black power hinders him from considering the ways in which such materials – Fanon, Baldwin, analogous freedom songs and other cultural resources – might be rewritten or translated in London. Popular resistance indebted to race-consciousness seems inexplicably immune from translative transformation, unable to beckon newness into the world or contribute to the metropolitan machinations of hybridity, impurity and intermingling.

As the riots begin, evidence quickly mounts which suggests the popular resistance on the street, in the Club Hot Wax and in the Brickhall Friends Meeting House is regressive. Dr Uhuru Simba dies in police custody under suspicious circumstances and the Granny Ripper strikes not long after, throwing into doubt the police's case. The police respond by suggesting that the latest murder has been committed by someone keen to copy Simba's crimes. Temperatures rise in Brickhall. 'Don't anybody cool off', declares Simba's brother Walcott; '[m]aintain your rage' (Rushdie 1988: 450). On the streets, 'young men and women maintained, and fanned, the slow flame of their anger, a shadow-flame, but one capable of blotting out the light' (450). When seven young Sikhs discover a 'bland, pale man of medium height and build' (453) under a canal bridge in southern Brickhall running from the body of an old woman, the riots begin, fuelled by rumours that the police are reluctant to charge the murderer. Rushdie synchronizes the riot with the cultural gatherings and energies of youth: 'It was at this point, at half-past eleven on a Saturday night, with the clubs and dance-halls beginning to yield up their excited, highly charged populations, that the divisional superintendent of police, in consultation with higher authority, declared that riot conditions now existed in central Brickhall' (453–4).

To one degree, the rioting of Brickhall's youth brings into the streets the frustration and anger which has been incubating in the Club Hot Wax, and the ensuing fires are (as in Johnson's work) clearly part of a political protest against 'higher authority'. Yet Rushdie is profoundly uneasy with the riots and casts doubt (as one might expect) on the conviction and righteousness of the revolt. Throughout the riot the impression is given that the violence witnessed in Brickhall is a flawed oppositional revolt which falls foul of 'hot certainties'. As Gibreel approaches the Shaandaar Café amidst the riot he notices that '[t]he street has become red hot, molten, a river the colour of blood' (462). The connection forged at this moment in the novel between Powell's infamous 'rivers of blood' speech cited earlier and the incendiary consequences of the riots implies a doubling between the persecutor and the persecuted – recalling too the Fanonian dialectic of native and settler – while also hinting that the riots give credence to Powell's proleptic racializing rhetoric. Earlier in the novel we learn that Jumpy Joshi has written poetry which uses Powell's image of the 'rivers of blood' in order to '[r]eclaim the metaphor' (186) and 'make it a think we can use' (186). Yet in contrast to this individual act of aesthetic transformation, the collective action of popular protest seems to be devoid of the propensity to reclaim and remake. The youthful rioters remain lost in shadow beyond the purview of the novel, locked in a flawed form of oppositional protest which Rushdie to an extent understands but ultimately cannot sanction. Popular violence is regarded as a misguided attempt to move from the position of the oppressed to that of the persecutor, and not an act of creative translation or metamorphosis. In a similar fashion to Kureishi, Rushdie cannot envisage riotous protest as significantly different from the violence of the persecutor turned back on itself, with oppressor and oppressed locked in cyclical and uncreative dialectic. This process of translative reclamation seems to be primarily the remit of the individualized figure of the writer – Jumpy Joshi and, presumably, Rushdie himself.

As the riot reaches its climax, the narrative focuses upon the encounter between Gibreel and Saladin in the burning building of the Shaandaar Café. Through their angelic and devilish incarnations and the rivalry which has been mounting, the novel has prepared us for their ultimate confrontation. It never comes, of course; as Saladin lies pinned beneath the burning wreckage of the café, Gibreel rescues his adversary and carries him through the fire to safety 'along the path of forgiveness into the hot night air; so that on a night when the city is at war, a night heavy with enmity and rage, there is this small redeeming victory of love' (468). At this moment, the city's riotous war receives its darkest judgement as a cauldron of aggression, anger and rage which destroys the redemptive possibilities figured in the advocacy of love. Love tempers and cools; Gibreel forges a path through the fire with 'a long, continuous exhalation of extraordinary duration, and as his breath blows towards the door it slices through the smoke and fire like a knife' (468). The smallness of Gibreel's act contrasts with the magnitude of the riot which is, as Hanif Johnson calls it, 'an event in the history of Britain' (Rushdie 1988: 469). But whereas Linton Kwesi Johnson applauded the Brixton rioters for 'Mekin Histri', in *The Satanic Verses* the 'process of change' (469) in which the rioters are caught is doomed to remain locked inside a recursive cycle of dialectical enmity which refuses to consider that 'victory, no matter how overwhelming, is never absolute' (467). The pursuit of absolutes – whether it be by the exiled Imam, Gibreel tropicalizing London or the rioters making the city melt down – destroy the possibility of love and meaningful change. *The Satanic Verses* ultimately does little to offer an alternative view of the riots, despite the discomfort expressed with unsympathetic depictions of London's youth 'burning their own streets'. For a novel which demands to be read as a set of irresolvable oxymorons or antinomies and which eschews 'hot certainties', it seems remarkably assured when broaching the issue of what constitutes legitimate social protest and meaningful cultural change.

As we have seen, the depiction of fiery protest in 1980s London serves a number of contrasting purposes. In Johnson's work the different fires of racism and revolt record London's 'hurting black story'. The incendiary actions of Brixton's black youth are contextualized in terms of the longer history of slave revolt in the Caribbean and the cultural energies of reggae music. These antecedents fan the flames of righteous protest in Brixton and fuel the Promethean, creative energies of youth who are 'Mekin Histri' amidst provocation and harassment. Crucially, in poems like 'New Craas Massakeh' Johnson suggests that the fires of racism and revolt are not equivalent: the 'fiery red' anger of black Britons comes from different sources and is not coincident with the violence of racism and the police. Like Johnson, Kureishi regards youth as possessing resistant and creative energies which can effect change in, and to, London, yet he remains sceptical towards riotous protest as enabling effective social revolt. *Sammy and Rosie Get Laid* suggests a continuum which connects both oppressive and anti-racist violence, and posits instead an idealized community of straggly kids as holding the possibility of meaningful change in their spatial practices despite gloomily depicting the lack of agency in Thatcher's Britain. Although Rushdie's *The Satanic Verses* celebrates a London translated and transformed by migrancy as its definitive condition, its attempt to bear witness to the city from the perspective of Brickhall is severely curtailed by Rushdie's reluctance to consider popular violence as a translative act. Instead, the rioters and their incendiary acts are deemed compromised by the 'hot certainties' of victory which ignore the redemptive possibilities of love – just as, in *Sammy and Rosie Get Laid*, Danny worries about the destruction of beauty amidst the flames. Both Kureishi and, to a greater degree, Rushdie remain uneasy with popular revolt in 1980s London. Like the mural which Ferdinand Dennis discovered on Brixton's Frontline in the winter of 1987, the work of each figure forges connections between images of fire, social resistance and cultural creativity. Yet the relations between each, and the representations of resistance which result, are significantly and revealingly different.

5 Millennial currents
David Dabydeen, Fred D'Aguiar and Bernardine Evaristo

In 1991, David Dabydeen contributed an essay entitled 'On Cultural Diversity' to a collection concerning the future of British cities. Published in association with the British Labour Party – at that time still the official Opposition in the House of Commons and fated to lose the 1992 General Election to John Major's Conservative Party – the collection featured contributions from a number of significant cultural figures, such as David Edgar, Mike Phillips, Ruth Rendell, Alison Fell and Naseem Khan. Conscious perhaps of the riotous social conflicts which impacted upon urban life in 1980s Britain, the contributors looked to the future of British cities and considered the role of the arts in reshaping and democratizing metropolitan culture and society in the decade to come. A sensitivity to variety – of urban cultural phenomena, modes of social affiliation, old and new ethnicities – was paramount. Several essays addressed themselves to the 'diversity of city life experienced by the women, the young, the elderly, those with disabilities, those with different ethnic cultures, [who] demanded more various ways of expressing local culture and identity' (Fisher 1991: 3). Although some contributors depicted British cities as conflicted spaces, divided and hostile, many looked to the future with optimism. The 1990s British city was linked to a transformative agency which might impact upon wider issues of cultural and national identity. As Mike Phillips put it in his contribution, '[s]cratch the Londoner and you uncover a loony living a British future in which the national project is reassessed, the interpretation of our history is a comparative exercise, citizenship is divorced from racial origins, and you can't tell an Englishman from an Indian or an African or a Chinese' (1991: 121–2).

Dabydeen's contribution was one of the less optimistic essays. It reflected upon the extent to which Caribbeans and their descendants had changed the city in the postwar decades (while also tracing London's long history as a location of arrival and settlement of black peoples overseas). In contrast to those who celebrated the metropolis as a site of transcultural melange, he struck a sobering note:

A city packs people in. They live on top of each other, alongside each other, sideways to each other. The city is a hive in this sense, but there are no inevitable passageways between one cell and another. And this has been the problem for West Indian culture in London – the white people who come to the West Indian cells for a while, to attend a carnival or to taste curried goat, return afterwards to their own cells. They don't spend long enough in the West Indian cells to appreciate the syntax, metre, chords, daubs, noises and smells created in these cells.

And they don't invite West Indians to visit *their* cells (called universities, banks, concert halls, theatres, arts councils, art galleries, Houses of Parliament, television studios) for a prolonged period either, or in any great numbers. The city is culturally diverse, but there is little cross-fertilization of cultures taking place. White people remain incarcerated in their own cells, afraid to venture out in case they are mugged by West Indians.

(1991: 104)

Writing in the wake of the so-called Rushdie Affair and perhaps with the violence of the 1980s riots still fresh in his mind, Dabydeen's essay outlined the continuing social and cultural divisions that characterized early 1990s London. His solemn depiction of a cellular city which enabled only superficial kinds of cross-cultural encounter paralleled a similar view offered in the same year by Harry Goulbourne of the nation in general. Goulbourne lamented the fact that the different peoples based in Britain enjoyed only a 'market relationship' with each other, as 'people of African, Asian and European backgrounds increasingly meet only where they buy and sell commodities' (1991: 231). In calling for a new kind of national consciousness in Britain which eschewed ethnicity as its central agglutinating factor, he warned that '[i]t is most unlikely that a series of mutually exclusive communities with little more than a vulgar market relationship between them would live together in peace and tranquillity' (232). Dabydeen seemed to share Goulbourne's sense of trepidation about the future of the nation. In looking to the decade to come, he projected a 'New World' in which white European culture would dominate and white racism continue, and wondered if British blacks 'will be largely excluded from the New World jamboree' or 'be able to adapt, modify and enrich our culture in the new environments' (1991: 106).

Looking back across the fortunes of London in the 1990s from the vantage of a new century, it is perhaps tempting to suggest that Dabydeen's pessimism and Goulbourne's trepidation have been subsequently challenged, while Mike Phillips's hopes for the reassessment of national culture in terms of London's diasporic melange have made significant headway –

especially if representations of London at the end of the decade are to be believed. On 25 June 2000 Yasmin Alibhai-Brown published an article in *The New York Times* entitled 'A magic carpet of multiple cultures in London' in which she explored with enthusiasm the city's vibrancy and diversity at the millennium. Citing the success of the British television comedy series *Goodness Gracious Me* written by and featuring a cast of British Asians including the novelist and actress Meera Syal, the art of Steve McQueen, and novels such as Zadie Smith's *White Teeth* (2000), Alibhai-Brown suggested that London's transformation in the 1990s was having an important impact on culture and society at large. Whereas the city had previously possessed localities seen as immigrant ghettoes, these days 'the flux has started to loosen these imagined barriers':

> Notting Hill is now clogged up with the white chattering classes who previously would have headed for Hampstead with its old money and unnatural calm. Brixton, Paddington and Shoreditch, which were once impoverished dumps, are places where dot.com millionaires, artists and designers want to live and play. Brick Lane in the east end, famous for its cruel penury and racial thuggery, now swarms with diners in sharp suits from the City. Multiracial London is coming of age, and it is this that is igniting such energy, buzz and creativity.
>
> (32)

Alibhai-Brown offered a mapping of the city in which its imagined geography is positively reconceptualized and remade as a consequence of 'multicultural' creative energies. Her sketch suggested that Dabydeen's notion of a cellular London, a hive devoid of inevitable passageways, was no longer appropriate at the turn of a new century. She acknowledged that 'ethnic and social divisions [still] exist', but firmly argued that 'evidence of real and irreversible integration is everywhere' (32). Although her depiction of 'diners in sharp suits' descending upon Brick Lane's Bengali restaurants might be regarded as evidence which paradoxically supports Dabydeen's vista (not least because it suggests the endurance of a 'market relationship' between ethnically different Londoners), the optimistic tone of the article points to an important and predominant way of thinking about London's fortunes in the 1990s which had become prevalent by the decade's end. But rather than constituting a complacent attitude towards London's millennial 'buzz', such sentiments about contemporary London culture were important political assertions concerning the city's social fortunes during the decade.

The political importance of what we might term 'millennial optimism' regarding London can be gauged by considering very briefly both the content and the critical reception of Zadie Smith's celebrated novel *White Teeth*, whose author was hailed by Alibhai-Brown in her article as the new literary voice of London. Described by one commentator as 'half-Jamaican', Smith was born in London in 1975 and grew up in Willesden before reading English at Cambridge. *White Teeth* was published in 2000 to huge commercial and critical acclaim – its first British edition featured ringing endorsements by Salman Rushdie on both the front and the back of the dust jacket. It offered a predominantly comic depiction of North-West London's multicultural urban milieu, bringing together characters from a number of religious faiths and with Indian, English and Jamaican backgrounds. According to Maya Jaggi, it was 'a serio-comic novel of great verve and distinction which offers its own corrective to England's distorting mirror, lending a keen ear to the fertile – often ignored – polyphony of postcolonial London' (2000: 11), while Caryl Phillips applauded its emphasis on the 'helpless heterogeneity' and 'dazzlingly complex world of cross-cultural fusion in modern-day London' (2001: 283). For these readers, Smith presented a view of London that acted as an affront to homogenizing and racially inclusive models of nationhood (England's 'distorting mirror') as well as evidencing by its very existence the verve, vitality and creativity of contemporary London highlighted by Alibhai-Brown.

Smith's novel offers a version of London in which the depressingly familiar social conflicts of previous decades are no longer primarily determining the formation of character and fortunes of plot. As Peter Brooker has perceptively noted, 'the novel is grounded, less in an identity crisis or divided ethnic consciousness, than in the quotidian period details of nineties North London and in a ready acceptance of the decentred mentalities of the now thoroughly decentred capital city' (2002: 89). This 'ready acceptance' might be thought of not so much as an avoidance of crises of identity or ethnicity but as an important and strategic cultural reaction to the social problems which continued to mount throughout the 1990s, epitomized by the racist murder of Stephen Lawrence in Eltham, South London, on 22 April 1993. After a considerable outcry about the inadequacy of the police and judicial system in responding to the killing specifically of a black Londoner, a public inquiry led to the publication in 1999 of the McPherson Report, in which the police and other organs of the state were found to be institutionally racist. It is my contention that we might regard Smith's 'serio-comic' novel *as well as its* advocacy by Alibhai-Brown, Caryl Phillips and others alongside other celebratory events, such as the 1998 fiftieth anniversary celebrations of the SS *Empire Windrush*, as vital cultural rejoinders to London's enduring social problems of racialization and discrimination. Many of Smith's advocates did not presume for one moment that London's conflicts had magically disappeared. Yasmin Alibhai-Brown gloomily commented elsewhere in 2000 that

> white Britons, especially in the metropolitan areas, started developing conflicting attitudes to the changes in the society. They opened up their stomachs and their sensory organs, but not, on the whole, their heads and hearts. Subtle moments, light racism flutter in and out of your face so often you barely notice. The evidence of prevailing discrimination, racial violence and abuse piles up daily.
>
> (2001: 9)

The staunchly optimistic representations of London which gather at the end of the 1990s may be legitimately considered as cheerful and politically vital declarations of tenure and change – ones which stubbornly reminded reactionary mentalities in London that their attempts to shore up the divisive borders of race, culture and ethnicity had spectacularly failed. In lauding *White Teeth* and the London of 'decentred mentalities' it depicts – however wilful or selective Smith's narrative may be – its advocates were making a political statement about the positive and creative processes of transformation wrought by multicultural energies.

That said, one potentially negative consequence of the novel's success – for which Smith is by no means responsible – has been to distract attention away from other representations of 1990s postcolonial London in which many of the issues raised by *White Teeth* also appear, but in different modes. It is not always acknowledged that *White Teeth* stands at the end of a busy decade of postcolonial London representations by such writers as Andrea Levy, Diran Adebayo, Bernardine Evaristo, Ferdinand Dennis, Atima Srivastava, Meera Syal, Alex Wheatle, Benjamin Zephaniah and others. In this chapter I want to direct attention towards some of these different currents in 1990s writing. This will involve me crossing the river away from Smith's Willesden and engaging with the poetry and fiction (and in one instance, the poetic fiction) of three figures, each with a connection to South (and) East London: David Dabydeen, Fred D'Aguiar and Bernardine Evaristo. Their work offers alternative aesthetic paths to Smith's familiar 'postimmigrant' style, while also adumbrating something of the heterogeneity of postcolonial London writing in the decade which has yet to be adequately acknowledged. In addition, the work of these figures propels us at times to a more sobering contemplation of the city's enduring and emerging problems at the end of the twentieth century while simultaneously pointing to new possibilities and modes of transformation at the beginning of the new millennium.

Since the publication of Paul Gilroy's important study *The Black Atlantic*

(1993), it has become increasingly popular to conceive of diasporic cultures in terms of aquatic metaphors. The fluidity and flux of the sea across which cultures, peoples and politics move have been appropriated as dynamic tropes of the restlessness, provisionality, adaptability and itinerant character of diasporic (especially black) cultures. In representing diasporic cultures in terms of transatlantic routes and in opposition to the sedentary politics of oppositional nationalist political movements, Gilroy recast aquatic metaphors as figuring the enabling political and cultural possibilities of 'creolisation, métissage, mestizaje, and hybridity' (1993a: 2). Prior to such initiatives, the application of aquatic metaphors to the effects of diaspora tended to buttress a sensationalized fear of immigration and settlement. In the postwar decades in particular, migrants have been described as constituting dangerous 'floods' and 'waves' that threaten the host community. One needs only to think of Powell's provocative reference to 'rivers of blood' or Margaret Thatcher's terrors of immigrants 'swamping' Britain as evidence of the centrality of such language in state and popular racism. Whether or not the turn to aquatic metaphors in the 1990s is a conscious appropriation and reinscription of one of racism's rhetorics, as we shall see below, images of water have proved vitally important in the cultural reimagining of notions of home, belonging and identity, as well as opening up new ways of identifying London's place on a larger transcultural map. In turning to three texts of the 1990s, we may see the emergence of different kinds of transcultural consciousness in London which similarly appropriate aquatic metaphors in an attempt to resist the border controls of exclusionary models of belonging and identity, and assert the migrational character of the city from which new ways of conceptualizing such models can be discovered. As we shall see, 1990s representations of London serve a radical and enabling purpose in contesting the divisive character of both city and nation.

Dabydeen's gloomy contemplation in 1991 of London's cellular cosmopolitan character at the beginning of the decade betrayed one way in which he regarded London, but in his first novel, *The Intended* (1991), a slightly different attitude towards the city's migrational and transcultural conditions can be discerned. An accomplished poet, essayist, critic and editor, Dabydeen was born in 1955 in Berbice, Guyana. In 1969 he moved to England to join his father who had travelled there a few years previously, having separated from Dabydeen's mother. As he told Wolfgang Binder, between the ages of fourteen to eighteen he lived 'in South London, a stone's throw away from Brixton . . . in the care of the local authorities, because my parents were divorced' (Binder 1997: 162). *The Intended* depicts the fortunes of a young Guyanese migrant in London and is partly indebted to Dabydeen's experiences of arrival. Set both in Balham in South London and in a village in Guyana, *The Intended* is the unnamed narrator's retro-spective account of his childhood and adolescent years, written after he has gained admission to Oxford University to study English. In London he has lived in the care of the local authority before renting his own flat. Many of the London scenes focus upon the narrator's relationship with his various friends. As a Guyanese child with ancestral connections to India, he finds himself part of a group consisting of children who also have a relationship with South Asia. Shaz and Naseem are from Pakistani families, while Patel's family is Indian. With the narrator they constitute 'the regrouping of the Asian diaspora in a South London schoolground' (Dabydeen 1992: 5). The narrator later meets Monica (a companion of Shaz) and Janet, both white girls; Mr Ali, his Pakistani landlord; and Joseph, an orphaned Rasta-farian boy who also lives at first in the care of the local authorities.

The portrait of the narrator as a young man emphasizes his quest to join the sanctified culture of England, symbolized by Oxford University, and escape both his Guyanese past which he considers shameful and his unhappy life in London. He succeeds in entering Oxford as an undergradu-ate but the retrospective narrative he eventually writes works significantly against the youthful ambitions of his younger self. The narrator's youthful and older personas are in tension throughout *The Intended*. At the novel's heart resides a conflict between the youthful narrator's desire to escape the untidiness and instability of migrant life epitomized by London, and his older self's account of his younger life which works to an opposite end by facilitating a narrative in which the transcultural character of 1990s London is retrospectively admitted and valued. Although *The Intended* is not a novel which articulates gleefully the transformative possibilities of London's transcultural conjunctions, the text formulates an optic shaped by the untidy concurrences of different times, peoples and places in the narrator's experience of the city.

As Margaret Fee has argued, '[t]he explicit focus of the novel is on the young narrator's desire to assimilate, to succeed in British terms by going to Oxford, becoming a famous writer, and marrying an upper-class white woman' (1993: 109). But as she acknowledges, this is *not* the narrative which the narrator ultimately provides. Instead, his passage through London – arriving from Guyana, leaving for Oxford – is cross-hatched with and offset by his memories of Guyana and the experiences of his London peers, especially Joseph who 'returns to haunt me' (Dabydeen 1992: 195) as the narrator sits in Oxford's University Library studying the fourteenth-century poem *Sir Gawain and the Green Knight*. The haunting presence of such stories disturbs the novel's 'explicit focus' and holds up for question both the narrator's desire to assimilate and his self-confessed shame at the behaviour of black Londoners. As Fee perfectly describes it, in writing the narrative of *The Intended*, with its deliberate 'irony and structural disjunctions', the narrator's adolescent 'struggle to jettison his shameful past is retroactively reconstructed by his self in such a way that re-visions that past, both in Guyana and in the slums of Balham, as valuable, as worth memorialising' (1993: 109). To borrow the novel's title, it is clear that the intentions of the adolescent, Balham-based version of the narrator are at odds with those of his older self. If the former is keen to expunge his 'messy' (Dabydeen 1992: 168) migrant and Guyanese past, then the latter deliberately admits it to the retrospective narrative he creates. Its consequent shape contributes to a vision of London connected to, not sundered from, seemingly distant yet firmly linked times and places and possessing an untidiness which the narrator as a young man had intended to extinguish in his quest for cultural belonging and purity. The primary index of this mature admission is the text's water imagery, in which both the quest for purity and the untidy transcultural consequences for London are figured.

From the novel's outset, London is represented in terms of aquatic metaphors. Sitting on a train, the narrator remarks that in 'the swift journey between Tooting Bec and Balham, we re-lived the passages from India to Britain, or India to the Caribbean to Britain, the long journeys of a previous century across unknown seas towards the shame of plantation labour' (16–17). One summer the narrator lands a job at Battersea Fun Fair where he works on the 'World Cruise' (75) attraction, which consists of a boat ride through an illuminated tunnel the walls of which feature 'painted scenes from various countries, in alphabetical order' (76). Such details keep in focus the transcultural relationship between London and the world beyond, with the sea or (mock) river acting as that which both divides and links disparate locations, and also underline London as a city of flux through which the presence and influence of myriad cultures have perpetually washed. Significantly, the substance of the water is untidy and full of mess, and it flows through a tunnel the walls of which are decorated with images of twenty-six nations – one for each letter of the alphabet. The waterway emphasizes London's transcultural history and character, and implies that the city is similarly 'messy': the passages of peoples through it have sometimes resulted in unpredictable and multifarious combinations of lives and loves, and new generations of Londoners. But this is by no means an idealizing or celebratory conception of a 'hybrid' London. The waterway also evidences the city's racial tensions: on one of the paintings '[s]omeone had scrawled "niggers out" on [a black woman's] body and had drawn a fat penis pointed at her mouth. The genitalia of the black men had also been elongated or smudged as if to erase them' (78).

In a detail which mirrors his youthful intention to expunge from his life the transcultural untidiness of his own migrational existence, the narrator is charged with the task of cleaning up the waterway of the World Cruise which some pleasure-seekers use for amorous pursuits, owing to the darkness of the tunnel and length of the ride. From the water he daily scoops 'an assortment of underclothing, male and female, abandoned between Fiji and Timbuktu' (77). The depiction of the youthful narrator cleaning the water underlines his general quest for purity while also positioning him at odds with London's contemporaneity. If the messy waterway symbolizes London's multicultural and multiracial legacy, the narrator's attempt to clean the water may be read as symptomatic of his agonized Naipaulian quest for cultural and national purity, epitomized by his study of canonical English literature at Oxford. The quest for purity is impossible in London, however, the waters of which are always muddied. Ironically, it is only when the narrator has left London and is reflecting upon Joseph at Oxford that he begins to reassess and value his life in terms not of a process of cultural purification but of the transcultural untidiness epitomized by the waterway.

Joseph's life evidences the migrational and diasporic history of London as well as the futile quest for purity which can never be satisfied. At Oxford the narrator comes to value the life of Joseph and those like him, as well as to re-evaluate purity as a meaningful or achievable goal. Benita Parry has described Joseph as 'the novel's figure of a utopian desire' (1997: 93). Joseph disturbs the narrator's youthful investment in the purity and sanctity of English culture, and offers an important critical perspective. He is described as a black Rastafarian aged 'seventeen or thereabouts' (Dabydeen 1992: 87) – he has no way of being sure. Like the narrator, he has been abandoned in London. Forgotten by his father, chewed up by welfare institutions and declared a criminal by the police, he has grown up in a number of institutions, including a Bethnal Green borstal and 'welfare hostels all over London' (81). Although he is illiterate, he is an accomplished guitarist; his sole aim in life is 'to give love to people' (88); and he is also an able literary critic despite his inability to read. While studying Conrad's *Heart of Darkness* (1899) the narrator becomes irritated at Joseph's frequent interruptions, although he finds that '[t]he sound of his guitar when he was in the next room was soothing, inspiring me to think and write in bursts of creativity' (83). Joseph's creative energy is in general simultaneously inspirational and disruptive. He listens to the narrator's reading of Conrad's novel and mounts his own critique of the text:

> No, it ain't, is about colours. You been saying is a novel 'bout the fall of man, but is really 'bout a dream. Beneath the surface is the dream. The white light of England and the Thames is the white sun over the Congo that can't mix with the green of the bush and the black skin of the people. All the colours struggling to curve against each other like a

rainbow, but instead white light want to blot out the black and the green and reduce the world to one blinding colour.

(98)

The 'white light' of the Thames and England challenges the 'rainbow' vision of Joseph, in which London and the Congo are envisaged as over-lapping in ways that contest the authority of metropolitan 'civilization'. Acting potentially as another Conrad, the narrator's quest for purity is recast by Joseph as an overarching white light which covers up the myriad colours that distinguish the landscape and exist harmoniously together. Joseph's simile of the rainbow is apt as a figure for the conjunction of differ-ences, especially when we recall that rainbows are created by the refraction of light through water. Only at Oxford will the narrator accept a 'rainbow' vision of London in place of his desire for purity and escape into a white English culture. Joseph's comment also reveals not just Conrad's novel but Dabydeen's contemporary London as bathed in an imperious white light – the white light of the authority of the nation and the institutions of the old Empire's heart of which Joseph is a perpetual victim. If the narrator uses Conrad to engage obediently with English culture, Joseph makes possible a dissident reading of the text which becomes part of an attempt to reinvent his contemporary urban milieu. It is towards Joseph's subversive propensity and counter-cultural creative energies that the older narrator becomes retrospectively drawn in telling his tale.

But Joseph is also drawn into his own search for purity as an agonized response to his experience of London's racism and treatment by the social services and the police, keen to criminalize him as a Rastafarian delin-quent. At first he is a wonderfully creative figure whose energies have the potential to reimagine London from a subaltern transcultural perspective. His inability to write makes him turn to music and especially film as the means to articulate his visions. 'I can't read nor write', he says, 'but I can see' (107). On Tooting Bec Common he attempts to film a version of *Heart of Darkness* and is undaunted by Shaz's comment that such a task is impos-sible: as he says, 'all you have to do is think about it. Everything in the world is there for us to take, we only have to do so' (108). He also uses the waterway of the World Cruise as a location for his film. But later, having abandoned the project, he turns to a more experimental and ambitious pro-ject by attempting to film 'nothingness, colourlessness, the sightlessness of air, wind, the pure space between trees' (133). In pursuing these 'pure spaces' in response to his experiences of racism, Joseph attempts to reach for an imaginative location where divisions of race no longer matter, one which is figured by images of pure water. Consider his response to the nar-rator's recital of Milton's 'Lycidas' (1638):

Lycidas dead and gone to a world where nowadays-things don't matter nothing, like white people against black people, like thieving and hustling and pimping and rioting, like slavery and all that kind of history. The man turn pure spirit, pure like flowing water, that's why it's all water talk, the theme thing is water. His body bathe and the spirit come out clean-clean and clear – not white or black but clear. All of we is music, all of we is clear underneath, inside.

(147–8)

Joseph's 'water talk' projects an idealized space where the social problems of London past and present lose their agency to define and delimit human activity. The political edge to this vision is underlined later when Joseph aims to film a montage of images accompanied by natural sounds that would be 'no less than a complete statement of the condition of England' (156). Yet the identification of this 'clear' world with death and the search for purity leads to difficulties. Joseph's attempts to make his film are thwarted by the police, who arrest him on Tooting Bec Common for hanging from a tree in order to film the wind and consequently damage the camera. Shaz attempts to revive his flagging spirits by getting Patel to employ him as a cameraman for a pornographic film, but on the set Joseph experiments with light and colour and is more interested in the filters and artificial lights rather than the 'gross actuality' (235) of the intercourse performed by the actors. Patel furiously dismisses him. Devoid of a camera and conscious perhaps that he is 'doomed to be a coon' (196) in an unsympathetic, economically divided and racist city, Joseph kills himself by pouring oil on his body and setting it alight. Like the narrator's attempts to clean the waterway, Joseph can never succeed in detaching himself from the city's corruption and mess suggested by the prejudicial police and sleazy pornography. Both the narrator and Joseph attempted to escape 'this dirt and shame called Balham, this coon condition' (230) by ascending to loftier, purer heights. Each fails – fatally in the case of Joseph, but redemptively for the narrator.

Joseph's interruptive presence – his critical reading of Conrad, his schemes for films, his guitar playing and inventive speeches – stops the narrative from being what its young narrator might have intended: a story of assimilation into and acceptance by white English society and culture. In telling of Joseph's tragedy the narrator comes to accept the impossibility of achieving purity and values Joseph's life as evidence of the migrational character of contemporary London, as well as appreciating the creative and critical energies of Joseph which call into question exclusionary notions of identity and belonging in which purity is prized. Consequently, the novel's narrative structure and substance, moving unexpectedly between Guyana and London, or Oxford and London, reflect the untidiness of diasporic London rather than the neatness and order epitomized by Janet and her family, whose 'stable community' (167) the young narrator had regarded with 'sullen envy' (168). Such idealized visions of English civilization, order and wholesomeness figured in images of pure water are unsustainable. Rather, it is the messy, murky waterway of the World Cruise which most closely resembles the reality of contemporary postcolonial London, and through which the narrator and those akin to him must navigate and embrace, rather than escape. In writing his retrospective narrative which calls into question his youthful intentions, the narrator takes his first hopeful steps towards a way of regarding his identity and multiple cultural affiliations based upon the transcultural conjunctions of postcolonial London. *The Intended* does not necessarily promote an idealized or enthusiastic vision of London as transcultural and hybrid – its description of the dreary and often sleazy underbelly of Balham puts paid to that. But Dabydeen's narrator ultimately faces London's messiness and disorder in order to find there the beginnings of a new way of regarding the capital and its culture which substitutes national regard with transcultural travails. And although *The Intended* is not an optimistic novel, the diasporic optic it negotiates soberly foreshadows the more overtly ebullient writing of the late 1990s, such as *White Teeth*, in which London's transculturality is considered as the city's proudest boast.

A more overtly positive and ebullient articulation of 1990s London is found in the poetry of Fred D'Aguiar, which also seizes upon images of water in rewriting and reimagining the city. Although he was born in London in 1960, D'Aguiar spent his early childhood in his parents' native land of Guyana. He returned to London in 1972, settling with his mother in Blackheath Hill. He records that his adolescence was spent in South and East London, specifically 'the area around Greenwich Park and Charlton School near the industrial estate where the Woolwich barrier is located. Throughout my time at Charlton School the barrier was under construction' (2000: 195). He remembers suffering racist abuse at school and grew up with a feeling that 'London did not belong to me, could never belong to me on account of my race, my minority status' (197). In contrast to Brixton-based Linton Kwesi Johnson, in Blackheath D'Aguiar did not feel part of a community of black Londoners from whom he might receive support and a sense of shared identity. Owing to his Guyanese accent he felt apart from other black children who spoke 'with a Cockney accent' (196), and he did not share their love of football, preferring instead the game of cricket (a particularly Caribbean passion, of course). There was little opportunity for D'Aguiar to indulge in the camaraderie of youth. He developed as a consequence a keen sense of apartness: from Guyana, from

London, and from other black Londoners. He felt disengaged from the city which seemed to him strange, yet as time went by he found himself 'falling in love with it' (196).

D'Aguiar's collection of poems *British Subjects* (1993) opens several perspectives on London voiced by a writer who remains consciously apart yet intimately engaged with the 'strange' city, and whose poetic voice 'cherishes privacy from the tribe' (2000: 198) rather than forging a radical and resistant communal 'wi'. His choice of the lyric form underwrites his care for the value of the individual perception and singular voice (in contrast to Grace Nichols, D'Aguiar's poetry is less experimental with the lyric). But this does not make his poetry any less politically sensitive or focused. At one level several of the collection's poems record the unhappy experiences of those, like him, living in a 'London [which] was spoiled by a definition of Britain which never took my presence into consideration' (2000: 200). At another level, however, the poetry attempts to mark and celebrate the changes nurtured in the city which have remarkable transformative potential. The consciousness of the speaking 'I' is bestowed with the vital capacity to effect change through their capacity to revision both self and city. In several such poems London becomes subject to imaginative transformation by a poetic persona who seems to share the wondrous and loving relationship with the city which D'Aguiar maintained as a younger man.

As D'Aguiar told Harald Leusmann, *British Subjects* was an attempt 'to re-examine what it means to be a British subject because it was shifting and changing because there were attempts to make the definition of Britishness more and more racially pure' (Leusmann 1998: 19). In the collection, such shifts and changes impact upon the aesthetic characteristics of several poems as social circumstances are opened up to the power of poetic revisioning. D'Aguiar frequently adopts an optimistic and positive tone which anticipates the millennial confidence and buoyancy we considered at the beginning of this chapter. The British subjects of his collection, often but not exclusively racially marginalized, possess the agency to contest the dominant scripts of British identity to which they are unhappily subjected. They also have the power to remap the city in a way which disrespects its racialized borders. In addition, and suitably for someone who grew up in the city while the flood barrier at Woolwich was being constructed, a recurring trope in these determined transformative visions of London is frequently the River Thames. As D'Aguiar put it to Leusmann, '[t]alking about the Thames is a way of talking about London' (20).

D'Aguiar's representation of the city where identities are in flux is glimpsed in two poems at the beginning of *British Subjects*, 'A Gift of a Rose' and 'Black Ink'. In 'A Gift of a Rose' the speaker records being beaten and verbally abused by two policemen who have taken exception to his 'black skin' (D'Aguiar 1993: 11). But the dramatic situation is not at first sight obvious. In sharp contrast to Linton Kwesi Johnson's 'Sonny's Lettah', which pointedly portrays racist aggression in its punchy rhythm and vivid choice of verbs depicting physical violence, D'Aguiar's poem recasts the incident in terms normally associated with affection, namely the giving of flowers. The 'bunch of red, red roses' which the speaker receives are un-expected images of the bruises he suffers during the beating and which 'liberally spread over my face and body' (11). The poem follows this conceit with relish. The speaker is told by some that his roses should be photo-graphed and logged as a statistic, while others suggest that the police should receive a similar gift – 'a rose for a rose' (11). The roses gradually disappear, but a 'rose memory' remains with the speaker, who learns to avoid the police on the street and fancies that 'I have a bouquet of my own for them' (11). The effects of the poem are several and instructive to a reading of the collection as a whole. As well as defamiliarizing racist violence through an unanticipated register, the choice of a rose as an image of bruising appropri-ates a national cliché in order to suggest that the assault on the street has connections to wider issues of state authority and national identity. The speaker is clearly being subjected to a certain exclusionary version of Britain in being assaulted. But most important, perhaps, is the very act of trans-forming the incident with recourse to the conceit of the rose. D'Aguiar will not allow the ugliness of racist violence to set the tone of his poem nor define its language; instead, the poetic transformation of the incident into a bizarre moment of gift-giving effects an occasion for invention in which the creative agency of the poet is foregrounded above the violent doings of the police. To a certain extent, the 'bouquet' which the speaker may subse-quently offer the police is not an anti-racist beating so much as the poem itself. D'Aguiar's collection prizes the individual's ability to find new ways of writing which resist the authority of officious representations of social marginality and illegitimacy; note that in the poem he does not take the advice of those who suggest several ways of responding to the incident.

The function of language as a mode of subjection complicit with politi-cal attitudes and social experience is rendered in 'Black Ink', which also includes an important reference to a rose – Umberto Eco's novel *The Name of the Rose* (1983), a medieval mystery story in which a number of Italian monks die as a consequence of licking their fingers while turning the pages of a manuscript of Aristotle's *Poetics* which are laced with poison. In a sim-ilar fashion, the poem explores the relations between writing, skin, the city and the poison of race. The speaker is wary of licking his fingers when reading Sunday national newspapers and washes his hands regularly, as if concerned by the poisonous language they carry. He uses cocoa-butter rather than soap as his skin reacts to the latter's detergents, but finds that this attracts more newsprint. His hands 'would shine ebony, // No blacker' (12) if he neglected to wash. The image of newsprint blackening the speaker's hands literalizes the ways in which the media is complicit in promoting a poisonous racializing rhetoric which converts an 'ebony' hand into part of a 'black' body, just as the rain insists on 'blackening this city's red brick walls' (12). The connection between self and city is important; each is made figuratively subject to noxious racialization. The racializing media hence use a form of trick ink 'which disappears as its dries' (12), the deception of which is the presentation of racial difference as a natural occurrence rather than a concocted divisive fiction. Such texts effect a process every bit as fatal as the poisoned pages of Aristotle's *Poetics*. D'Aguiar's poem appropriates the image of newsprint as a central conceit in order to reveal its racializing ruse and resist its social agency. Furthermore, the parallel between the 'Black Ink' of the poem's title and the 'trick ink' of its final stanza also hints obliquely at the dangers of writing resistance with the recourse to a racialized rhetoric or identity. The social articulation of 'black' can only ever be a grotesque confidence trick.

The connection briefly mooted in 'Black Ink' between self and city is explored in more detail in two important poems, 'Home' and 'Dread'. 'Home' concerns the speaker's arrival at Heathrow Airport in West London and subsequent journey to his house in the city. In contrast to migrant arrivals in the city, the poem marks a return to a familiar urbanscape. As the speaker confesses, while staying overseas the sight of a red telephone box can make him 'miss here more than anything I can name' (14). His difficulties with naming are important: the disjunctive twinning of the poem's title, 'Home', and the use of 'here' in the first stanza marks the predicament of the racialized Londoner who is not allowed to consider 'here' as a legitimate home. It also captures the poem's determination to challenge the officious interdiction of those who attempt to keep 'home' and 'here' apart, denying the legitimacy of the speaker's emotional relationship to London. On arriving at his front door the speaker's progress is impaired by a pile of junk mail – more intrusive texts – which causes the door to stick. But he will not be barred from entry; he gives his key an 'extra / twist and fall[s] forwards over the threshold' (14). The speaker returns to London fully cognisant and expectant of the cool reception to come: the usual inquisition of Customs Officers at the airport, and the chatter of the 'cockney cab driver [who] can't or won't steer clear of race' (14). The speaker's response to such potential barriers to entry often combines determination with imagination and wit. At the airport's Customs desk, and despite sporting a valid passport, he is exposed to the racist gaze of an officer who assumes, in Sarah Lawson Welsh's words about the poem, 'that skin colour and ethnicity are key factors in determining who is British and who is not [and] uncovers the normative biases of this particular form of boundary control' (1996: 50). The speaker takes the officer's hostility to his presence 'like an English middleweight / with a questionable chin' (14). As well as appearing difficult to knock down, he makes a mockery of the officer's racialized sense of British identity by calling subtle attention to English middleweight boxers, of whom most in recent years have been black. It is a similar scenario in the taxi. When the driver turns the conversation towards race, the speaker reveals that he lives with an Asian and locks eyes with him in the rear-view mirror. His confrontational response is resolute, while the presence of the mirror underlines racism as a 'rear view', a way of seeing which looks backwards and refuses to embrace the new. In its closing moments 'Home' ultimately looks forwards to the beginnings of something new nurtured in the city. It ends with the speaker responding to London's grey light, 'chokey streets, roundabouts and streetlamps / with tyres chucked round them' by declaring 'I love you' (14).

While the greyness of London so disconcerted Selvon's migrant lonely Londoners, D'Aguiar's speaker's cherishing of the city's humdrum aspects reveals both his intimacy and his sense of connection. To love grey London is to be accustomed to its everyday milieu. His loving evocation of a city which is pointedly *not* seen in idealized or mythic terms is a crucial rehearsal of tenure, one that contests the construction of him as an outsider who belongs primarily to 'elsewhere' (14). The speaker refuses to bow to the interdiction of state authority and popular racism. In possession of legal tender – a British passport, money, a front-door key – his determined arrival celebrates the propensity of both self and city to survive and contest the racializing rhetoric at the heart of discourses of British subjectivity, while also suggesting that the loving declaration of tenure in London requires repeating if change is to be secured. As the final line of the poem soberly puts is, '[w]e must all sing for our suppers or else' (15).

The significance of song to the revisioning of London as a site that nurtures racially inclusive forms of national identity is underlined in 'Dread', perhaps the most impressive poem in *British Subjects*. In this poem the Thames is imagined as a significant transformative location. Inspired perhaps by the sleeve art of Jamaican reggae artist Bob Marley's 1980 album *Uprising*, the speaker watches a magical vision from the banks of the Thames as the dreadlocked Marley rises like a colossus from the river to deliver a speech, before slipping back below the surface. The poem inscribes a history of London as a colonial centre as well as a site of postcolonial resistance. It intimates London's significance as the heart of imperial trade in previous centuries through several telling references. As Marley begins to rise the speaker sees the river's waves 'roping off into strands / that combine to make a fat rope' (16). These eventually form to make Marley's dreadlocks, but also recall the ropes of bondage, servitude and slavery, wound from London's implication in the slave trade. This is supplemented by the refer-ence to the City of London and the 'stocks and shares at the Exchange' (16). We are reminded that London functioned as a point of 'exchange' during the colonial period in both economic and cultural terms, and grew prosperous in part through the trading and shipping of slaves bound by ropes and locked in 'stocks'. Another reference to colonial history is made when the speaker remembers a Marley concert at the Crystal Palace Bowl. This location recalls the site of the Great Exhibition of 1851. Nineteenth-century colonial displays like the Great Exhibition gathered manifold peoples under one 'colonial' umbrella by putting them collectively on display as sub-servient to the singular authority of the British Empire (Greenhalgh 1988). It arguably epitomized nineteenth-century British confidence in the colo-nial enterprise, Western civilization and industrial might.

The reference to the Crystal Palace Bowl acts as a hinge between London's colonial past which still resonates in the present, and the dias-pora communities and cultures which are being built upon its ruins. Some of the descendants of those objectified and placed on display in the Great Exhibition have become, over one hundred years later, subjects of a new society and have introduced to the city innovative cultural forms, in this instance the reggae concert. Bob Marley is the icon of this novel and youthful London which poses a direct challenge to the colonial legacies of the past. The presence of the Jamaican-born reggae artist in London, rising up from the Thames and chanting down Babylon to the consternation of the city stockbrokers, breaches the boundaries both of city space and the space of the nation. In shaking his dreadlocks Marley sends a tremor through the City of London, 'knocking points' (16) off the value of stocks and shares, and when he begins to skank in the river his 'big steps threat-ened to make the water / breach its banks, Barrier or no Barrier' (16). As in other poems in the collection, the Thames flood barrier at Woolwich sym-bolizes the divisive and static racial boundaries of the city which echo notions of British national identity, while the river is appropriated as an image of transcultural melange, creativity and dissidence. The popular cul-tural energies of Marley's song and dance impact upon London's agencies of high culture – the ripples he creates threaten to mark 'new heights on the South Bank' (16) – and its social conflicts. 'This was the dance of the war-rior' (16), declares the speaker. In the poem's final lines the unruly motion of the river is foregrounded as Marley's head disappears under the 'waves I mistook / for plaits doing and undoing themselves' (16) in perpetual, con-tradictory motion. Such undoings contrast with the poem's opening lines which depict separate strands combining to make 'one fat rope', and suggests that in London the enduring legacy of slavery is similarly coming apart with the advent of communities of diasporic Londoners. Above all, the final lines enshrine a vision of the river's endless flux which comes to epitomize the energy and agency of popular cultural creativity conjured by Marley. Just as the Great Exhibition has given way to the reggae concert at the Crystal Palace Bowl, so too the imperial metropolis has given in to the city's endless flux and is constantly changing and transforming as people come, go, and settle.

The Thames functions similarly in other poems as an important figure of postcolonial transformation and symbol of the perpetual conflicts which occur in the city, in which past and present combine. In 'Domestic Flight' the speaker looks upon London while flying over the city at night. In lovingly recording the beauty of London studded by its lights which resemble 'pearl necklaces' and 'diamonds' from the vantage of 3,000 feet, the speaker acknowledges that such idealized visions of the city can only be indulged from a distance while also staking a claim to the city through the joyous celebration of its wonder. In the final stanza, writing and water are connected through an image of the Thames which appears like 'sanskrit in black ink / scribbling away into the dark, / turning over with each tide' (26). The reference to the Indic language of Sanskrit locates and treasures the influence of many different cultures at the heart of the city; yet the phrase 'black ink' recalls the enquiry into race in the eponymous poem considered previously and serves as a reminder of the unhappy realities to be found on the ground. London is presented in the poem as a site of contestatory 'scribbling', caught between the influence of cultural difference which brings new language and the racialized scripts written in 'black ink'. Like the Thames, London is constantly in motion, 'turning over with each tide' of arrivants who bring new initiatives which have the capacity to change a city already divided by hostility. Ultimately, London's transformative potential resides in its refusal to stay still, to defy barriers which divide the waters and control the tides. As D'Aguiar would have it, flux is best considered to be London's inevitable condition, its unstoppable and definitive characteristic.

The 'giant soup' of the Thames is also the concern of 'Greenwich Reach', the title of which makes reference to a section of the Thames east of the city (near to where the ill-fated Millennium Dome can now be found). With the West India docks on its northern bank, this part of London has a long nautical history and enjoys many sea-faring associations. The poem both provokes and confounds an allegorical interpretation of its dramatic situation, namely the speaker's act of fishing in the river. It proceeds from the speaker's uncertainty concerning the quality of his catch as he sits with his line cast into the water: 'How do I know for sure you're fish / and not pieces of old rubbish?' (27). The predicament implies that the Thames is full of unknowable and manifold matter, yet only those con-sidered worthy of capture – the fish – are deemed to count. Considering the collection's portrayal of the Thames as a symbol of the city's hetero-geneity, flux and transcultural admixture, it is tempting to read the begin-ning of 'Greenwich Reach' as raising obliquely issues of legitimacy and belonging in London. The act of fishing is an attempt to separate the fish from the rubbish, to sort out the matter which turns the river into a 'giant soup'. The poem proceeds to make reference to 'Old Nick' who is also 'The Fisher of Men', and whose fishing rod is a 'big death-dealing stick' (27). These phrases conjure myriad associations. The reference to the Fisher King indexes T. S. Eliot's poem 'The Waste Land' (1922) which imagina-tively casts London as a city of the dead, while 'Old Nick' is another name for the devil. Such details raise the spectre of the city as a 'London Aver-nus', a dangerous and hellish location. 'Old Nick' might also be an allusion to a colloquial term for the police, which would make the 'death-dealing stick' appear as a truncheon. This allusion recalls the fatal history of police brutality in postwar London which we considered in Chapter 4. Notably, the figure of Old Nick wishes to rejuvenate the Thames by relocating people. Like the Customs Officers at Heathrow, perhaps, Old Nick appears as a figure of authority intent on catching those deemed unwelcome. In the poem's terms, then, to be caught by the officious 'Fisher of Men' heralds destruction and death; the fish are removed from the river and re-located elsewhere. This is part of the 'fish's nightmare' (27) mooted in the final stanzas. The fishing of the river exposes the fish to the deathly ele-ment of air, suspended from the water and remote from its flux and restless tides. Similarly, deaths have resulted from the actions of those keen to re-locate racialized constituencies of Londoners. The mention of a school of fish in the penultimate stanza introduces notions of group identity or belonging based on assumptions of kind. Such ways of classifying fish are represented as divisive and against the fluid motion of the river, just as the 'stranded fins' (27) of the flood barrier at Woolwich sit motionless in the water, partly suspended in air. Although 'Greenwich Reach' is delightful in its complexity and rich in associative resonances which defy schematiza-tion, it is fair to say that the poem charts both the presence and the impos-sibility of divisive notions of citizenship and belonging. Just as the fluidity and viscosity of the river's teeming 'giant soup' make a mockery of those deathly attempts to fish out its apparently unwanted matter, so too is the divisive logic that believes in homogeneous 'schools' and attempts to secure firm barriers in the water doomed to failure. As in previous poems, D'Aguiar mobilizes the Thames as a symbol of the city's inevitable tran-scultural flux which renders impossible the officious and divisive death-dealing of 'Old Nick'.

D'Aguiar's poetry pits the potential of London's 'giant soup' against the social divisions which continue in contemporary London. His conception of the Thames as a figure for transcultural transformation is also shared by Bernardine Evaristo in *Lara*. Born to an English mother and a Nigerian father in Eltham, South-East London in 1959, Evaristo lived in Woolwich as a child. Her mother was a schoolteacher; her father worked as a welder and was active in socialist politics, taking the children on a number of anti-racist marches in London during the 1970s. One of eight children, Evaristo was raised as a Catholic and received her primary education at a local convent before attending Eltham Hill Girls Grammar School. Attracted to the theatre from an early age, she joined the Greenwich Young People's Theatre aged twelve. After leaving school she enrolled at the Rose Bruford College of Speech and Drama where she studied acting and community theatre arts (not surprisingly, Evaristo's early work was for the theatre). After travelling extensively – she lived in Spain and Turkey between 1988 and 1990 – she returned to London and began writing *Lara*.

Evaristo's three published works to date include a collection of poetry, *Island of Abraham* (1994), and two novels, *Lara* (1997) and *The Emperor's Babe* (2001). The conventional generic borders between drama, fiction and poetry are especially permeable in Evaristo's writing. She told Alistair Niven in 2001 that when writing for the theatre, 'I always wrote choreo-poems, dramatic poems. I have always found it very hard to get away from writing poetry and in the last ten years I have been increasingly interested in telling a story through poetry' (Niven 2001: 17). Consequently, both *Lara* and *The Emperor's Babe* are novels-in-verse rather than dramatic poems. Even if the title page of *The Emperor's Babe* firmly defines the ensuing narrative as 'a novel', Evaristo's particular fictional form defies adequate categorization and points more generally towards the difficulties in labelling both her work and her position as a writer. Mindful of the label 'black writing' as constructing a literary ghetto, and no doubt influenced by her family heritage, Evaristo does not always welcome approaches to her work which 'can't see beyond race' (18). She has striven to show that the fortunes of black peoples in history are not marginal or of interest only to black readers, but play a central part in the wider historical narrative of the British isles and make a mockery of notions of cultural and racial purity. For example, inspired by a stint at the Museum of London in 1999 as Poet in Residence, Evaristo's most recent novel, *The Emperor's Babe*, wittily fictionalizes third-century Londinium in order to call attention to London's multiracial history which stretches back over nearly two millennia (McLeod 2001).

In uncovering London's long transcultural history in *Lara* and *The Emperor's Babe*, Evaristo seeks to reshape a racist city in her work into a utopian (yet never idealized) space of cultural admixture and part of a wider transcultural web that connects London to related locations overseas. The social and political future of the British isles rests upon the ability of its conflicted population to reconceive of Britain's past and present in transcultural terms, recognizing and prizing the unruly rhythms of arrival, settlement and departure which London particularly, but not exclusively, exemplifies. Although it is dangerous to harmonize London's fortunes with those of the nation as we have considered earlier in this book, *Lara* invites readers to reimagine Britain in terms of the circuits and conjunctions which link London to other times and places. Evaristo's work reinscribes London's long migrant history and contests the reactionary anxieties about the nation through the delightful buoyancy, wit and daring of her creative imagination.

Traversing three continents and two centuries, *Lara* is at its heart the story of its eponymous heroine's exploration of her family's past. Lara shares several similarities with her creator. Born in 1962 in Westmount Road in Eltham, Lara is the fourth of eight children conceived by Taiwo and Ellen da Costa. Her parents met in London in 1949 and married to the disapproval of Ellen's mother, Edith. Taiwo migrated from Lagos, Nigeria, after the Second World War and has ancestral connections to plantation slaves in Brazil during the nineteenth century, and to the Yoruba tribes of West Africa. Ellen is descended from 'Emma of the O'Donoghue clan' who in 1888 arrived in London from the southern Ireland garrison town of Birr with her daughter Mary Jane whom she conceived with 'her dearly departed husband of the great British Army' (Evaristo 1997: 12). As a young girl growing up in London in the 1960s and 1970s, Lara knows little about her ancestral inheritance. Edith's initial unhappiness in Ellen's marriage drives a wedge between their generations, while Taiwo remains reticent about his family partly as a traumatized response to his experiences of racism in postwar London and to receiving word in 1953 that his twin sister, Kehinde, has died: 'I must erase their memory in order to live' (57). Upset and disconcerted by her own experiences of discrimination as a young girl, Lara begins to uncover and explore her family's past in a lengthy process which takes her imaginatively (and later literally) to Nigeria and Brazil. In so doing she begins to piece together a new way of conceiving her identity and place which breaks beyond, in Paul Gilroy's words, 'the constraints of ethnicity and national particularity' (1993a: 19). Her travails between different pasts and places are echoed in the structure of *Lara* which similarly moves unexpectedly back and forth across history and nation, plaiting together different strands of culture and ancestry into a linked yet by no means homogenizing narrative which approximates to the transcultural character both of Lara and of contemporary London.

Evaristo emphasizes from the novel's very beginning London's existence as a meaningful location on a wider transcultural circuit which inseparably links the city to the fortunes of places overseas. However, as in *The Intended*, a transcultural form of consciousness for its central character is approached only after a certain struggle. There are at least three modes of imagining London's links to the world beyond which are explored in *Lara*. In the first which is perpetuated in different ways by both Taiwo and Ellen, London is conceived in colonial terms as the centre of the Empire and a beacon of civilization. In the second, which Lara is made to confront as a young girl, London appears as a racialized city which designates certain citizens as black, demonizes their blackness and questions their rights of abode. Lara must come to consciousness of a third, transcultural perception of London conceived of as a 'rainbow metropolis' (137) similar to other cities such as Rio de Janeiro, a location of admixture and melange where 'one culture [is] orchestrated by another' (139). It is this third view of London which the novel celebrates and ultimately pits against outmoded and divisive ways of conceiving of both the city and the British isles through the optics of race, ethnicity and nation – and which anticipates much of the millennial optimism of the decade's end.

The first of *Lara*'s different conceptions of London is familiar to us from the texts of migrants to the city in the 1950s and 1960s. As he boards ship in Lagos Taiwo remembers listening to radio broadcasts from the BBC's Broadcasting House. As a child he had dreamed of London, imagining '[h]ow he'd stroll / through the City with bowler and brolly, amble into a pub, / "A pint of ale, my man," white froth fringing his top lip' (132). On arriving in London he is amazed by its size yet disappointed by the mean circumstances and deathliness of the city – 'the streets are quiet / as cemeteries' (5), he remarks. Like others from the Empire, he has been sold a golden myth of London and has willingly travelled to replace the 'fallen dead' (6) and rebuild a city 'burnt out from doodlebug / and Luftwaffe' (6). Yet London has effected an unhappy translation of his identity: he is racially abused in the street and adopts the name of Bill in order to find accommodation because 'an African name closes doors' (5). Yet popular cultural locations make new relationships possible. While congregating with other arrivants in the Commonwealth dance hall and the Catholic Overseas Club, Victoria, Taiwo encounters young white women, including Ellen, his future wife. Ellen's interaction with London's latest newcomers is also shaped by a colonial dream, in this instance a benevolent attitude to Africa and Africans encouraged by the missionary zeal of her Catholic education. Her attraction to Taiwo and desire to be his wife make possible dreams 'of a huge brood of / children so lots of souls could be saved in heaven' (9). Gradually Ellen is drawn into the subcultural underside of London and responds to 'Soho's tempting finger [which] beckoned on busy Friday nights / to Hi-life basement dives replete with emigres and sailors' (9).

Although the problematic dreams of Empire bring together Ellen and Taiwo, Evaristo is careful to point out the immeasurable value of their union. Ellen refuses to endorse her mother's racism – 'Oh!, He's not too dark, is he?' (29), Edith asks – and that of their neighbours, and marries Taiwo in the face of uncomfortable social disapproval. Their relationship makes available to Taiwo an experience of London different from the cool reception afforded to many newcomers. Ellen involves him in the city's pleasures and 'revealed the goodies of a country [Taiwo had] only known / a stranger peering through snug windows on icy nights' (9). Importantly, Ellen's father refuses to grant significance to Taiwo's Nigerian origins: 'I don't care where you're from, just look after my Ellen' (37). Above all, the scenes when the couple have sex are remarkably loving and tender. Ellen perceives Taiwo as a 'gentle lion' (41), while her husband revels in her comforting body and 'drown[s] in her' (41). As their coupling reaches its climax, Ellen's feelings are clear: 'I love him' (41). Their union and act of love are significant to the novel as a whole. Evaristo demonstrates that although the circumstances of upbringing and history have led Taiwo and Ellen to each other, they cannot fully contain or define the interpersonal relationships subsequently created. While Ellen may be drawn to the Catholic Overseas Club because of her misplaced missionary benevolence, she comes to know Taiwo beyond the confines of a colonial perspective on Africans and does not care about the social *faux pas* their relationship risks. London makes possible unanticipated conjunctions which have the propensity to challenge and disrupt the dominant ideological climate of the time.

Frequently in *Lara*, sex and desire are celebrated as profoundly creative forces which, as with Ellen and Taiwo's union, productively antagonize the divisive discourses of race and nation. It is significant that the representation of desire often mobilizes images of water. When Ellen and Taiwo explore London together as part of their courting they enjoy 'boating on the Serpentine's waveless waters' (19), while their romantic bicycle rides follow 'the controlled curve of the Thames / from the Tower to the glamorous lights of Chelsea Bridge' (9). Taiwo loves the fact that Ellen refuses to despise him for his colour and lovingly compares her to 'spring water' (39), while Ellen embraces him with 'feline fluidity' (39). As desire prickles her flesh she feels as if she is floating 'tensionless, / on water, safe, bobbing, open to the swirls of gravity' (39). And immediately after Taiwo happily 'drowns' in Ellen's body, we hear the voice of Lara narrating her own birth in terms connected to fluidity:

I shot into creation as sperm from my father's penis
slept in my mother's womb for eight months and ten days
then sludged out her dilated hole as if on a muddy slide:
my entry to this island was messy, impatient, and dramatic . . .
[W]hen a gloved hand smacked my wrinkled bum I bawled
air into activated lungs, grieving the sea I'd left behind.
They named me Omilara, 'the family are like water,'
and my crumpled mother wept joy at my perfection
for amid all the soup, snot and cord I was proportioned:

(43)

'The family are like water.' As well as emphasizing the trope of fluidity,
Lara's full first name calls subtle attention to the waters which her ancestors
have criss-crossed, the Irish Sea and the Atlantic Ocean. The fundamentally creative aspect of these crossings is captured and sustained in the
novel's repeated use of images of water which repeatedly stress fertility,
desire and change. In contrast, destructive and intolerant attitudes to cross-
cultural and inter-racial exchange are linked to sterility. Edith's horror at
Ellen's proposed marriage leaves her feeling like 'a kettle – screaming, dried
out, explosive' (38).

Lara is born into a city where a significant proportion of the population
does not regard her creation in terms that match Ellen's joy at her daughter's 'perfection'. Edith's neighbours consider that her children will be
'half-breeds, mongrels. / It's not right bringing them into the world, it isn't'
(33). As a young girl Lara confronts a similar range of attitudes which, as
with her father, make for her a racialized identity which renders her incom-
plete, split and problematically cleaved. These attitudes construct and
corrupt the second London of the novel: Lara attempts to live in a city that
refuses to recognize the legitimacy of her presence. 'Home', she muses as a
ten-year-old; 'I searched but could not find myself, / not on the screen, bill-
boards, books, magazines, / and first and last not in the mirror, my demon,
my love / which faded my brownness into a Bardot likeness' (69). As in
D'Aguiar's poem 'Home', London-born Lara is not allowed to enjoy the
'here' of London as her legitimate home. Even her well-meaning best
friend, Susie, does not recognize London as Lara's home despite her birth in
Eltham, and asks 'where are you from, y'know orginally [*sic*]?' (65). As
Caryl Phillips has remarked, this kind of enquiry is '[t]he problem question
for those of us who have grown up in societies which define themselves
by excluding others. Usually us. A coded question. Are you one of us?
Are you one of ours? Where are you from? Where are you *really* from?'
(2000: 98). When Lara describes her parentage, Susie calls her a 'half-
caste' (Evaristo 1997: 65) and asks if Africa is near Jamaica (the island from

which Susie's father imagines Lara to hail). Although she ultimately regrets hurting Lara, who bursts into tears, Susie cannot escape the rhetoric of race. Valorizing Lara with the comment 'as far as / I'm concerned you're nearly white, alright?' (65), she attempts to smooth troubled waters by challenging Lara to a contest: 'Race you to the tuck shop' (65). The rhyming of 'white' with 'alright' reminds us that colour plays a crucial role in the legitimacy of identity in London, while the proposed running contest is an ironic indication of the ways in which Lara is locked into a race contest not of her making.

As she begins to explore London, Lara navigates a racialized city which offers little hope of her completing her search for the valuing and accommodation of herself. Susie's grotesque boyfriend racially abuses Lara as a 'nig nog' (68), while the activities of the local National Front bring trepidation and fear. She takes to avoiding her father in public as 'it was bloody embarrassing having a black dad' (70). When she begins art school in 1981 as a nineteen-year-old, she begins to explore Brixton, notable for its 'vivacious tableaux of Atlantic faces' (88), with her Nigerian boyfriend Josh. The relationship with Josh enables Lara to experience the excitements and energies of sex, and once again Evaristo reaches for oceanic metaphors in representing their coupling: 'Josh, your limbs were waves. I swam. / Your myriad hands smooth licked me. The sea' (88). Yet despite the creative potential implied by its figurative register, Lara's time with Josh is one of several false starts she experiences as a young woman looking for the means to anchor her identity. Josh chides Lara's ignorance of Nigerian ways – her inability to distinguish 'Jolof rice' (90) will make her a 'sorry wife' (90) – and playfully yet insightfully accuses her of spending time with him purely because of his ethnicity: 'It's obvious, you hope some of it will rub off on you' (90). The relationship breaks down when she discovers Josh with another woman in a Portobello pub.

Derided by white Londoners and betrayed by her Nigerian boyfriend, Lara's response is interesting. At first she seems to appropriate the radical language of gender and racial oppositional politics and respond with aggression to her surroundings:

> I was a walking irradiated automated diatribe, saw
> the rapist in every homme, worms in every phallus,
> the bigot in all whites, the victim in every black
> woman, London was my war zone, I sautéed
> my speech with expletives, detonated explosives
> under the custard arses of those who dared detour
> from my arty political dictates, I divorced my honky
> mother, rubbished the globe for its self-destruct sins,

and then flung open the Hammer House gates
of my Rocky Horror Hades,
and tossed the key.

(92)

The divisive and lonely consequences of Lara's 'arty political dictates' is emphasized in the schematization of white people and black women into the conflicted Manichean opposition of oppressor and victim, as well as her sundering of familial connections. As well as racializing and divorcing her 'honky' mother Lara denounces her 'patriarchal father' (92). Locked inside a hellish Hades of her own making, her angry response to the puzzle of her identity is ultimately futile. By her own admission she regurgitates appropriated ideas 'like closing-time vomit' (92). The language of radical oppositional politics which demands severance rather than negotiation and transculturation is clearly rejected in *Lara* as leading only to emotional and identitarian narcosis. In the pages following the aforementioned lines Lara begins to drink heavily, choosing intoxication as a means of escape from the pain of living in London. The sterility of this response is underlined by a disconcerting dream that Lara experiences, in which she is dressed luridly in a PVC mini-skirt with 'black fishnet / stocks, crotchless satin knicks, red-light thigh highs' (94) and engaged in a sado-masochistic encounter with a man who whips her with a 'cat o' nine tails' (94), perversely recalling her slave ancestry. Soon the dream shifts and Lara finds herself being 'stoned into rivers' (94). She awakes relieved but 'dehydrated' (94) – at odds, of course, with the liquid associations of her name.

As a young woman Lara may not be fully conscious of her ancestral inheritance which links London to seemingly distant times and places, yet throughout the novel Evaristo keeps before her readers a vision of the city mediated through a transcultural optic. On a number of occasions London is described in such a way as to yoke together its landscape with that of distant lands. For example, the beginning of the 1969 section offers a flamboyant description of dawn over the city: 'a silver flash of Thames / emerged from darkness under the insipid eyes / of giraffes which lined the deserted embankments. / Battersea Power station loomed incongrous [*sic*], Peruvian / temple of energy, magnetising bleary-eyed men / who approached it' (49). As well as anticipating Lara's imaginative and physical journey to South America, this way of looking at London highlights a transformative transcultural consciousness which Lara requires but lacks. Another important location is Atlantico, home to the da Costa family, which echoes in its name the Atlantic Ocean across which generations of Lara's family have criss-crossed. It sits 'behind Nightingale Vale, / on the bend of long Arundel Road which ambles / towards the bleak wasteland of

Woolwich Common' (46). Its proximity to wasteland recalls several similar ruinous locations which postcolonial Londoners have settled and transformed, building upon the often forgotten and neglected spaces of the city. Significantly, Atlantico also stands near the river 'which sulks / like a dirty industrial puddle on the border of Woolwich'. The house is also, and suitably, moist: four staircases run from the 'dank basement' (46) to the attic bedrooms (one of which is Lara's). It is also situated next to Notre Dame Convent, which keeps in focus Lara's Catholic inheritance and links her both to Ireland on her mother's side and to South America on her father's. Finally, the 'untended terraced field' (46) at the bottom of the garden recalls the wild countryside where Ellen was evacuated during the Second World War. Atlantico enshrines connections and memories that characterize Lara's ancestry, and is specifically liminal. Standing near the edge of the Thames, and close to wasteland, it is also a 'wild mix of town and country' (46). It is here that Lara first sees the 'Daddy People' (48), ghostly reminders of a part of her unacknowledged ancestry who haunt her life in London. Indeed, Atlantico is the major trope for the transcultural London which Lara has yet to discover.

Lara's coming to consciousness of her family's past involves her in a quest of 'tomb raiding' (79), gradually excavating the memories enshrined at Atlantico and questioning her parents about their pasts. As a young girl in 1972 she had climbed sadly on to the roof of Atlantico 'where in the silence of the sky I longed for an image, / a story, to speak me, describe me, birth me whole' (69). Yet Evaristo suggests that help may be at hand not in the contemplation of the silent sky but in the depths of the house:

> Hidden in the moist entrails of Atlantico,
> the basement passage was body-wide, mildewed,
> one medieval wooden door, arched onto the coal hole,
> now populated with a miscellany of saws, shovels,
> sinks, enamel potties, antique telephones and lamps
> which hung on the stone walls like exhibits in a museum . . .
> black bic biros, a plastic replica of the Eiffel Tower,
> framed wedding photographs and two sullen Yoruba carvings,
> his n'hers, side by side and grey with dust foundation.
>
> (79)

Recalling Salman Rushdie's comment that London has 'foundations' rather than roots, Atlantico's basement evidences the transcultural travails at the heart of its history. The juxtaposed Yoruba carvings and plastic Eiffel Tower beckon the presence of other places, while the wedding photograph (if not the basement 'museum' as a whole) emphasizes the unanticipated conjunctions created by the vicissitudes of history. Among the mildewed miscellany of relics are objects which suggest communication, such as the biro pens and the antique telephone, while the presence of the 'enamel potties' wittily suggest that these seeming waste products of history rotting in Atlantico's 'moist entrails' may be more valuable than one suspects. If the sky of London's present affords Lara only silence, Atlantico's basement entombs a past which has the potential to speak vocally and valuably to Lara, equipping her with a new way of seeing her self and her city beyond the confines of race and nation.

Lara's gradual awakening to her past involves her exploration of her ancestors' stories. She begins to question Taiwo closely about his Nigerian background and uncovers an ancestral connection to Brazil. On visiting her grandmother Edith, who remains uncomfortable with Ellen's marriage, she learns about the unhappy atmosphere which her parents have endured since their first meeting, and gains knowledge about her mother's side of the family. These encounters stress both connection and displacement. Taiwo chides Lara that she 'does not really know anything' (80) about Nigeria, the Yoruba and Brazil, while Lara remains uncomfortable with Edith's racism – when Lara mentions a desire to see Nigeria for herself, Edith asks her what 'do you want to go there for? You'll come back looking like a nigger-man, dear' (84). Ellen tries to defend her mother with recourse to her old age, but Lara is steadfast: 'Not all old people are like that. / Age has nothing to do with it' (84). Lara is drawn into a complex relationship with the past in which she acknowledges both a connection to and disconnection from other people, times and places. Lara cannot define herself with singular categories of national identity such as English, Irish, Nigerian, Brazilian, as she exceeds their exclusive parameters. Rather, definition emerges from the conjunction of these strands epitomized by her very creation in London. Lara reconceives of London in this fashion by taking a series of travels, both physical and imaginative, the terminus of which is the city, suitably re-envisioned and transformed.

A central aspect of Lara's imaginative journeys is her love of stories. As well as searching out the stories of her father and grandmother, she reads the books of Thor Heyerdahl, the Norwegian explorer and archaeologist who spent much of his life in Polynesia and provocatively suggested that American Indians had once migrated to the region from Peru and British Columbia (Heyerdahl 1952). Lara's reading transforms her vision of London. When she catches the Woolwich Ferry she imagines she is riding 'across turbulent / seas to Silvertown, coconut palms and coral reefs. / . . . I watched the Thames drift into the South Pacific void / as trade winds guided my balsa raft from the Americas / to the remote Marquesas when I caught the ferry home' (Evaristo 1997: 71). Lara's capacity to reimagine the city takes place while crossing water, and emphasizes the River Thames as an important waterway which links London to other island-based cultures and makes the British isles part of a wider transcultural archipelago. This moment also moves Lara's consciousness closer to the narrator's, who had previously represented Battersea Power Station in terms of a Peruvian temple. 'Books enlarged my world' (71), claims Lara. Yet she represses her love of language, storing away the new words she learns. When she begins to travel the world, however, the treasures of the past and the creative powers of language become an invaluable resource.

Aged thirty-one, in 1993 Lara accompanies her father to Lagos, another island city with watery connections – Taiwo explains that its name comes from the Portuguese word 'lagoon'. This is the first of several journeys which will reveal to Lara the complexity and transculturality of her past. Visiting Lagos cannot be considered a homecoming for her, of course, although she muses 'I wonder if I could belong' (104). But the local children shout at her 'Oyinbo!' which her father translates as 'Whitey!' (104), while Lara betrays her European upbringing amidst the heat of Lagos: 'What I'd give for a cappuccino and croissant right now' (107). While snoozing in the 'West Indian Quarter' (109) of Lagos she is visited by the ghost of her grandmother, Zenobia, who reveals Lara's line of descent from the slaves of Brazil. In the proceeding pages the narrative passes between generations; at one point Lara's great-grandfather Baba Agbuda tells of his birth in 1839 as a chattel owned by Senhor Fernandés da Costa, whose name has passed down the line and across oceans to Lara's birth in London in 1962. Baba's is not the oldest voice in the novel. In his narrative he makes reference to his mother Tolulopé, with whose voice the text opens, and also to the stories of an unnamed 'lady in the old country' (124) which is presumably Yorubaland in West Africa. This figure has the power of language, 'churning stories into a babbling stream of poetry oratory' in which can be discovered 'the lives, loves, wars / of our ancestors' (124). Suitably these stories were famously told 'by the quiet sea' where 'she voyaged back to the early time' (124). If water is often used as a trope of fertility and desire, in Baba's narrative it becomes linked to the value and creativity of storytelling. It is the capacity of stories to transport and transform which Lara learns in the novel's closing sections. As captured by the image of the 'babbling stream' of the Yoruba storyteller's words, stories do not flow from a single source or point of origin, but are indebted to other tales. It is worth remembering at this point the Yoruba proverb which prefaces the novel: 'However far the stream flows, it never forgets its source.' As *Lara* subsequently suggests, a stream can have many sources, of which the flow of storytelling – the 'babbling stream' of oratory – enables the remembering. The novel sets against the schematic certainties of familial lineage, stable origins and secure roots an alternative way of rendering history which emphasizes fluidity and flow, and foregrounds the creative and transformative changes which occur from generation to generation. Water is the central complex trope of the novel's revisioning of history, with the Thames the epitome of London's existence as the contemporary conduit of manifold ancestral transcultural stories.

Lara's imaginative encounter with her transcultural legacy is followed by a trip she makes in 1995 to South America, where she is given ample evidence of the cultural conjunctions and hybridizing circumstances of her past. In Rio de Janeiro she marvels at 'this sexing city' which is described as a 'rainbow metropolis' (137). As in Joseph's critique of Conrad in Dabydeen's *The Intended*, the rainbow is a sign of the harmonious concurrence of cultural differences. In *Lara* it seems especially suitable to the novel's use of water as a trope of fertility and creativity. Lara's view of Rio is by no means idealized or depoliticized: she worries bout the 'favela shacks' that are 'homes for the disempowered' (137). As she travels further, she takes a trip along the Amazon river and docks at a remote settlement on Palm Sunday where she discovers a hilltop church with an Indian congregation singing 'Catholic hymns hybridized by drums' (139). Lara describes this as 'one culture being orchestrated by another' (139) and finds in it a template for social and cultural creativity and change. She imagines returning to London in the novel's final page ready to regard and recreate the city as a transcultural 'rainbow metropolis':

> I savour living in the world, planet of growth, of decay,
> think of my island – the 'Great' Tippexed out of it –
> tiny amid massive floating continents, the African one –
> an embryo within me – I will wing back to Nigeria again
> and again, excitedly swoop over a zig-zag of amber lights
> signalling the higgledy energy of Lagos.
> It is time to leave.
> Back to London, across international time zones,
> I step out of Heathrow and into my future.
>
> (140)

The 'higgledy energy' and 'zig-zag' patterns of light suggest something of the unpredictable and agreeably untidy journeys to come, in which borders marked by international time zones are rendered porous. With the world reclaimed and reconceived in such terms, London is celebrated in the final lines as a place of accommodation, and of both arrival and departure. Lara will return to London to transform it imaginatively, perhaps writing a book like the one in which she appears – which suitably crosses generic boundaries, unpredictably passes the narrative voice between generations, and criss-crosses time and space. In a detail which recalls the conclusion of MacInnes's *Absolute Beginners*, London's airport at Heathrow appears at the book's end as a point of both departure and arrival. Yet unlike the Africans who arrive in MacInnes's novel, Lara will 'step out' into a city she already knows. At the end of the novel, having journeyed imaginatively and in person across oceans, Lara is ready to begin.

The image of London which ultimately emerges from *Lara* is like the narrator: confident, cognisant of its transcultural past, optimistic, full of creative energies nurtured from the conjunction of different times and places in both city and self. Some of these energies can be detected too in the exuberance and wit of Zadie Smith's *White Teeth*, but they do not originate there. Dabydeen and D'Aguiar also proffer revisionings of London which, despite their tonal differences, none the less suggest a new way of regarding the city in relation to the myriad peoples and cultures which have washed up there, and will continue to do so. If Dabydeen began the decade by reflecting gloomily upon the city's cellular nature which organized London's different cultures into discrete units, closed off from each other, the three texts we have explored in this chapter perhaps suggest new routes and passageways in the city, alternative spatial practices that resituate, remap and transform London. The optimism they enshrine is exquisitely postcolonial: it bears witness to the achievements of Londoners in making the city accommodating for all, not just a select and officious few, while looking ahead positively and demanding further changes. The London of these texts is not the migrants' dream of the 1950s and 1960s, or the apocalyptic and turbulent neighbourhoods of the 1970s and 1980s, although it remains indebted to them. At the turn of a new century, these writers and others look to the future with robust confidence, determination and renewed resolve. Their cheerful determination is a sign of the dedication to the perpetual recreation of London in the face of resistance and prejudice, and constitutes its own cultural contribution to the progression of social change. As Evaristo's Lara so powerfully puts it, 'the future means transformation' (139).

Coda
'No fenky-fenky road'

Simon Schama opens his exploration of the relations between environment and the imagination, *Landscape and Memory* (1995), by remembering travelling across the River Thames as a young boy:

> When I took a boat trip with my father from Gravesend to Tower Bridge, the docks at Wapping and Rotherhithe still had big cargo ships at berth rather than upmarket grillrooms and corporate headquarters. But my mind's eye saw the generations of the wharves, bristling with masts and cranes as if in a print by Hollar, the bridges top-heavy and overhung across their whole span with rickety timber houses, alive with the great antswarm of the imperial city.
>
> (4)

Schama's admittedly nostalgic view of the Thames in terms of its imperial traffic gestures to the colonial facticity of London, its central role in the pursuit of Empire, as well as the ways in which one always looks at the city through previous representations made of it. As a child, his view of the Thames looked backwards romantically to the generations of nautical traffic which brought people and goods from overseas to fill the wharves. In remembering that childhood moment from the vantage of the 1990s, he adumbrates the Thames as it appears to him at the end of the century no longer as a centre for shipping but the site of dockland developments and corporate headquarters. In looking simultaneously at the past and the present, Schama layers on top of each other a number of images of the Thames from different moments which suggest some of the changes which have happened in London as it has turned from an imperial metropolis into a globalized world city. What of the future?

The views of London which we have encountered in *Postcolonial London* portray the fortunes of the city through the representations and impressions made by a diverse body of writers with links to such places as Australia,

Guyana, Jamaica, India, New Zealand, Nigeria, Pakistan, South Africa, and Trinidad. Their visions of London, which delineate the oppressive obliga-tions of place as well as the creative and resistant revisionings of space, collectively constitute a heterogeneous series of layers, a body of texts which tell no single story but instead bear witness to the different routes through the city, and their consequences, from a perspective similar to Gabriel Gbadamosi's depiction of Brixton market which we considered in the Introduction. These texts often tell a sombre tale of struggle, hostility and violence; yet above all they emphasize the vital creative potential of postwar London's postcolonial settlers and their children – from Sam Selvon's spatial creolization of London's unwelcoming streets to Bernardine Evaristo's transcultural heroine Lara, whose hybrid identity offers a particu-larly educative mirror for London's migrant history and multicultural contemporaneity. The frequent utopianism found in postcolonial London writing which dares to reinvent London in defiance of those who would deny the city's latest transformations is a measure of its political efficacy and predominant commitment to social change. Rather than glibly cheer-leading cultural difference, the representations of postcolonial London we have explored in this book invest centrally in the painful and at times violent fortunes of postwar London in which it occurs and to which it con-tributes – even if, as in the case of V. S. Naipaul's 1960s writing or Rushdie's depiction of popular riotous protest, such changes provoke unsettling feel-ings of disappointment or despair.

In several of these texts, as we have seen, postcolonial London has emerged in those locations often forgotten or neglected by most Londoners – derelict streets, neglected neighbourhoods, bomb-sites and ruins. In Colin MacInnes's *City of Spades* Johnny Fortune first meets Billy Whispers at a Brixton house which 'stood all by itself among ruins of what I suppose was wartime damages, much like one tooth left sticking in an old man's jaw' (1993: 26); and the Moorhen pub where Montgomery Pew hears Lord Alexander's calypso stands opposite 'the brick fence that lined the bombed-out site' (48). Both Doris Lessing's depiction of the typist writing amidst West London's bombed-out ruins and Buchi Emecheta's portrayal of Adah's efforts to secure accommodation for herself and her family amongst the derelict streets of 1960s Kentish Town take us to neglected and disused environments in which new narratives are written and new communities emerge. Such locations might be understood in terms of de Certeau's con-ceptualization of spatial stories, as the city is changed by the uses to which it is put by those often forced to improvize – like Mangohead and Hotboy in Selvon's 'Calypso in London' – with only the meagre means at their dis-posal. In contradistinction to the shocked response of Sheila Patterson, who encountered such a space when she turned off the main high street in

Brixton in 1955, the writers we have explored offer different renderings of such spaces as locations where, in Rushdie's important phrase which echoes throughout *The Satanic Verses*, newness comes into the world.

At the vanguard of London's newness has been the city's young, drawn from those with ancestral connections to once-colonized countries and the enthusiastic members of the so-called host nation keen to engage with the cultural initiatives of a multicultural city. Selvon's 'boys', MacInnes's teenagers, Lessing's confused West London Rose, Linton Kwesi Johnson's 'yout', Hanif Kureishi's multiracial community of straggly kids, David Dabydeen's teenage schoolboys, Bernardine Evaristo's Lara – London's envisioned transformation has so frequently been bound up with the optimism, promise and naivety of youth. London's young have made possible an engagement not only with other cultures but also with fresh cultural forms, bringing together (as in the sensibility of Hanif Kureishi) popular cultural energies with the 'noble' pursuits of fiction and poetry. Just as Dabydeen's Rastafarian orphan Joseph can turn his hand equally to the guitar and literary criticism despite being able to read neither music nor language, so too has postcolonial London writing searched for innovative and unexpected generic juxtapositions in order to bear witness to the experiences of settling, and being unsettled, in London. We have witnessed several examples of this, including Selvon's calypsonian approach to both the novel and society; MacInnes's critical adulation of the world of pop songs and teenagers which poises his novels between the gravity of documentary and fiction, and the levity of pop songs, teenagers and skaz; Frame's morbid vision of London which devours the fictional form within which it is articulated; Grace Nichols's innovative lyrics of the Fat Black Woman; Linton Kwesi Johnson's dub aesthetic which fuses poetry and reggae in the context of Brixton's youthful milieu; Bernardine Evaristo's novel-in-verse which (like Lara) modulates between generic categories which cannot fully contain it.

The fertility and dynamism of popular and frequently youthful visions of London, negotiated and explored in the cultural sphere, offer tempting and transformative social models of postwar and contemporary London which potentially resource the political contestation of those discourses – race, nation, gender – which attempt to deny tenure to those who have made London their home. As Paul Gilroy has argued in the context of popular music, 'the informal, long-term processes through which different groups have negotiated each other have intermittently created a "two-tone" sensibility which celebrates its hybrid origins and has provided a significant opposition to "common-sense" racialism' (1993b: 35). Popular cultural initiatives have often suggested new spaces of social autonomy which are no less pragmatic for their utopianism, and which energize much of the postcolonial London writing we have considered. Indeed, many such texts enable one to think critically about these spaces, and at times raise concerns over the difficult task of translating the progressive aspects of cultural endeavour into the social practices of everyday life – Emecheta's Adah struggles in *Second-Class Citizen* to establish a space for social autonomy through the imaginative transcultural travails which open new ways of thinking about her race and gender; and in *Sammy and Rosie Get Laid* Kureishi's community of kids is evicted from its caravan-site and forced to seek out new spaces in London.

Looking beyond the city's limits, can representations of postcolonial London offer transformative resources not only for the city's social conditions but also to the imagining of the nation-state within which it resides? Do the transcultural and transnational aspects of postcolonial London's facticity productively confront both the exclusionary consolidation of national culture and identity increasingly grounded in a notion of racialized whiteness and the cellular balkanization of the nation's (not just London's) multicultural communities? According to a recent report commissioned by the Runnymede Trust on the future of multi-ethnic Britain, chaired by Bikhu Parekh:

> expunging the traces of an imperial mentality from the national culture, particularly those that involved seeing the white British as a superior race, is a ... difficult task. This mentality penetrated everyday life, popular culture and consciousness. It remains active in projected fantasies and fears about difference, and in racialised stereotypes of otherness. The unstated assumption remains that Britishness and whiteness go together, like roast beef and Yorkshire pudding. There has been no collective working through of this imperial experience. The absence from the national curriculum of a rewritten history of Britain as an imperial force, involving dominance in Ireland as well as in Africa, the Caribbean and Asia, is proving from this perspective to be an unmitigated disaster.
>
> (Parekh *et al.* 2000: 24–5)

Postcolonial London writing assists in the task of reorienting the narration of the nation by recontextualizing culture and society in relation to Empire and its legacy, and challenging the projected fantasies of cultural otherness and apartness which have manifested themselves in institutionalized and popular racism at the levels of both state and street. It may well afford an opportunity for some to begin to work through the consequences of the end of Empire which, as Stuart Ward has persuasively argued, only *seems* to have had minimal impact in the postwar decades (Ward 2001) – whether it

be Naipaul's ambivalent rendering of the relations between Englishness
and imperialism or Lessing's undemonstrative account of the racializing
turn in postwar notions of national identity. In foregrounding the cultural
and social admixture of London, its problems but also its possibilities, postcolonial London writing demands that received notions of the nation be
recast in terms of the transcultural travails explored, for example, in Dabydeen's and Evaristo's work – and perhaps offers new ways of thinking about
identity, belonging and citizenship which are sensitive to the multiple affiliations and emotional connections of transnational consciousness. Rather
than dispensing with the concepts of nation and national culture – such
things are not easily given up – and adopting a postnational optic, an attention to postcolonial London writing affords not an escape from national
issues but a confrontation with them. It enables a vital opportunity for *re-
appraisal* through which the imperial relations between Britain and its
(former) colonies are made admissible to the narration of national history
and the reading, and constitution, of national culture. Considered in this
way, postcolonial London suggests democratizing and culturally sensitive
models of national identity and culture which admit the transformative
presence of transcultural creativity. In this regard, perhaps, the utopian
propensity of much of the postcolonial London writing we have explored
in this book is more pragmatic than idealist, and remains politically
important as a new century for London, and for Britain, proceeds. If, as
Mike Phillips has argued, 'the identity of London and Londoners has now
become a major plank in the secret agenda of national anxiety about the
future of the country' (1991: 121), then postcolonial London writing
affords the opportunity to address and overcome those anxieties and, as in
the last pages of Evaristo's *Lara*, project new and exciting ways of conceptualizing Britain with 'the "Great" Tippexed out of it – tiny amid massive
floating continents' (1997: 140).

So how to find the future? Turn the corner. Take a walk. Go with the
Grenadan poet and short-story writer Merle Collins to Tottenham. Explore
the names of the streets, the sights and smells of the market; listen to the
different languages layering history upon history, passage upon passage. Sit
down with her in the High Road barber shop which is

> not far from Bruce Grove, tongue curving and cutting a
> cadence with a word announcing Dominica, St Lucia, Côte d'Ivoire
>
> names that suggest a story bigger than the Tottenham space
> Hear the teteh music of the tongue telling about Ghana
> Check that pambere swing to words that speaks of Zimbabwe

And nowadays, you hear the sound of Bosnia
The mix changing again on the green and in the grove

One day, I walk without even knowing it into this place called
    Tottenham
No court, no fenky-fenky road, but a history of islands, continents
(Collins 2000: 16)

As the above extract from Collins's poem 'Tottenham' reveals, to her mind this postcolonial London space contains a conjunction of passages which breach its boundaries, opening up London to the names, sounds and words of other islands and continents. The sound of Bosnia reminds us that this is by no means an idealized space beyond the conflicts of the present which have forced some from their native lands to cities like London in search of accommodation, respite and asylum. It is not cheerfully hybrid and hetero-glot. Perpetually restless, inevitably pluralized and endlessly transforming, the mix changes with each layer of history, each arrival, departure and settlement, modulating between pain and possibility, the cut and the curve. In Collins's Tottenham, tongues delightfully entwine, producing modes and means of representation which make new the city while they too are changed. It is a hopeful vision, a utopian expression of transcultural engage-ment upon which the future might rest.

Like so many of the writers we have explored in *Postcolonial London*, Collins demands that we become or remain sensitive to the migratory spa-tial stories of the city which persistently breach the tidy boundaries of place. The cultural consequences of those histories are vital. As we have seen – and as we continue to see in the work of writers such as Monica Ali, Ferdinand Dennis and Zadie Smith – London ain't no fenky-fenky road.

Bibliography

Ahmad, A. (1992) In Theory: Classes, Nations, Literatures, London: Verso.

Alibhai-Brown, Y. (2000) 'A magic carpet of multiple cultures in London', New York Times, Sunday 25 June, 30–2.

—— (2001) [2000] Imagining the New Britain, New York: Routledge.

Alomes, S. (1999) When London Calls: The Expatriation of Australian Creative Artists to Britain, Cambridge: Cambridge University Press.

Appadurai, A. (1996) Modernity at Large: Cultural Dimensions of Globalization, Minneapolis and London: University of Minnesota Press.

Appignanesi, L. and Maitland, S. (eds) (1989) The Rushdie File, London: Fourth Estate.

Ashcroft, B. (2001) Post-Colonial Transformation, London and New York: Routledge.

Ashcroft, B., Griffiths, G. and Tiffin, H. (eds) (1989) The Empire Writes Back: Theory and Practice in Post-colonial Literatures, London: Routledge.

Augé, M. (1995) Non-Places: Introduction to an Anthropology of Supermodernity, trans. by John Howe, London: Verso.

Bachelard, G. (1994) The Poetics of Space, trans. by Maria Jolas, Boston, MA: Beacon Press.

Batt, C. (1999) 'Post-colonial London, by way of medieval romance: V. S. Naipaul's Mr Stone and the Knights Companion', Kunapipi, 21.2, 66–74.

Baucom, I. (1999) Out of Place: Englishness, Empire and the Locations of Identity, Princeton, NJ: Princeton University Press.

Bhabha, H. K. (1994) The Location of Culture, London and New York: Routledge.

—— (2000) 'The vernacular cosmopolitan', in F. Dennis and N. Khan (eds) Voices of the Crossing: The Impact of Britain on Writers from Asia, the Caribbean and Africa, London: Serpent's Tail, 133–42.

Binder, W. (1997) 'Interview with David Dabydeen', in K. Grant, (ed.) The Art of David Dabydeen, Leeds: Peepal Tree, 159–76.

Boehmer, E. (2002) Empire, the National, and the Postcolonial, 1890–1920: Resistance in Interaction, Oxford: Oxford University Press.

Brennan, T. (1989) Salman Rushdie and the Third World: Myths of the Nation, Basingstoke: Macmillan.

—— (1997) *At Home in the World: Cosmopolitanism Now*, Cambridge, MA: Harvard University Press.

Brooker, P. (2002), *Modernity and Metropolis: Writing, Film and Urban Formations*, Basingstoke: Palgrave.

Brown, L. W. (1981) *Women Writers in Black Africa*, Westport, CT: Greenwood Press.

Bryan, B., Dadzie, S. and Scarfe, S. (eds) (1985) *The Heart of the Race: Black Women's Lives in Britain*, London: Virago.

Centre for Contemporary Cultural Studies (1982) *The Empire Strikes Back: Race and Racism in 70s Britain*, London: Hutchinson.

Certeau, M. de (1984) *The Practice of Everyday Life*, trans. by Steven Rendall, Berkeley: University of California Press.

Chambers, I. (1990) *Border Dialogues: Journeys in Postmodernity*, London and New York: Routledge.

—— (1994) *Migrancy, Culture, Identity*, London and New York: Routledge.

Chaudhuri, N. C. (1966) [1959] *A Passage to England*, London: Macmillan.

Chrisman, L. (2003) *Postcolonial Contraventions: Cultural Readings of Race, Imperialism and Nationalism*, Manchester: Manchester University Press.

Cohen, R. (1994) *Frontiers of Identity: The British and the Others*, London and New York: Longman.

Collins, M. (2000) 'Tottenham', in C. Newland and K. Sesay (eds) *IC3: the Penguin Book of New Black Writing in Britain*, London: Penguin, 15–16.

Connor, S. (1996) *The English Novel in History 1950–1995*, London and New York: Routledge.

Constantine, L. (1954) *Colour Bar*, London: S. Paul.

Cowley, J. (1996) *Carnival, Canboulay and Calypso: Traditions in the Making*, Cambridge: Cambridge University Press.

Dabydeen, D. (1991) 'On cultural diversity', in M. Fisher and U. Owen (eds) *Whose Cities?* London: Penguin, 97–106.

—— (1992) [1991] *The Intended*, London: Minerva.

D'Aguiar, F. (1993) *British Subjects*, Newcastle: Bloodaxe Books.

—— (2000) 'Home is always elsewhere: individual and communal regenerative capacities of loss', in K. Owusu (ed.) *Black British Culture and Society: A Text Reader*, London and New York: Routledge, 195–206.

Dance, D. C. (1992) *New World Adams: Conversations with Contemporary West Indian Writers*, Leeds: Peepal Tree.

Dasenbrock, R. and Jussawalla, F. (1995) 'Interview with Sam Selvon', in S. Nasta and A. Rutherford (eds) *Tiger's Triumph: Celebrating Sam Selvon*, Armidale Hebden Bridge: Dangaroo 114–25.

Delrez, M. (2002) *Manifold Utopia: The Novels of Janet Frame*, New York and Amsterdam: Rodopi.

Dennis, F. (1988) *Behind the Frontlines: Journey into Afro-Britain*, London: Victor Gollancz.

Donald, J. (1999) *Imagining the Modern City*, London: The Athlone Press.

Donnell, A. (ed.) (2002) *The Routledge Companion to Contemporary Black British Culture*, London and New York: Routledge.

Eade, J. (2000) *Placing London: From Imperial Capital to Global City*, New York and Oxford: Berghahn Books.

Edmond, R. (1995) '"In search of the lost tribe": Janet Frame's England', in A. R. Lee, (ed.) *Other Britain, Other British: Contemporary Multicultural Fiction*, London: Pluto Press, 161–73.

Emecheta, B. (1989) [1974] *Second-Class Citizen*, London: Hodder and Stoughton.

—— (1994a) [1972] *In the Ditch*, Oxford: Heinemann.

—— (1994b) [1974] *Second-Class Citizen*, Oxford: Heinemann.

—— (1994c) *Head Above Water: An Autobiography*, Oxford: Heinemann.

Evaristo, B. (1994) *Island of Abraham*, Leeds: Peepal Tree.

—— (1997) *Lara*, Tunbridge Wells: Angela Royal Publishing.

—— (2001) *The Emperor's Babe*, London: Hamish Hamilton.

Fanon, F. (1990) [1963] *The Wretched of the Earth*, trans. by Constance Farrington, London: Penguin.

Farson, D. (1993) [1987] *Soho in the Fifties*, introduction by George Melly, London: Pimlico.

Fee, M. (1993) 'Resistance and complicity in David Dabydeen's *The Intended*', *ARIEL* 24.1, 109–26.

Fisher, M. (1991) 'Introduction', in M. Fisher and U. Owen (eds) *Whose Cities?* London: Penguin, 1–7.

Foucault, M. (1990) [1978], *The History of Sexuality: An Introduction*, trans. by Robert Hurley, Harmondsworth: Penguin.

Frame, J. (1962) *The Edge of the Alphabet*, London: W. H. Allen.

—— (1979) *Living in the Maniototo*, New York: G. Braziller.

—— (1990) *The Complete Autobiography*, London: The Women's Press.

Fryer, P. (1984) *Staying Power: The History Of Black People in Britain*, London: Pluto.

Gandhi, L. (1998) *Postcolonial Theory: A Critical Introduction*, Edinburgh: Edinburgh University Press.

Gane, G. (2002), 'Migrancy, the cosmopolitan intellectual, and the global city in *The Satanic Verses*', *Modern Fiction Studies*, 48.1, 18–49.

Gbadamosi, G. (1999) 'The road to Brixton Market: a post-colonial travelogue', in S. Clark (ed.) *Travel Writing and Empire: Postcolonial Theory in Transit*, London and New York: Zed Books, 185–94.

Geiss, I. (1974) *The Pan-African Movement*, trans. by Ann Keep, London: Methuen.

Gerzina, G. (1995) *Black London: Life before Emancipation*, New Brunswick, NJ: Rutgers University Press.

Gikandi, S. (1992) *Writing in Limbo: Modernism and Caribbean Literature*, Ithaca, NY, and London: Cornell University Press.

—— (1996) *Maps of Englishness: Writing Identity in the Culture of Colonialism*, New York: Columbia University Press.

—— (2000) 'Pan-Africanism and cosmopolitanism: the case of Jomo Kenyatta', *English Studies in Africa*, 43.1, 3–27.

Gilroy, P. (1991) [1987], *'There Ain't No Black in the Union Jack': The Cultural Politics of Race and Nation*, London: Routledge.

—— (1993a) *The Black Atlantic: Modernity and Double Consciousness*, London and New York: Verso.

—— (1993b) *Small Acts: Thoughts on the Politics of Black Cultures*, London: Serpent's Tail.

—— (1999) 'A London sumpting dis . . .', *Critical Quarterly*, 41.3, 57–69.

—— (2000) *Between Camps: Nations, Cultures and the Allure of Race*, London: Allen Lane.

Glass, R. (1960) *Newcomers: The West Indians in London*, assisted by Harold Pollins, London: Centre for Urban Studies and George Allen and Unwin.

Gohrisch, J. (2001) 'Uncovering a hidden reality and raising the possibility of change: Joan Riley's novels', in B. Neumeier (ed.) *Engendering Realism and Postmodernism: Contemporary Women Writers in Britain*, Amsterdam and New York: Rodopi, 279–89.

Goulbourne, H. (1991) *Ethnicity and Nationalism in Post-Imperial Britain*, Cambridge: Cambridge University Press.

Gould, T. (1993) [1983] *Inside Outsider: The Life and Times of Colin MacInnes*, London: Alison and Busby.

Greenhalgh, P. (1988) *Ephemeral Vistas: The Expositions Universelles, Great Exhibitions and World's Fairs 1851–1939*, Manchester: Manchester University Press.

Grewal, S., Kay, J., Landor, L., Lewis, G. and Parmar, P. (eds) (1988) *Charting the Journey: Writings by Black and Third World Women*, London: Sheba.

Habekost, C. (1993) *Verbal Riddim: The Politics and Aesthetics of African-Caribbean Dub Poetry*, Amsterdam and Atlanta, GA: Rodopi.

Hall, S. (1996) 'When was "the post-colonial"? Thinking at the limit', in I. Chambers and L. Curti (eds) *The Post-Colonial Question: Divided Skies, Common Horizons*, London: Routledge, 242–60.

—— (2002) 'Calypso kings', *The Guardian*, Friday 28 June.

Harlow, B. (1987) *Resistance Literature*, London and New York: Methuen.

Hebdige, D. (1979) *Subculture: The Meaning of Style*, London: Methuen.

Heyerdahl, T. (1952) *American Indians in the Pacific: The Theory behind the Kon-Tiki Expedition*, London: Allen and Unwin.

hooks, b. (1982) *Ain't I a Woman: Black Women and Feminism*, London: Pluto.

Huggan, G. (2001) *The Postcolonial Exotic: Marketing the Margins*, London and New York: Routledge.

Huxley, E. (1964) *Back Street New Worlds: A Look at Immigrants in Britain*, London: Chatto and Windus/Punch.

gton, E. (1988) *Beyond the Mother Country: West Indians and the Notting Hill*
hite Riots, London: I. B. Tauris.

, E. J. (1969) *Freedom and Reality*, ed. by John Wood, Kingswood, Surrey:
erfronts.

J. (ed.) (2000) *Writing Black Britain 1948–1998: An Interdisciplinary Anthol-*
Manchester: Manchester University Press.

03) *Dwelling Places: Postwar Black British Writing*, Manchester: Manchester
rsity Press.

A. (2000) *Postcolonialism: Theory, Practice or Process?* Oxford: Polity

(1999) *Reinventing Britain: 500 Years of Black and Asian History*, London:

R. (2002) *Hanif Kureishi*, Plymouth: Northcote House.

5) *The Unbelonging*, London: The Women's Press.

Waiting in the Twilight, London: The Women's Press.

Romance, London: The Women's Press.

A Kindness to the Children, London: The Women's Press.

Writing reality in a hostile environment', *Kunapipi*, 16.1, 547–52.

994) *The Myth of Aunt Jemima: Representations of Race and Region*,
New York: Routledge.

90) *Calypso and Society in Pre-Independence Trinidad*, Port of Spain:
ehr.

8) *The Satanic Verses*, London: Viking Penguin.

inary Homelands: Essays and Criticism 1981–1991, London: Granta/

[1983] *The World, the Text, and the Critic*, London: Vintage.

e and Imperialism, London: Vintage.

scape to an Autumn Pavement, London: Hutchinson.

8) *Beyond Postcolonial Theory*, New York: St Martin's Press.

ondon Calling: How Black and Asian Writers Imagined a City,
ollins.

) [1981] *The Scarman Report: the Brixton Disorders 10–12 April*
orth: Pelican.

dscape and Memory, London: Fontana.

ndon 1900: The Imperial Metropolis, New Haven, CT, and
rsity Press.

Housing Lark, London: McGibbon and Kee.

s of Sunlight, London: Longman Caribbean.

s Ascending, Heinemann: Oxford.

onely Londoners, Harlow: Longman.

do West One, Leeds: Peepal Tree.

ne can't go: East Indian, Trinidadian, West Indian', in

Innes, C. L. (2002) *A History of Black and Asian Writing in Britain, 1700–2000*,
Cambridge: Cambridge University Press.

Jacobs, J. M. (1996) *Edge of Empire: Postcolonialism and the City*, London and New
York: Routledge.

Jacobson, D. (1958) 'After Notting Hill', *Encounter*, 11.6, 3–10.

—— (1962) [1959] *The Evidence of Love*, Harmondsworth: Penguin.

—— (1986) [1985] *Time and Time Again: Autobiographies*, London: Flamingo.

Jaggi, M. (2000) 'In a strange land', *The Guardian*, Saturday 22 January.

Johnson, L. K. (1999) 'In conversation with John La Rose', in R. Harris and
S. White (eds) *Changing Britannia: Life Experience within Britain*, London: New
Beacon Books/George Padmore Institute, 50–79.

—— (2002) *Mi Revalueshanary Fren: Selected Poems*, with an introduction by Fred
D'Aguiar, London: Penguin.

Keith, M. (1993) *Race, Riots and Policing: Lore and Disorder in a Multi-racist Society*,
London: UCL Press.

Keith, M. and Cross, M. (1993) 'Racism and the postmodern city', in M. Cross and
M. Keith (eds) *Racism, the City and the State*, London: Routledge, 1–30.

Kenyon, O. (1991) *Writing Women: Contemporary Women Novelists*, London:
Pluto.

King, A. D. (1990) *Global Cities: Post-Imperialism and the Internationalization of
London*, London and New York: Routledge.

Kureishi, H. (1988) *Sammy and Rosie Get Laid: The Script and the Diary*, London:
Faber and Faber.

—— (1990) *The Buddha of Suburbia*, London: Faber and Faber.

—— (2002) *Dreaming and Scheming: Reflections on Writing and Politics*, London:
Faber and Faber.

Kureishi, H. and Savage, J. (eds) (1995) *The Faber Book of Pop*, London: Faber and
Faber.

Lamming, G. (1954) *The Emigrants*, London: Michael Joseph.

—— (1960) *The Pleasures of Exile*, London: Michael Joseph.

—— (1998) 'The coldest spring in fifty years: thoughts on Sam Selvon and
London', *Kunapipi*, 20.1, 4–10.

Lefebvre, H. (1991) *The Production of Space*, trans. by Donald Nicholson-Smith,
Oxford: Blackwell.

Lessing, D. (1950) *The Grass is Singing*, London: Michael Joseph.

—— (1993) [1960], *In Pursuit of the English: A Documentary*, London: Flamingo.

—— (1997) *Walking in the Shade: Volume Two of My Autobiography, 1949–1962*,
London: HarperCollins.

Leusmann, H. (1998) 'Interview: Fred D'Aguiar talks to Harald Leusmann',
Wasafiri, 28, 17–21.

Loomba, A. (1998) *Colonialism/Postcolonialism*, London: Routledge.

Low, G. (2002) '"Finding the centre?" Publishing Commonwealth writing in

London: the case of anglophone Caribbean writing 1950–1965', *Journal of Commonwealth Literature*, 37.2, 21–38.

MacCabe, C. (1999) 'Interview: Hanif Kureishi on London', *Critical Quarterly*, 41.3, 37–56.

MacInnes, C. (1962) *London: City of Any Dream*, London: Thames and Hudson.

—— (1966) [1961] *England, Half English: A Polyphoto of the Fifties*, Harmondsworth: Penguin.

—— (1967) *Sweet Saturday Night*, London: MacGibbon and Kee.

—— (1969) *Visions of London: City of Spades, Absolute Beginners, Mr Love and Justice*, with an introduction by Francis Wyndham, London: MacGibbon and Kee.

—— (1979) *Out of the Way: Later Essays*, London: Martin Brian and O'Keefe.

—— (1985) [1966] *All Day Saturday*, London: The Hogarth Press.

—— (1992) [1959] *Absolute Beginners*, London: Allison and Busby.

—— (1993) [1957] *City of Spades*, London: Allison and Busby.

McLeod, J. (ed.) (1999) 'Post-colonial London', special issue of *Kunapipi*, 22.1.

—— (2000) *Beginning Postcolonialism*, Manchester: Manchester University Press.

—— (2001) 'Bernardine Evaristo, *The Emperor's Babe*', *Wasafiri*, 34, 60–1.

—— (2002a) 'A night at "the Cosmopolitan": axes of transnational encounter in the 1930s and 1940s', *Interventions: International Journal of Postcolonial Studies*, 4.1, 53–67.

—— (2002b) 'Naipaul's London: *Mr Stone and the Knights Companion*', *Moving Worlds: A Journal of Transcultural Writings*, 2.1, 42–50.

—— (2003) 'Reflections on the Thames, Westminster', *Kunapipi*, 25.1, 141–7.

McNaughton, H. (1993) 'Fraying the edge of an alphabet', *SPAN*, 36.1, 131–43.

McPherson, Sir W. (1999) *The Stephen Lawrence Inquiry: Report of an Inquiry by Sir William McPherson of Cluny* (Cm 4262-I), London: The Stationery Office.

Mama, A. (1997) 'Black women, the economic crisis and the British state', in H. S. Mirza (ed.) *Black British Feminism: A Reader*, London and New York: Routledge, 36–41.

Manring, M. M. (1998) *Slave in a Box: The Strange Career of Aunt Jemima*, Charlottesville: University Press of Virginia.

Merriman, N. and Visram, R. (1993) 'The world in a city', in N. Merriman (ed.), *The Peopling of London: Fifteen Thousand Years of Settlement from Overseas*, London: Museum of London/Reaktion Books, 3–27.

Mirza, H. S. (1997) 'Introduction: mapping a genealogy of Black British feminism', in H. S. Mirza (ed.) *Black British Feminism: A Reader*, London and New York: Routledge, 1–28.

Moore-Gilbert, B. (1997) *Postcolonial Theory: Contexts, Practices, Politics*, London and New York: Verso.

—— (1999) 'London in Hanif Kureishi's films: Hanif Kureishi in interview with Bart Moore-Gilbert', *Kunapipi*, 21.2, 5–14.

—— (2001) *Hanif Kureishi*, Manchester: Manchester University Press.

Naipaul, V. S. (1961) *A House for Mr Biswas*, London: An

—— (1962) *The Middle Passage: Impressions of Five SoDutch, in the West Indies and South America*, London:

—— (1968) [1964] *An Area of Darkness*, Harmondswor

—— (1969) [1967] *The Mimic Men*, London: Penguin

—— (1972) *The Overcrowded Barracoon and Ot*
Deutsch.

—— (1980) [1979] *A Bend in the River*, Harmondsv

—— (1987) *The Enigma of Arrival*, Harmondswor'

—— (1988) [1963] *Mr Stone and the Knights Com*

—— (1999) *Letters between a Father and Son*, wit
Aitken, London: Abacus.

Nasta, S. (2002) *Home Truths: Fictions of the S*
stoke: Palgrave.

Nasta, S. and Rutherford, A. (eds) (1995) *7*
Armidale/Hebden Bridge: Dangaroo Pr

Nichols, G. (1983) *i is a long memoried wo*

—— (1984) *The Fat Black Woman's Poen*

Niven, A. (2001) 'In conversation wit
The Emperor's Babe', *Wasafiri*, 34, 1°

Nixon, R. (1992) *London Calling: V.*
and London: Oxford University F

Parekh, B. *et al.* (2000) *The Future*
on the Future of Multi-ethnic Brit

Parry, B. (1997), 'The Intended',
Leeds: Peepal Tree, 89–97.

Patterson, S. (1965) [1963] *D*
Harmondsworth: Pelican.

Paul, K. (1997) *Whitewashing*
NY, and London: Cornel'

Phillips, C. (2000) *The Atla*

—— (2001) *A New World*

Phillips, C. and Phillips,
and Wishart.

Phillips, M. (1991) 'L
Whose Cities? Lond

—— (2001) *London*
Continuum.

Phillips, M. and P
Britain, Londor

Pichler, S. (200
Trier: Wisser

Pilki

W
Powel

Pap
Procter
ogy,

—— (20
Univ
Quayson,
Press.
Ramdin, R
Pluto.
Ranasinha,
Riley, J. (19

—— (1987)

—— (1988)

—— (1992)

—— (1994)
Roberts, D. (1
London and
Rohlehr, G. (1
Gordon Roh
Rushdie, S. (198

—— (1991) *Imag*
Penguin.
Said, E. W. (1991

—— (1993) *Cultu*
Salkey, A. (1960) *E*
San Juan, Jr, E. (19
Sandhu, S. (2003)
London: HarperC
Scarman, Lord (1982
1981, Harmondsw
Schama, S. (1995) *La*
Schneer, J. (1999) *Lo*
London: Yale Univ
Selvon, Sam (1965) *Th*

—— (1973) [1957] *Th*

—— (1984) [1975] *Way*

—— (1985) [1956] *Mose*

—— (1988) [1956] *The I*

—— (1989) [1969] *Eldord*

—— (1989) 'Three into

K. Ramchand and S. Nasta, (eds) *Foreday Morning: Selected Prose 1946–1980*, Harlow: Longman, 211–25.

—— (1995) 'Finding West Indian identity in London', in S. Nasta and A. Rutherford (eds) *Tiger's Triumph: Celebrating Sam Selvon*, Armidale/Hebden Bridge: Dangaroo Press, 58–61.

Sinfield, A. (1989) *Literature, Politics and Culture in Postwar Britain*, Oxford: Blackwell.

Sivanandan, A. (1982) *A Different Hunger: Writings on Black Resistance*, London: Pluto.

Sizemore, C. W. (1996) 'The London novels of Buchi Emecheta' in M. Umeh (ed.) *Emerging Perspectives on Buchi Emecheta*, Trenton and Asmara: Africa World Press, 367–85.

Smith, A. M. (1994) *New Right Discourse on Race and Sexuality: Britain, 1968–1990*, Cambridge: Cambridge University Press.

Smith, Z. (2000) *White Teeth*, London: Hamish Hamilton.

Sougou, O. (1990) 'The experience of an African woman in Britain: a reading of Buchi Emecheta's *Second Class Citizen*', in G. V. Davis and H. Maes-Jelinek (eds) *Crisis and Creativity in the New Literatures in English*, Amsterdam and Atlanta, GA: Rodopi, 511–22.

Spivak, G. C. (1993) *Outside in the Teaching Machine*, London and New York: Routledge.

Stein, M. (2001) 'Black city of words: London in the popular novel', in P. Lucko and J. Schlaeger (eds) *Anglistentag 2000 Berlin: Proceedings*, Trier: Wissenschaftlicher Verlag Trier, 155–65.

Thieme, J. (1987) *The Web of Tradition: Uses of Allusion in V. S. Naipaul's Fiction*, London: Dangaroo/Hansib.

Umeh, M. (ed.) (1996) *Emerging Perspectives on Buchi Emecheta*, Trenton, NJ, and Asmara: Africa World Press.

Visram, R. (1986) *Ayahs, Lascars and Princes: Indians in Britain 1700–1947*, London: Pluto.

—— (2003) *Asians in Britain: 400 Years of History*, London: Pluto.

Walder, D. (1998) *Post-Colonial Literatures in English: History, Language, Theory*, Oxford: Blackwell.

Walmsley, A. (1992) *The Caribbean Artists Movement 1966–1972: A Literary and Cultural History*, London and Port of Spain: New Beacon Books.

Walvin, J. (1984) *Passage to Britain: Immigration in British History and Politics*, Harmondsworth: Penguin.

Ward, S. (ed.) (2001) *British Culture and the End of Empire*, Manchester: Manchester University Press.

Webster, W. (1998) *Imagining Home: Gender, 'Race' and National Identity, 1945–64*, London: UCL Press.

Welsh, S. L. (1996) '(Un)belonging citizens, unmapped territory: black immigration and British identity in the post-1945 period', in S. Murray, (ed.) *Not on Any Map: Essays on Postcoloniality and Cultural Nationalism*, Exeter: University of Exeter Press, 43–66.

Westwood, S. and Phizaklea, A. (2000) *Trans-nationalism and the Politics of Belonging*, London and New York: Routledge.

White, J. (2001) *London in the Twentieth Century: A City and Its People*, London: Viking.

White, L. (1975) *V. S. Naipaul: A Critical Introduction*, London: Macmillan.

Wolfreys, J. (1998) *Writing London: The Trace of the Urban Text from Blake to Dickens*, Basingstoke and London: Macmillan.

Wyke, C. (1991) *Sam Selvon's Dialectal Style and Fictional Strategy*, Vancouver: University of British Columbia Press.

Yelin, L. (1998) *From the Margins of Empire: Christina Stead, Doris Lessing, Nadine Gordimer*, Ithaca, NY, and London: Cornell University Press.

Young, R. J. C. (1995) *Colonial Desire: Hybridity in Theory, Culture and Race*, London and New York: Routledge.

—— (2001) *Postcolonialism: An Historical Introduction*, Oxford: Blackwell.

Index